SPORTS TV

This book offers an introductory guide to sports TV, its history in the United States, the genre's defining characteristics, and analysis of its critical significance for the business practices, formal properties, and social, cultural, and political meanings of the medium.

Victoria E. Johnson discusses a range of examples, from textual analysis of programs such as *Monday Night Football* and *Being Serena* to examination of television rights details, to sports TV's technological innovations and engagement of critical political debates. Johnson examines sports TV from its introduction to the ESPN+ era. She proposes that sports, as seen on TV in all of its iterations, is the central cultural forum for working through questions of community ideals, struggles over national and regional mythologies, and questions of representative citizenship.

This book is an ideal guide for students and scholars of television, media, and cultural studies as well as those with an interest in television genre, sports TV history, and contemporary sport and media culture.

Victoria E. Johnson is Professor of Film and Media Studies and African American Studies at the University of California, Irvine. Her *Heartland TV: Prime Time Television and the Struggle for U.S. Identity* (2008) was awarded the Society for Cinema and Media Studies Katherine Singer Kovacs Book Award in 2009. She writes about the cultural history of US television by examining its popular geographic mythologies, representations of race and place, and sports media.

ROUTLEDGE TELEVISION GUIDEBOOKS

The Routledge Television Guidebooks offer an introduction to and overview of key television genres and formats. Each guidebook contains an introduction, including a brief history; defining characteristics and major series; key debates surrounding themes, formats, genres, and audiences; questions for discussion; and a bibliography of further reading and watching.

POLITICAL TV
Chuck Tryon

LIFESTYLE TV
Laurie Ouellette

REALITY TV
Jonathan Kraszewski

THE SITCOM
Jeremy Butler

FAIRY-TALE TV
Jill Terry Rudy and Pauline Greenhill

SPORTS TV
Victoria E. Johnson

SPORTS TV

Victoria E. Johnson

Routledge
Taylor & Francis Group

NEW YORK AND LONDON

First published 2021
by Routledge
52 Vanderbilt Avenue, New York, NY 10017

and by Routledge
2 Park Square, Milton Park, Abingdon, Oxon, OX14 4RN

Routledge is an imprint of the Taylor & Francis Group, an informa business

© 2021 Taylor & Francis

Library of Congress Cataloging-in-Publication Data
A catalog record for this title has been requested

ISBN: 978-0-415-72293-3 (hbk)
ISBN: 978-0-415-72294-0 (pbk)
ISBN: 978-1-315-85799-2 (ebk)

Typeset in Perpetua
by Apex CoVantage, LLC

In memory of

Karen E. Johnson (1940–2016) and David C. Johnson (1937–2017)

For everything—including encouraging me to play sports, and to become a TV Professor

And for Chris Davis: You are an Ironman

CONTENTS

FIGURES

ACKNOWLEDGMENTS

All thanks are due to Erica Wetter for initiating the Routledge Television Guidebooks series and for her exceptional support, kindness, and patience when an unfathomable series of unexpected life-events happened between *Sports TV*'s initial contracting and its submission. During and after Erica's tenure at Routledge, Emma Sherriff has been exceptional to work with and I thank the entire production team.

I am privileged to be in the company of fellow series authors who have also been wonderful interlocutors regarding the work, not to mention terrific friends. These include Laurie Ouellette, Jon Kraszewski, Ellen Seiter, and Ron Becker. I thank the following colleagues for encouraging earlier publications, inviting talks, or joining in conference panels or workshops regarding sports media and the media industries, each of which informed this project and shaped its contours: Aaron Baker, Sarah Banet-Weiser, Mary Beltrán, Branden Buehler, Michael Butterworth, CL Cole, Lester Friedman, Herman Gray, Hollis Griffin, Jennifer Holt, Amanda Lotz, Helen Morgan Parmett, Roopali Mukherjee, Thomas Oates, Alisa Perren, Tim Piper, Yeidy Rivero, Steven Secular, Samantha N. Sheppard, Markus Stauff, Ethan Tussey, and Lawrence Wenner.

I am particularly grateful for conversations and collaborations with Jon Kraszewski that led me to first write about sports TV. An early discussion with Reece Peck helped illuminate key questions around which all of my subsequent writing about sports have turned. And, across many years and venues, the keen insights and unparalleled expertise and encouragement of Travis Vogan have been invaluable and inspirational. Thank you to Anne Bergman, Bridget Cooks, Jen Holt, and Kristen Hatch for ongoing local support and wisdom.

Portions of Chapter 4 pertaining to LeBron James's "decision" to leave Cleveland were published in an extended form, copyright 2019 as "More Than a Game: LeBron James and the Affective Economy of Place," in *Racism Postrace*, eds. Roopali Mukherjee, Sarah Banet-Weiser, and Herman Gray (Durham, NC: Duke University Press, 2019), 154–177, and are reproduced here by permission of Duke University Press. Special acknowledgement is due to the Humanities Commons at the University of California, Irvine, which provided crucial grant support to secure permissions for included images. At UCI, a few of the courses I have been privileged to teach include "Race, Sports, Media" and "Writing About Sports Media." I am indebted to the students from these courses, in particular, for their enthusiasm, adventurousness, expertise, and engagement with the questions and issues raised in what follows.

INTRODUCTION

Sports have been integral to US TV from the medium's introduction to the public at the 1939 World's Fair in New York—where demonstrations featured live telecasts of college baseball and professional football—to contemporary mobile apps such as ESPN+, which provide streaming sports "TV everywhere." From its inception to the present, sports TV has helped to define the medium's industrial structure (through scheduling), support (through advertising), and viability (through broadcast rights packages and network branding). It has advanced the medium's textual, or formal, audio-visual developments (such as instant replay, slow motion, and onscreen graphics), and it has driven audience adoption of and engagement with the medium (from its earliest appearances in taverns to its latest extensions in high-definition and immersive environments). Sports have been both a constant, stable cornerstone and a supple, ever-adaptable entity, critical to the medium's transitions from the "classical" network era of broadcasting (1950s–1980s) to the growth of cable and satellite delivery of TV (1980s–2000s), to the current addition of "connected viewing" (2010s–present).[1] As US television transitioned "from the one-to-many distribution strategies of the broadcast networks to a moment 'characterized by interactive exchanges, multiple sites of productivity, and diverse modes of interpretation and use,'"[2] sports TV has emerged as the ideal "multiplatform entertainment experience," seamlessly integrating "digital technology and socially networked communication with traditional screen media practices."[3]

Perhaps more than any other genre, sports TV reminds us that broadcast television, cable and satellite-delivered television, and nonlinear or internet-protocol distributed "over-the-top" television continue to coexist and overlap rather than supplant each other.[4] The present television landscape challenges us to continue to recognize those audiences and practices that appear *resistant* to niche TV, economically, technologically, and in racial, generational, and geographic terms.[5] In the 2018 calendar year, for example, 88 of the top-100 most-viewed telecasts were sports events.[6] National Football League (NFL) telecasts "accounted for 37 of the year's top 50 broadcasts, or nearly three-quarters (74 percent) of the most-watched programs on TV."[7] According to NFL Commissioner Roger Goodell, the league believes that broadcast television "is best for our fans because it is the most broadly distributed. The big events continue to be on broadcast television and they amass the biggest audience."[8]

Sports is the primary genre—with local news, spoiler-sensitive reality TV, and events such as awards shows—where the ethos of broadcast television not only still exists but thrives. Though Elihu Katz argued as early as 1996 that with "the rapid multiplication of channels, television has all but ceased to function as a shared public space,"[9] sports remain an important day-to-day *and* big event attraction where shared television culture continues to captivate conjoined audiences. As critic Matt Zoller-Seitz has argued, "image-driven entertainment" such as sports represent "the works that have the power to unite large sections of an otherwise fragmented society" and, as such, "are more reminiscent of television as we've always known it"[10] (at least, for those who still remember the broadcast era). And yet, though sports epitomize "legacy" TV's ideals of service to a broad public, sports TV is also privileged content for the newest modes of "connected viewing" off the edges of the traditional TV screen. What follows proposes that digital and mobile extensions of sports TV actually represent a continuation and renewal that is complementary and additive to traditional TV platforms.[11]

Sports TV thus understands sports to be a critical, industrial, textual, and cultural "ecosystem."[12] Everyday life is now infused so thoroughly with sports media that even when one is *not* a sports fan, it has become imperative to understand this ecosystem. Brett Hutchins and David Rowe have described this context as a "media sport economy" wherein "the traditional conception of sport *and* media has given way to sports *as* media within a broader leisure framework."[13] As communications law scholar Susan Crawford states, "In many ways, the subject of sports programming crystallizes all the convergence stories of the twenty-first century."[14]

Beyond examining deal-making and profits and noting sports television's aesthetic achievements and technological bells and whistles, however, *Sports TV* proposes that sports, as seen on TV, is *the* central, shared venue for working through questions of community ideals, struggles over national and regional mythologies, and questions of representative citizenship. Sports is a field of deeply *affective* cultural and political resonance, recalling and epitomizing Horace Newcomb's and Paul M. Hirsch's definition of television as a "cultural forum"—a key site for "the collective, cultural view of the social construction and negotiation of reality, or the creation of . . . 'public thought.'"[15] Televised sports offer a shared cultural realm through which we safely encounter and struggle with "our most prevalent concerns, our deepest dilemmas."[16] It is where "our most traditional views, . . . as well as those that are subversive and emancipatory, are upheld, examined, maintained, and transformed."[17] More than any other genre, televised sports programming actively engages and encourages shared discussions of community identity and ideals. Sports TV explicitly references race, gender, age, sexuality, and regional "difference" in ways that appear "safely" displaced onto the field of play but that, effectively, represent the shared, ritual site for significant interrogation of these culturally constructed categories. As former ESPN producer Dennis Deninger notes, "Sports is television that matters to people in ways that no other entertainment can."[18] And, sports TV represents and engages these concerns and investments through the most advanced audio-visual and technological means in screen culture, with texts whose richness and complexity encourage close analysis and the media literacy skills such analysis requires. Yet, in spite of sports and TV's always intertwined history and sports TV's visibility as an everyday site of impassioned engagement and, even, flashpoint for critical debates in media culture, still, remarkably little scholarship exists that studies US sports TV from a TV studies perspective.[19] The project of this book is to argue for the critical value and necessity that a television studies approach to industry, text, and reception context can and must offer to the study of sports TV and to the broader sports-media ecosystem at large.

TV Studies . . . Without Sports?

Jonathan Gray and Amanda Lotz have recently proposed that while there are many scholarly studies of television, television *studies* is "an *approach* to studying media" that has an identifiable "set of methods and theories" in the humanities since the 1990s—an approach that considers television to be a social institution that is best analyzed as an interconnected web of industry, text, and audience in historical and cultural context.[20] Lynn Spigel has outlined the genealogy of this approach, noting that

> [a]s it developed in the 1970s and 1980s . . . television studies drew upon at least five critical paradigms: (1) the "mass society" critique associated with the Frankfurt School and postwar intellectuals such as Dwight McDonald; (2) a textual tradition (to borrow John Hartley's term) associated with literary and film theory and, by the late 1970s, with feminist theories of spectatorship; (3) a journalistic tradition associated especially with theater criticism . . . (4) qualitative and quantitative mass communications research on audiences and content; and (5) cultural studies approaches to media and their audiences.[21]

The television studies to which Gray and Lotz refer and with which *Sports TV* is aligned emerged in the academy primarily through the second of these paradigms and became particularly identified with the last paradigm Spigel describes. Along the way, the other three traditions for studying TV came to be associated with social science methodologies and, particularly, communication studies, journalism studies, and sociological research and scholarship.

Notably, in the 1970s and 1980s, key film- and literary studies–trained scholars—many of whom are considered foundational figures in television studies—included sports in their analyses of television, its texts, audiences, and social importance.[22] These scholars' works are incorporated throughout *Sports TV* for their interventions in thinking carefully about sports TV's distinctive textual aesthetics, audience address, and affective power. And yet, by the 1990s, with few critical exceptions, sports TV had largely disappeared from TV studies–focused publications, conference panels, and course offerings.[23] During this same period, sports found a home in social science–focused communications and sociology where it has thrived in its own subfield, the sociology of sport.

Why did television studies, generally, neglect sports TV? As described earlier, a split developed in media studies in the academy whereby literature and film / media departments focused study on "fictional forms" while nonfiction TV became "the province of sociologists" and journalism studies.[24] Beyond these now-conventional—but never given—field boundaries, however, sports TV's historic omission from humanistic television studies relates to broadly shared apprehensions regarding sports' relation to capital, its presumed gender biases, and its sheer scope. As regards questions of capital or cultural status and value, the everyday ordinariness of most sports TV and its association with arguably "non-serious" pursuits (play, leisure) have contributed to gaps in its study. Treating sports as a "low" cultural object has had significant consequences.[25] This lack of scholarship can lead to the impression that—much as TV at large is generally dismissed by other scholarly fields—everyone already understands sports due to its familiar omnipresence. This discourages examination of sports' multiplicity and complexity.[26] In other words, sports is *both* culturally omnipresent *and* academically marginal.

Significantly, such oversimplifications and oversights have often historically been premised in active *antagonism* as much as benign neglect.

5

From this perspective, sports are presumed to be an anti-intellectual realm that is inherently conservative (both culturally and politically) and explicitly masculine, allied with white, cis-gendered, heteronormative patriarchal capitalist, dominant cultural ideals. Jonathan Gray's definition of the "antifan" as someone who is actively expressive of his/her/their hatred of "a given text, personality, or genre"[27] is particularly helpful here. Throughout most of its history, TV studies scholars have largely assumed the role of antifans of sports TV and sports culture more broadly. Further, those who shun sports TV often do so by invoking *moral* claims—particularly in relation to almost exclusively male, violent contact sports such as the top-rated National Football League. Here, sports TV appears aligned with "forms of ethically contested media, such as pornography" by which "it is sometimes argued that the audience's attention" and, by extension, the attention of scholars, "amounts to complicity in exploitation."[28] Such perspective extends beyond academia to TV industry and popular discourse as well. Reinforcing this sentiment, for example, lauded TV producer Jill Soloway recently stated, "men watching men do things of interest to mostly men. . . . There is NOTHING close to equality while this thing called SPORTS dominates."[29]

Henry Jenkins has opened up a critical conversation regarding such presumptions and absences, reflecting on ways in which fan and audience studies developed within television studies to share "blind spots" that "reflect the field's starting points."[30] Jenkins notes that fan studies historically has emphasized fan production and "cult" TV genres and focused "on fans who are resistant and transgressive rather than negotiating or accommodating; to celebrate fans who transform the original over fans who are more affirmational."[31] Within TV studies, fan and audience studies have rarely focused on mainstream texts. Further, as Jenkins importantly acknowledges, this work has overwhelmingly excluded "fans of color."[32] By contrast, sports TV more often than not is considered broadly mainstream and its audience is strikingly diverse across categories of gender, race, geography, and generation.

A persistent and central question of gender has also discouraged television studies scholarship and approaches to studying sports media. Throughout *Sports TV*—as addressed most thoroughly in Chapters 2, 3, and 4—gender is understood to be a social *construct* while sex-identity is a presumptively (if also contested) biological assignation. In what follows, the biological is *not* presumed to be "fixed" or "either/or." However, these binaries are referenced here as they persistently inform the literature on spectatorship and gender with respect to film and television at the emergence of TV studies. As such, these foundational models for thinking about and explaining the real social power of "ways of seeing" still carry tremendous weight in scholarship and teaching about popular media.[33] Most significant to this literature and its critiques is the idea that one's sex-identity does not necessarily conform to one's gender identification. Female-identifying or non-binary-identifying TV viewers can occupy a "masculine" gaze in relation to the text. Male-identifying or non-binary-identifying TV viewers can occupy a "feminine" gaze in relation to the text. Critics and scholars have understood TV genres to be "gendered" based on their narrative structure (featuring "closed," "masculine" resolutions versus "open," "feminine" enigmas), aesthetic conventions (e.g., a "masculine" proclivity for medium long shots, allowing an anchored, overview of the action versus the "feminine" close-up's emphasis on reading individuals' emotions and reactions) and audience engagement with the text's "flow" (e.g., with an attentive "gaze" versus a distracted, multitasking "glance").[34] *Sports TV* re-examines and critiques these frameworks to emphasize that sports television has always *confounded* such theoretical assumptions, thus establishing the genre as an outlier to the project of TV studies at its inception. Significantly, however, as TV studies moved away from such psychoanalytically influenced and literary analyses of TV texts, the omission of sports was still not meaningfully redressed.

Indeed, while sports media has been understood to be a presumptively "masculine" domain, largely reiterating and reinforcing such gendered "ideals" as dominant within the culture, TV studies' humanistic origins, foundational texts, and methodological perspectives overwhelmingly have been rooted in *feminist* perspectives and praxis. While television studies scholars of the 1980s and 1990s actively wrote against traditional academic disrespect of popular media and its pleasures, they did so by studying TV from an explicitly feminist and cultural studies perspective focused, for example, on soap operas and their "feminized" address. These scholars explicitly recuperated previously disdained texts and audiences for critical and historical study but did so with methodological and political commitments to writing female audiences and "feminine" texts back into the history of TV and academic research and publication more broadly. US television studies' signal interventions of the 1980s and 1990s thus focused on the pleasures of presumptively "feminine" genres, cis-gendered female audiences, middle-class domestic space, and the viewing context of the home.[35] This was and remains absolutely essential work. However, more generally, this commitment to revolutionize the study of everyday media in gendered terms and to depose the convention of valorizing media through masculinized frames and understandings of spectatorship led humanities-based TV studies to *excise* sports from its purview. Margaret Morse's groundbreaking essay, "Sport on Television: Replay and Display," from 1983, discussed in Chapter 2, is a clear exception in this period, as an explicitly feminist examination of sports TV aesthetics and the "gendered" gaze that underscores the constructed nature and *fragility* of masculine ideals in sports media discourse.

Here lies a critical dividing line: *Sports* studies scholars who write about media through cultural studies frames often focus on sports as a realm of "hegemonic masculinity," characterized by an "ideology of hypermasculinity . . . an exaggerated ideal of manhood linked mythically and practically to the role of the warrior"[36] in order to interrogate dominant cultural mythologies and their real social power. As sociologist Lois Bryson has noted, "For many feminists, sport has, quite rightly, been identified as a supremely male activity and therefore eschewed, both in practice and as a topic of interest."[37] And yet, as Bryson argues, "it is only through understanding and confronting"[38] such hegemonic dominance that it can be challenged. Thus, the sociology of sport has been notable for the extensive work of feminist scholars of sports and media culture, notably including CL Cole, Susan Birrell, Cheryl Cooky, and Sarah K. Fields, among others. In the spirit of such scholarship, *Sports TV* proposes that not only can one be a feminist scholar of sports media but that feminist analysis is *required* to do such work. As Tania Modleski has encouraged in her work on mainstream, Hollywood cinema:

> It is useless to deplore . . . texts for their omissions, distortions, and conservative affirmations. It is crucial to understand them: to let their very omissions and distortions speak, informing us of the contradictions they are meant to conceal and, equally importantly, of the fears that lie behind them.[39]

As regards racial, gendered, and geographic identity, sports TV is a central site for visualizing struggles over the presumptively "normative" *and* transformative at once.[40] As Todd Boyd notes, sports are "one of the few places in American society where there is a consistent racial discourse . . . race, directly or indirectly *is* the conversation, at all times."[41] Further, particularly since the mid-1990s, there has been a "sea change in gender norms that is principally evident in sports"[42] largely due to socio-cultural shifts in the decades following the passage of Title IX of the Education Act of 1972,[43] and related to the "recent development of a male beauty culture and the marketing of the male body."[44] These transformations and conversations have occurred in a "postfeminist," "postracial," neoliberal context which has recast the concepts of rights, commodity culture, corporate identity, and individual responsibility in ways that have encouraged an explosion in participation in sports and have supported sports leagues' development into full-fledged media institutions. Sports television thus exists at the intersection of industry, texts, and publics as a dynamic set of practices. Through analysis of these intersections and practices we can begin to trace the ways in which sports TV "contribute[s] to constraining" but also *challenging* "representations of gender, sexuality, race, class and ethnicity"[45] as well as geographic identity at critical historical moments within US culture. *Sports TV* asks, what is the broader potential of *instability* and *ambivalence* in sports TV?[46]

To return to Amanda D. Lotz and Jonathan Gray's definition, then, television studies

9

conceives of television as a repository for meanings and a site where cultural values are articulated. It assumes television is a key part of lived, everyday culture in contemporary society and one which may allow us to understand large parts of that culture. It is also an industrial entity produced under specific conditions that require analysis precisely because it is one of our prime storytellers, a resource tool for learning, deliberation, debate, and persuasion, and a site wherein power and ideology operate.[47]

Television is, here, understood to be a key social institution in dialogue with other sites of power, knowledge, and authority in US culture. If, in the previous passage, you were to replace "television" with "sports," it becomes clear that sports is analogous with TV as a social institution which—according to sociologist Harry Edwards' *Sociology of Sport*—while "not directly involved in political implementation, it does share with the polity the function of disseminating and reinforcing values that are influential in defining societal means and determining acceptable solutions to problems, that is, goals to be attained."[48]

While sports and television may be understood to be analogous institutions, Sut Jhally has proposed that sports represent a distinctly different *type* of TV from other program forms because,

> unlike other media messages (e.g., the news), sports also involves us in other ways. There are *passions* involved, emotional entanglements with the events that we witness. . . . Sports, perhaps more than any other cultural phenomenon, lies at this *tension* between consciousness and subjectivity, between "way of life" and "structure of feeling."[49]

Here, Jhally is pointing to the fact that sports involve our deepest sense of identification, often originating with allegiances to teams associated with where we were born or fandoms handed down within families for generations. For example, what it means to be a North Carolina Tar Heel fan as opposed to being a Duke Blue Devil fan is wrapped up with subjectivities forged by family and geographic ties, educational and economic distinctions, and the rivalry's extensive history. While Tar Heel fans and Blue Devil followers can share dedicated fandoms of variety, drama, and comedy series such as *Dancing With the Stars* (ABC, 2005–present), *Better Call Saul* (AMC, 2015–present), or *The Good Place* (NBC, 2016–2020), no Tar Heel fan could ever root for the Blue Devils, and vice versa. Due to this passionate attachment by which sports are a way of life, sports have been compared, variously, to a secular religion or a "magical" realm.[50] Sports have also been called a rare realm of "absolute truth," sincerity, and authenticity in an otherwise inauthentic day-to-day context.[51] If we live in an era that some assume is overrun with "fake news," it seems that sports "don't lie."[52] This expectation that sports are "true" (and, by extension, are a potentially *ethical* realm) is based in the idea that—in spite of the genre being the most technologically advanced and *mediated*—there is nowhere to "hide" on the field of play. An athlete either makes a shot or she does not. The team wins or loses. This need to believe in a space that feels intimate *and* communal, affective and authentic, explains a great deal of sports' allure. Though we can critique this sensibility, it is foundational to sports' cultural power and relevance. Indeed, sports TV energizes water-cooler discussion of the very real, everyday social stakes it raises while it simultaneously encourages our investment in its *utopian* promise—"the image of 'something better' to escape into, or something we want deeply that our day-to-day lives don't provide."[53]

Humanities-based television studies and critical studies of sports across disciplines are thus most productively conjoined in the perspective and methodology of cultural studies that emerged in post–World War II Britain in the wake of political and social upheavals to break from conceptualizing "Culture" as the "best" that has been thought and said—tied, significantly, to hierarchical, class-based access to education, economic and social capital—to attention to *everyday* life and culture characterized by an increasingly democratized understanding of "culture" as that which people "make and do." Cultural studies is not celebratory about popular culture and its meanings and pleasures but, rather, is concerned to unpack the relationships between culture and power at the site of the everyday and its engagement, particularly in hegemonic terms. Hegemony can be described as a kind of cultural commonsense whereby some ideas and values achieve dominance in a given society. As Justin Lewis has recently outlined,

> hegemony is not merely a description but a process, one that makes the dominance of certain groups or ideas in society seem normal, natural, or inexorable—even to those in subordinate positions. Hegemony often involves masking or solidifying various forms of inequality so that they seem part of everyday life, making customs and contrivances that favor some people over others *appear to be* common sense. Indeed, hegemony is often at its most effective when it is least visible, when ideological work goes on without noticing it.[54]

And yet, as Stuart Hall and George Lipsitz remind us, "'hegemonizing is hard work.' . . . It requires concessions to aggrieved populations. It mandates the construction and maintenance of alliances among antagonistic groups, and it always runs the risk of unraveling when lived experiences conflict with legitimating ideologies."[55] In the pages that follow, I propose that sports TV is a unique site within US media culture in which the hard work of hegemonizing often becomes *visible*, exposing instabilities in dominant ideals regarding race, gender, sexuality, and geography. These instabilities can open up productive engagement regarding "shared" values and the work of television as a continuing site of community and its interrogation.

Defining Paradoxes, and Chapters

Sports are inherently paradoxical: They are national and even global in reach but intensely regional and local in emotional connection. They offer community at its most "real" or deeply felt and experienced and at its most fantastic, imagined, or idealized. Industrially, as noted earlier, sports TV epitomizes both "old," broadcast TV ideals (its live broadcasts are DVR-resistant; its audiences remain the most "mass," demographically diversified in the medium), *and* it is the ideal content for streaming media's individually targeted extensions. Sports TV is television at its most spectacular, as is best exemplified by the Super Bowl or the Olympics. It is also the substance of the most everyday, aesthetically mundane, talking head programming, as seen in sports radio talk shows on TV such as *The Dan Patrick Show* (Peacock, 2020–present), or in most nightly sportscasts on local news. Sports TV also shares attributes of a variety of program forms: from incorporating elements of news (ESPN's *SportsCenter* [1979–present], roundtable talk shows, weekly highlight programs), to characteristics of reality TV (HBO's *Hard Knocks*, 2001–present), to aspects of game shows (*Pros v. Joes*, TNT, 2006–2010), to the logics of "quality" TV and "cinematic" series (*Friday Night Lights*, NBC, 2006–2011; *Playmakers*, ESPN, 2003; HBO Sports' Documentary series; ESPN's *30 for 30* [2009–present]). Sports TV is idealistically concerned with common cause, while it simultaneously celebrates individualism. It is interactive and participatory as well as contemplative and observational. It is quantifiably statistical and ineffably passionate—its discourses are both scientific and balletic. Sports TV reinforces dominant masculine cultural ideals, but it is also dismissed as "low" and trivial engagement in ways that have been historically associated with the "feminine." It is, in this respect, arguably the central daily site for both the fortification of hegemonic masculinity and the most public venue for exposing masculine subjectivity in crisis. Sports exemplifies the myth of the "level playing field" while it also makes visible institutional racism and gender biases on a broad scale. Here, particularly Black American sports figures represent "racial iconicity" while they simultaneously face "racial precarity," as profit creators for overwhelmingly white institutions *and* threats to these same structures.[56] In what follows, I focus on the following premises in order to consider the productivity of sports TV's paradoxes: Industrially, sports TV structures network schedules and "flow" and defines institutional identity and well-being; textually, sports TV drives audio-visual and temporal advances and

Figure I.1 Sports' "melodramatic mode" is not limited to fictional TV series and movies such as the classic *Brian's Song* (James Caan and Billy Dee Williams as Brian Piccolo and Gale Sayers [ABC, 1971])

Source: ABC TV/Photofest © ABC

technological development; and, though sports TV spans a continuum of program types, its dominant mode is fundamentally *melodramatic*.

Sports TV examines why television continues to be so important in spite of technological and cultural transitions.[57] *Sports TV* starts from the perspective that sports television is a *practice* that is cultural and experiential as well as economic and textual. Similarly, we can best understand and analyze the history, theory, and functions of US television when we think of TV as a practice—as something people do in particular historical contexts.[58] Thinking about television in this way encourages us to keep the always-interrelated voices and sites of industry, text, and context in dialogue with one another rather than isolating and compartmentalizing them.[59] As analogous and interrelated social institutions, sports and television can only be interpreted discursively, at the intersection or conjuncture of industry, text, social context, and audience engagement in key historical moments. By examining archival collections, legislative and policy documents, network rights deals, program scheduling and content (aesthetics and address), and public discourses about each of these (as reconstructed from trade industry press, news and popular press and websites), we can begin to "read" sports TV as a discursive field within which different interests struggle for authority.[60] And yet, where does one begin?

As a media ecosystem that is centrally seen on "traditional," in-home television sets, but is also at home across television's mobile and internet-enabled extensions as well as being a prominent brick-and-mortar public experience,[61] sports TV's vastness in scope and daily ever-presence is daunting. How do we define or delimit sports television and approach it from a contemporary, TV studies perspective? Though Chapters 1 and 2, and 5 in particular, examine US sports TV's broader history, *Sports TV*'s primary focus is particularly on the period following the Telecommunications Act of 1996, subsequent shifts resulting from the post-2009 transition to broadcast digital television, and the expansion of internet-protocol distribution from 2010 onward. As Jennifer Holt has argued, "The Telecommunications Act of 1996 was the ultimate deregulatory initiative to complete the structural convergence of the media industries that began during the 1980s."[62] Arguably, the television and sports industries have transformed more in the years since the Telecommunications Act than in their conjoined history prior to 1996. At the same time, while certainly players such as Comcast, Disney, and leagues such as the NFL and National Basketball Association (NBA) continue to change the overall sports TV landscape, current over-the-top portals (such as Netflix, Hulu, and broadcast and cable apps such as Fox Sports Go and ESPN+) and mobile viewing device options (tablet and smartphone technologies, in particular) have reached a new, if tentative, stability for the near future. Critical to further transformations, however, will be the fact that sports *content*—its ownership, production, and distribution—is essential to the industry, its aesthetics and address, and to audience engagement. Success in the contemporary media landscape requires a coherent, "insatiable content stream" that can consistently provide thrills and break through clutter, sustaining interest over years' worth of time.[63] The Marvel Cinematic Universe is an example of the type of content that succeeds because it can "keep audiences on the hook, constantly craving the dopamine rush that comes with narrative closure, even when it proves to be temporary, just a setup for the next cliffhanger."[64] Sports is a similarly ever-resolving (games are won, championships earned), ever-renewing (there's always next season) content universe, with its "franchise" properties (leagues, teams, stars, games, fantasy deals, wagers, and stats) having become thoroughly intertwined *as* media.

Sports TV's analysis of programming focuses particularly on everyday game coverage, special events, and documentary series, leaving out recurring fiction series, TV movies, reality series, or competition programs. Here, I have chosen to focus only on program forms that currently appear across the entire spectrum of TV—from linear, network TV to streaming websites, portals, and mobile apps. These are also the best-resourced and most-watched forms of sports TV. Further, most of the examples studied here are available for readers to view online, to compare their own readings and analyses with those in each chapter.

Finally, while any scholarship should be cautioned against reproducing a parochial, national emphasis when dealing with the global phenomenon that is sports culture, this book purposefully focuses on the idiosyncratic context of US sports TV in order to address complexities and specificities of the medium, genre, and contextually specific meanings that often drop out of studies with a more macro-political, global media lens. More pragmatically, focusing specifically on rights, policy, television programming, and broader discourses regarding US-based "stick-and-ball" sports, major professional sports leagues, and prominent US-based sports figures and controversies allows that *Sports TV* may be both thorough and meaningfully delimited.

Chapter 1, "'Not a Traditional Business': Sports TV as For-Profit Public Good?" is an historical examination of how sports structure the business of television, particularly as regards broadcast rights and policy, network brand identity, and audience cultivation. Using a critical media industry studies lens, this chapter is guided by the understanding that "policy decisions are . . . designed by those in power and, as such, policy study ultimately becomes a study in how social and political power is enacted, mobilized, and embedded in our media's structure and content."[65] This chapter examines the historical link made between sports television as a profit-making and institution-building entity alongside recurring rhetorical claims that sports are a public good allied with broadcast television's public service mandate. Securing the rights to telecast major US professional sports has transformed network identity and value in each era of TV's development, from ABC in the classic network era to FOX in the multichannel era, to Comcast/NBCUniversal's streaming era strength. Such institutional transformation was enabled by the passage of the Sports Broadcasting Act of 1961 (SBA), which remains foundational in conceptualizing professional sports' leagues as both cartels *and* public trustees. Focusing particularly on the conventionalization of professional sports leagues' broadcast network rights deals following passage of the SBA, the chapter illustrates that law and policy are *cultural* entities that shape definitions of public service, geographic value, equitable access to programming, and market imperatives. Where once TV transformed sports—facilitating, for example, the viability and national growth of all four major US professional sports leagues—following the Telecommunications Act of 1996, sports are now requisite to TV industry survival. In the streaming era, each of the major professional sports leagues themselves have become full-fledged media conglomerates. This trajectory is exemplified here by tracing the National Hockey League (NHL) from its early struggles for local and regional coverage to its cross-country expansion in the multichannel era and its new profitability following the Comcast/NBCUniversal merger. In conclusion, this chapter addresses a defining paradox of the streaming era: the increasing loss of "free TV" access to local sports teams, accompanied by increased availability of subscription-based out-of-market coverage; these phenomena literally re-map and reimagine sports markets and their fan communities.

Chapters 2 and 3 use television studies' analytical approaches to the *formal* properties of sports programming to analyze the genre's textual and aesthetic hybridity. Sports TV exemplifies both narrative and documentary conventions within TV's "flow." Chapter 2, "Sportvision: The Texts and Tech of Sports TV," examines the history and current context of the "bells and whistles" that make sports TV programming, generally, the most visually striking and innovative programming across the TV landscape. This chapter posits that the texts of sports TV are so successful and compelling, in large part, because of the simultaneously contrasting *and* conjoined tension in-game programming sustains between narrative entertainment conventions and technical appeals to confirmable "truths" that align sports TV with news and scientific discourses. The chapter focuses on key graphic inventions (e.g., the "glow puck" and "1st & Ten Line") as well as most recent developments in onscreen overlays (including TopTracer's PGA golf shot tracker) to chart sports TV's aesthetic transformations from the broadcast era to the present. The chapter focuses on the conventionalization, by the 1970s, of the "Arledge aesthetic," which describes a set of conventions developed by ABC's Roone Arledge for *Wide World of Sports* (ABC, 1961–1998) and *Monday Night Football* (ABC, 1970–2005; ESPN, 2005–present) that quickly became the standard for "up close and personal" sports coverage across TV. Though the Arledge aesthetic continues to thrive, Chapter 2 also examines further transitions in sports TV's look and sound during the multichannel era, exemplifying what John Caldwell has called the industrial practice of "televisuality," emergent in the early 1990s, and seen, particularly, in the example of FOX's sports coverage.[66] Finally, the chapter examines current trends in videogame-graphic sports aesthetics of the "EA Sports era," as seen, particularly, in the Professional Golf Association's incorporation of onscreen "tracker" graphics and the larger gamification of sports TV in attempts to attract new generations across television platforms.

Chapter 3, "Generation IX: Sports TV, Gender and Voice," continues Chapter 2's discussion of the formal properties of TV texts and their meanings by focusing on sports' institutional and textual association with "quality" TV and its cultivation of new audiences for networks undergoing transition. It takes up a key debate in feminist studies of sports media that often foregrounds the question of "voice": Whose commentary underscores and guides coverage of female athletes? How is female athletic achievement often either undermined through conventional objectification and fetishization *or* qualified and made "safe" through reference to maternity and heteronormative coupling? As the first full post–Title IX generation reached adulthood, a new image of the female athlete emerged that, arguably, challenged the hegemonic masculinity thesis by intervening in and destabilizing historic practices of objectification and gendered norms. Specifically, this chapter focuses on ESPN/espnW's *Nine for IX* (2013) and the HBO Sports' mini-series *Being Serena* (2018) as sites of struggle over questions of contemporary voice, authorship, and gendered athletic identity. It proposes that the post–Title IX athlete/author "voice" must be analyzed through competing tensions and struggles between popular feminist and postfeminist discourses. How is the athlete's voice simultaneously revolutionary *and* constrained? This chapter examines *Nine for IX*'s pedagogical discourse and expressed second-wave feminist commitments in contrast to Serena Williams's "authorship" of *Being Serena* and her broader star text—particularly as seen on Instagram—to analyze how these texts both productively challenge and re-inscribe sports' prevailing hegemonic ideals.

Chapter 4, "The Level Playing Field? Sports TV and Cultural Debate," analyzes perhaps sports TV's most significant paradox: it is simultaneously considered to be an "apolitical" sphere and is the most visible, broadly shared daily site of politically charged debate. While, ideally, sports has been hailed as the soul of democracy and a "level playing field," it is also a site that regularly exposes larger social inequities and reveals or tests the limits of "community standards." In what moments, this chapter asks, is sports cast as political speech? What broader social or political concerns does sports mobilize in these examples? Theorizing sports TV through the lenses of melodrama and populist aesthetics, the chapter examines a *policy* conflict, with public outcry over Janet Jackson's "wardrobe malfunction" during the halftime show (produced by MTV) of Super Bowl XXXVIII (CBS, 2004); a *textual* conflict, with LeBron James's broadcast "Decision" to take his "talents to South Beach" (ESPN, 2010) and critical vitriol over that event's blurring of breaking news and reality TV conventions; and, finally, the broader *contextual* conflicts that have, particularly since spring of 2020, positioned sports TV as the most prominent daily site of civic debate, athlete activism, and dialogue regarding systemic racism and, particularly, the Black Lives Matter movement. Each of these moments amplified sport's resonance as a site for the construction and contestation of local, regional, and national sensibilities regarding identity, and each emphasized the way sports stars and sports media function both as the crucible for nostalgic hopes for the tenacity of *older* forms of community in the face of drastic structural transformations, *and* as vehicles to re-examine community in the context of contemporary transitions. These cases of sporting controversy allow readers to consider both the "limits" of genre expression and the intersection of sports and celebrity culture, and to query the broader socio-cultural and political questions and debates that sports TV inspires.

The final chapter considers the out-of-home or *public* history of sports TV and the built-environment of the "new media sport order."[67] "The Sports Media Ecosystem: Sports TV's Out-of-Home Communities" examines sports' broader intimate, affective *and* social, communal significance in everyday US life, particularly in the contemporary context of the "sportification" of place.[68] Sports historically have been a local concern with teams, media coverage, and fandoms each representative of and emotionally connected to specific places. Paradoxically, in an ostensibly global and streaming media delivery era, sense of place has renewed resonance. Particularly in the 2000s, several cities have been reshaped by new stadium and lifestyle developments that prominently feature TV viewing as a communal activity and television as an integral element in "live/work/play" architectural design. In this same period, local loyalties can increasingly travel with fans who are far from home, via out-of-market mobile and subscription TV services (e.g., Major League Baseball's MLB Extra Innings, or the NHL's Center Ice package). The chapter traces the history of out-of-home sports TV particularly as illuminated by scholars Michele Hilmes, Anna McCarthy, and Jon Krazsewski (through their work on theater TV, tavern TV, and sports bars, respectively). The continued importance of out-of-home sports TV is illustrated in the example of the Philly Phans of OC (Orange County), who gather for the NFL's Eagles' football watch parties at a bar in Costa Mesa, California. The chapter concludes with analysis of the broader context of sports *as* mediated environment through the example of St. Louis, Missouri's Ballpark Village and its promise of shared, communal experiences with baseball as the vehicle for conjoined community and focus of urban renewal.

The Sports Ecosystem and Its Stakes

In his 2017 *Football and Manliness: An Unauthorized Feminist Account of the NFL*, Thomas P. Oates notes that his study of sports culture "is based on the assumption that patriarchy and white supremacy are not marginal and anomalous but rather ordinary, everyday, and routine—their logistics and frameworks embedded in everyday life."[69] In sports, "white, male, middle-class heterosexual identities" are "central norms in relation to which all other identities must be understood."[70] And yet, given sports' consistent visualization of the potential *vulnerability* of these norms, sports as seen on TV is a site that is rare in its ability to expose and "highlight the instability and contingency of this formation."[71] In one of the most inflammatory and widely known examples of this paradox, in 2016, San Francisco 49er quarterback Colin Kaepernick sat and, later, kneeled during the pregame playing of the "Star Spangled Banner" in silent protest of systemic violence, institutional racism, and ongoing genocide of African American citizens at the hands of police. Public figures from the President of the United States to National Football League executives attempted to cast Kaepernick's protest—and the activism of those who joined him—as "unpatriotic," and a sign of disrespect of US armed forces at home and abroad. These voices portrayed Kaepernick and his allies as outsiders within the NFL and broader US, suggesting that critique, dialogue, and debate were violations of socially integrative values as they were imagined through the most vivid shorthand symbols of nationalism and militarism (the flag, soldiers, military families). And yet, Kaepernick's protest activated and energized broad public debate across television and its social media extensions as well as at dinner tables, in classrooms, and in offices. "Standing with Colin" also led to displays of support through consumption, as his jersey became the NFL's top-seller for the 2016 season.

Indeed, sports as seen on TV are a high-profile site for political expression that both upholds conservative, traditional ideals and also exposes the fissures in that "consensus," expressing potentially challenging alternatives. During presidential election cycles, US voters have increasingly been imagined and categorized through sporting demographics (e.g., referencing the importance of the "NASCAR Dad," "hockey Mom," or "roller derby woman" vote). Recently, the 2018 Women's National Basketball Association (WNBA) season was themed, "Take a Seat, Take a Stand," with ticket proceeds benefitting one of six partner organizations, each selected for their advocacy on behalf of girls and women;[72] the National Hockey League and National Hockey League Players' Association had concluded their fifth season as partners with the You Can Play Project, an advocacy organization seeking to eliminate homophobia in sports; and, in Major League Baseball, 25 of the league's 30 teams hosted LGBT Pride night events at local ballparks.[73] It is perhaps not hyperbolic that National Basketball Association (NBA) Commissioner David Silver recently stated,

> through sports, we have the ability to bring people together, increasingly people on a global basis together, to frankly do what governments, in many cases, are no longer able or willing to do. We uphold important values, like integrity, and fair play, respect, tolerance and inclusion, that's our industry.[74]

As Travis Vogan notes, "commercial sports media never merely depict sport."[75]

With the notable exceptions addressed here, in the general *absence* of most televised sports during the COVID-19 pandemic of 2020, the value of its provision of a rare, shared space for conversation and common-ground (no matter how tenuous) has been made even more apparent. Indeed, this book proposes that sports TV's significance is rooted in its identity as our preeminent day-to-day site for the explicit visualization of how much *work* is required to prop "normative" values up. As Judith Butler has argued (specifically in the context of women's sports), "ideals are not static, but constitute norms or standards that are surpassable and revisable."[76] While the gains of activism and social change do not necessarily follow from increased visibility or market-based actions such as the purchase of a jersey or a game ticket, in what follows, *Sports TV* aims to use the models, driving questions, and tools of television studies to examine how historically, institutionally, textually, and in broader cultural context, sports television is *the* critical site for thinking through raced, gendered, and geographic *instability* and contingency, containment, and resistance in late capitalism.

In sum, *Sports TV* proposes that critical study of sports from a humanistic, television studies perspective must be a crucial concern and practice within cultural studies, television and media studies, the sociology of sport, gender/sexuality and critical race studies, cultural geography, and critical communication studies, and to the study of popular culture, consumer culture, and media literacy at large. Though it is not possible to offer an exhaustively comprehensive examination of the breadth of US sports TV, it is hoped that the methodological approaches modeled, the questions raised, and the examples that follow will lead readers to take up further studies to expand this work and fill in its gaps, particularly as regards taking a more global focus and extending analysis beyond "stick-and-ball" leagues and sports icons to emergent sports, extreme sports, and the broader "sportification" of lifestyle and place.

Notes

1. Jennifer Holt and Kevin Sanson, eds., *Connected Viewing: Selling, Streaming, & Sharing Media in the Digital Era* (New York: Routledge, 2014). Holt and Sanson use the term "connected viewing" to describe the contemporary multiplatform entertainment experience which integrates existing traditional screen media practices with social media and internet protocol television to make up a broader, digitally enabled "ecosystem." Over-air broadcast media and cable and satellite TV are still integral to this ecosystem.

2. Quoting Michael Curtin in Jennifer Holt and Kevin Sanson, "Introduction: Mapping Connections," in *Connected Viewing: Selling, Streaming, & Sharing Media in the Digital Era*, eds. Jennifer Holt and Kevin Sanson (New York: Routledge, 2014), 1.

3. Holt and Sanson, *Connected Viewing*, 4.

4. As Amanda Lotz notes, "over-the-top" TV is enabled by internet protocol technologies "to deliver personally-selected content from an industrially curated library," distinguishing it from "communication that traveled—or went 'over' networks built and managed by telecommunication providers." See Amanda D. Lotz, *Portals: A Treatise on Internet-Distributed Television* (Ann Arbor: Michigan Publishing, 2017), http://dx.doi.org/10.3998/mpub.9699689

5. See my own larger argument about this in Victoria E. Johnson, "Historicizing TV Networking: Broadcasting, Cable, and the Case of ESPN," in *Media Industries: History, Theory, and Method*, eds. Jennifer Holt and Alisa Perren (Malden, MA: Wiley-Blackwell, 2009), 57–68.

6. Austin Kapp, "Sports Maintain Dominant Viewership," *Sports Business Journal*, January 14–20, 2019, 16.

7. Anthony Crupi, "Despite Another Ratings Slump, the NFL Remains TV's Top Dog," *Ad Age*, January 2, 2018.

8. Meg James, "Fox Scores NFL 'Thursday Night Football' in Five-Year Deal for More Than $3 Billion," *The Los Angeles Times*, January 31, 2018.

9. Elihu Katz, "And Deliver Us from Segmentation," *Annals* 546 (July 1996): 22.

10. Matt Zoller Seitz, "Avengers, MCU, Game of Thrones, and the Content Endgame," *RogerEbert.com*, April 29, 2019, www.rogerebert.com/mzs/avengers-mcu-and-the-content-endgame

11. This idea of renewal and enhancement is explored in Jostein Gripsrud, "Broadcast Television: The Chances of Its Survival in a Digital Age," in *Television After TV: Essays on a Medium in Transition*, eds. Lynn Spigel and Jan Olsson (Durham, NC: Duke University Press, 2004), 215; and Ethan Tussey, *The Procrastination Economy: The Big Business of Downtime* (New York: New York University Press, 2018).

12. Holt and Sanson, *Connected Viewing*, 1.

13. Brett Hutchins and David Rowe, "Introduction," in *Digital Media Sport: Technology, Power and Culture in the Network Society*, eds. Brett Hutchins, David Rowe, Peter Morris, and Riki Therivel (New York: Routledge, 2013), 2.

14. Susan Crawford, *Captive Audience: The Telecom Industry and Monopoly Power in the New Gilded Age* (New Haven, CT: Yale University Press, 2013), 141, 142.

15. Horace Newcomb and Paul M. Hirsch, "Television as Cultural Forum," in *Television: The Critical View*, 4th edition, ed. Horace Newcomb (New York: Oxford University Press, 1987), 505.

16. Newcomb and Hirsch, "Television as Cultural Forum," 505.

17. Newcomb and Hirsch, 506.

18. Dennis Deninger, *Sports on Television: The How and Why Behind What You See* (New York: Routledge, 2012), 2.

19. Though critical progress in such scholarship is evidenced throughout this book and its Bibliography, particularly as seen in contributions by Nicole Fleetwood, Jennifer McClearen, Thomas P. Oates, Helen Morgan Parmett and Kate

Ranachan, Steven Secular, Samantha N. Sheppard, Markus Stauff, and Travis Vogan.

20. Jonathan Gray and Amanda D. Lotz, *Television Studies* (Malden, MA: Polity Press, 2012), 3.

21. Lynn Spigel, "TV's Next Season?" *Cinema Journal* 45, no. 1 (Fall 2005): 83.

22. See, for example: John Fiske's *Television Culture* (New York: Routledge, 1989) on professional wrestling and "masculine" TV texts; John Fiske and John Hartley, *Reading Television* (New York: Routledge, 1990) on "competition" television; Sut Jhally, "The Spectacle of Accumulation: Material and Cultural Factors in the Evolution of the Sports/Media Complex," *Insurgent Sociologist* 12, no. 3 (July 1984): 41–57; Margaret Morse, "Sport on Television: Replay and Display," in *Regarding Television: Critical Approaches—An Anthology*, ed. E. Ann Kaplan (Frederick, MD: University Publications of America, Inc., 1983), 44–66 on sports TV's challenge to film studies' premises regarding gendered spectatorship and objectification; Horace Newcomb, *TV: The Most Popular Art* (New York: Anchor Books, 1974); Michael R. Real, "Super Bowl: Mythic Spectacle," *Journal of Communication* 25, no. 1 (Winter 1975): 31–43; Elayne Rapping, *The Looking Glass World of Nonfiction TV* (Boston, MA: South End Press, 1987); and Lawrence A. Wenner, ed., *Media, Sports, & Society* (Newbury Park, CA: Sage Publications, 1989).

23. Key exceptions from television studies scholars in this period include: Aaron Baker and Todd Boyd, eds., *Out of Bounds: Sports, Media, and the Politics of Identity* (Bloomington: Indiana University Press, 1997); Sarah Banet-Weiser, "Hoop Dreams: Professional Basketball and the Politics of Race and Gender," *Journal of Sport & Social Issues* 23, no. 4 (November 1999): 403–420; Todd Boyd, *Am I Black Enough for You? Popular Culture from the 'Hood and Beyond* (Bloomington: Indiana University Press, 1997); and Toby Miller, *Sportsex* (Philadelphia, PA: Temple University Press, 2001).

24. Rapping, *The Looking Glass World of Nonfiction TV*, 7.

25. Jennifer Hargreaves, "Theorising Sport: An Introduction," in *Sport, Culture, and Ideology*, ed. Jennifer Hargreaves (London: Routledge & Kegan Paul, 1982), 17.

26. Hargreaves, "Theorising Sport," 9.

27. Jonathan Gray, "Antifandom and the Moral Text: Television Without Pity and Textual Dislike," *American Behavioral Scientist* 48, no. 7 (2005): 840.

28. Michael Z. Newman, "Is Football Our Fault?" *Antenna*, September 17, 2014, http://blogcommarts.wisc.edu/2014/09/17/Is-football-our-fault/

29. Jill Soloway, "The Female Gaze," *TIFF Master Class*, September 11, 2016, www.toppleproductions.com/the-female-gaze

30. Henry Jenkins, "Fan," in *Keywords in Media Studies*, eds. Laurie Ouellette and Jonathan Gray (New York: New York University Press, 2017), 67.

31. Jenkins, "Fan," 67.

32. Jenkins, 67. For recent interventions redressing such gaps regarding mainstream, widely popular TV genres (featuring, especially, reality TV but also prime-time drama), social media's significance, and fan communities of color, in particular, see Racquel Gates, *Double Negative: The Black Image and Popular Culture* (Durham, NC: Duke University Press, 2018); Elizabeth Elcessor, "Tweeting @feliciaday:

Online Social Media, Convergence, and Subcultural Stardom," *Cinema Journal* 51, no. 2 (2012): 46–68; Kristen J. Warner, "ABC's 'Scandal' and Black Women's Fandom," in *Cupcakes, Pinterest, and Ladyporn: Feminized Popular Culture in the Early Twenty-First Century*, ed. Elana Levine (Urbana, IL: University of Illinois Press, 2015), 32–50; and Rebecca Wanzo, "African American Acafandom and Other Strangers: New Genealogies of Fan Studies," *Transformative Works and Cultures* 20 (2015), http://journal.transformativeworks.org

33. John Berger, *Ways of Seeing* (New York: Penguin Books, 1972). Berger's study, with Laura Mulvey's foundational "Visual Pleasure and Narrative Cinema," *Screen* 16, no. 3 (1975): 6–18 outline visual culture's gendered "ways of seeing" and its theorization as it has largely been taken up in film and media studies in the US humanities.

34. See, particularly: Tania Modleski, "The Rhythms of Reception: Daytime Television and Women's Work," in *Regarding Television: Critical Approaches-An Anthology*, ed. E. Ann Kaplan (Frederick, MD: University Publications of America, Inc., 1983), 67–78; and Fiske, *Television Culture*.

35. See, for example: Newcomb and Hirsch's discussion of different reading possibilities in relation to *Father Knows Best*'s "Betty: Girl Engineer" episode in their "Television as Cultural Forum" essay; Lynn Spigel, *Make Room for TV: Television and the Family Ideal in Postwar America* (Chicago, IL: University of Chicago Press, 1992); E. Ann Kaplan, ed., *Regarding Television: Critical Approaches-An Anthology* (Frederick, MD: University Publications of America, Inc., 1983); Lynn Spigel and Denise Mann, eds., *Private Screenings: Television and the Female Consumer* (Minneapolis: University of Minnesota Press, 1992).

36. Varda Burstyn, "Sport as Secular Sacrament," in *Sport and Contemporary Society*, ed. Stanley Eitzen (Boulder, CO: Paradigm Publishers, 2005), 11–20. And, see Michael L. Butterworth and Stormi D. Moskal, "American Football, Flags, and 'Fun': The Bell Helicopter Armed Forces Bowl and the Rhetorical Production of Militarism," *Communication, Culture, & Critique* 2 (2009): 411–433; Real, "Super Bowl: Mythic Spectacle."

37. Lois Bryson, "Sport and the Maintenance of Masculine Hegemony," in *Women, Sport, and Culture*, eds. Susan Birrell and C.L. Cole (Champaign, IL: Human Kinetics, 1994), 47.

38. Bryson, "Sport and the Maintenance of Masculine Hegemony," 47.

39. Tania Modleski, *Loving With a Vengeance: Mass-Produced Fantasies for Women*, 2nd edition (New York: Routledge, 2008) Kindle Edition, 20. See also: Tania Modleski, *Feminism Without Women: Culture and Criticism in a 'Postfeminist' Age* (New York: Routledge, 1991); and, Tania Modleski, "Misogynist Films: Teaching 'Top Gun'," *Cinema Journal* 47, no. 1 (Autumn 2007): 101–105.

40. See this same dynamic in the overwhelmingly male realm of videogame development and play, as analyzed and challenged in Bonnie Ruberg, *Video Games Have Always Been Queer* (New York: New York University Press, 2019).

41. Todd Boyd, "Mo' Money, Mo' Problems: Keepin' It Real in the Post-Jordan Era," in *Basketball Jones: America Above the Rim*, eds. Todd Boyd and Kenneth L. Shropshire (New York: New York University Press, 2000), 60.

42. Miller, *Sportsex*, 2.
43. Title IX allows that "No person in the United States shall, on the basis of sex, be excluded from participation in, be denied the benefits of, or be subjected to discrimination under any education program or activity receiving Federal financial assistance." See Nicole Mitchell and Lisa Ennis, *Encyclopedia of Title IX and Sports* (Westport, CT: Greenwood Press, 2007).
44. Leslie Heywood and Shari L. Dworkin, *Built to Win: The Female Athlete as Cultural Icon* (Minneapolis: University of Minnesota Press, 2003), xxiv.
45. Julie D'Acci, "Defining Women: The Case of 'Cagney and Lacey'," in *Private Screenings: Television and the Female Consumer*, eds. Lynn Spigel and Denise Mann (Minneapolis: University of Minnesota Press, 1992), 194.
46. Sarah Banet-Weiser has proposed that, particularly in the circulation of appeals to "empowerment" in popular media—of which sports and athleticism are central sites—that we "take seriously the cultural value of emotion, affect, and desire, . . . and think about these values in terms of the *potential* of ambivalence, its generative power." See Sarah Banet-Weiser, "Keynote Address: Media, Markets, Gender-Economies of Visibility in a Neoliberal Market," *The Communication Review* 18, no. 1 (2015): 68.
47. Gray and Lotz, *Television Studies*, 22.
48. Harry Edwards, *Sociology of Sport* (Homewood, IL: The Dorsey Press, 1973), 91.
49. Sut Jhally, "Cultural Studies and the Sports/Media Complex," in *Media, Sport, & Society*, ed. Lawrence A. Wenner (Newbury Park, CA: Sage Publications, 1989), 73, 74.
50. Burstyn, "Sport as Secular Sacrament," 11, 12.
51. Bill Plaschke, "Finding Our United State," *The Los Angeles Times*, January 11, 2017.
52. I am particularly grateful to Reece Peck and to Seth Perlow for discussions regarding the perceived "truth" of sports and the question of the "sincere" and the ethical in contemporary media.
53. Richard Dyer, *Only Entertainment* (New York: Routledge, 2002), 20.
54. Justin Lewis, "Hegemony," in *Keywords for Media Studies*, eds. Laurie Ouellette and Jonathan Gray (New York: New York University Press, 2017), 88.
55. George Lipsitz, "The Struggle for Hegemony," *The Journal of American History* 75, no. 1 (June 1988): 147.
56. Nicole Fleetwood, *On Racial Icons: Blackness and the Public Imagination* (New Brunswick, NJ: Rutgers University Press, 2015).
57. Horace Newcomb, "Studying Television: Same Questions, Different Contexts," *Cinema Journal* 45, no. 1 (Autumn 2005): 111.
58. Tom Streeter, *Selling the Air: A Critique of the Policy of Commercial Broadcasting in the United States* (Chicago, IL: University of Chicago Press, 1996), 3.
59. John Thornton Caldwell, "Critical Industrial Practice: Branding, Repurposing, and the Migratory Power of Industrial Texts," *Television & New Media* 7, no. 2 (May 2006): 101.
60. This methodological approach is exemplified, particularly, in: Julie D'Acci, *Defining Women: Television and the Case of Cagney & Lacey* (Chapel Hill: University of North Carolina Press, 1994); Herman Gray, *Watching Race: Television and the*

Struggle for 'Blackness' (Minneapolis: University of Minnesota Press, 1995); Victoria E. Johnson, *Heartland TV: Prime Time Television and the Struggle for US Identity* (New York: New York University Press, 2008); and Spigel, *Make Room for TV.*

61. As explored particularly in Chapter 5, sports TV and a broader sports experience economy are thoroughly integrated at stadiums and arenas as well as at sports-themed destination districts such as St. Louis's Ballpark Village or Philadelphia's Xfinity Live! See also Joseph B. Pine, II. and James H. Gilmore, *The Experience Economy* (Boston, MA: Harvard Business Review Press, 2011).

62. Jennifer Holt, *Empires of Entertainment: Media Industries and the Politics of Deregulation, 1980–1996* (New Brunswick, NJ: Rutgers University Press, 2011), 165.

63. Zoller-Seitz, "Avengers, MCU, Game of Thrones, and the Content Endgame."

64. Zoller-Seitz. The Marvel Cinematic Universe refers to Marvel Studios and the Walt Disney Company's series of films and TV series featuring Marvel Comics superheroes. Examples include films *Iron Man* (2008), and TV's *Agents of S.H.I.E.L.D* (ABC, 2013–present).

65. Jennifer Holt, "A History of Broadcast Regulations: Principles and Perspectives," in *A Companion to the History of American Broadcasting*, ed. Aniko Bodroghkozy (Hoboken, NJ: John Wiley & Sons, 2018), 171.

66. John Thornton Caldwell, *Televisuality: Style, Crisis, and Authority in American Television* (New Brunswick, NJ: Rutgers University Press, 1995).

67. Brett Hutchins and David Rowe, *Sport Beyond Television: The Internet, Digital Media and the Rise of Networked Media Sport* (New York: Routledge, 2012), 4.

68. Ivo Jirásek and Geoffrey Zain Kohe, "Readjusting Our Sporting Sites/Sight: Sportification and the Theatricality of Social Life," *Sport, Ethics and Philosophy* 9, no. 3 (July 3, 2015): 257–270, https://doi.org/10.1080/17511321.2015.1065 433 and Kate Ranachan and Helen Morgan Parmett, "Fortune Favors the Braves? Race and the Suburban Rebranding of Baseball in Atlanta." (Paper presented at the annual meeting of the Society for Cinema and Media Studies, Atlanta, GA, April 2, 2016).

69. Thomas P. Oates, *Football and Manliness: An Unauthorized Feminist Account of the NFL* (Urbana, IL: University of Illinois Press, 2017), 20.

70. Oates, *Football and Manliness*, 20.

71. Oates, 20.

72. These organizations included Bright Pink (focused on breast and ovarian health), GLSEN (Gay, Lesbian and Straight Education Network), It's On Us (national movement to stop sexual assault), MENTOR (national mentoring partnership), Planned Parenthood (sexual and reproductive health), and the United State of Women (women's equality organization).

73. As of this writing, only two MLB organizations had never held a Pride event: the Los Angeles Angels of Anaheim, and the New York Yankees.

74. Quoted in Abraham Madkour, "Forum," *Sports Business Journal*, June 3–9, 2019, 4.

75. Travis Vogan, *ESPN: The Making of a Sports Media Empire* (Urbana, IL: University of Illinois Press, 2015), 5.

76. Judith Butler, "Athletic Genders: Hyperbolic Instance and/or the Overcoming of Sexual Binarism," *Stanford Humanities Review* 6, no. 2 (1998).

1

"NOT A TRADITIONAL BUSINESS"

Sports TV as For-Profit Public Good?

Communication historian Robert W. McChesney has traced the "symbiotic relationship"[1] between sports and mass media from the mid-1800s, when both daily newspapers and sports developed as local and regional cultural institutions. With the emergence of radio and the broadcast era in the 1920s, alongside corresponding improvements in transportation, social mobility, and increasingly national markets, "sport assumed its modern position as a cornerstone of US culture."[2] To a significant degree, modern sports and broadcasting are analogous institutions. Both rest "upon a foundation of individual stations," or teams "that give voice to local communities, promoting the values of citizenship and the unique character of local cultures."[3] Both are also integral to "post–World War II ideologies of the 'national' that [each] coincided with and contributed to."[4] As the broadcast era (of radio, then television) began in the US, so too did the professionalization of sports. Just as television became a truly national medium integral to everyday life by the 1960s, the big four sports leagues expanded to be truly cross-country phenomena. Commercially sponsored TV of the broadcast network era took the form of an oligopoly, with NBC, CBS, and ABC in control of the market. Simultaneously, professional sports leagues took the form of cartels, with the MLB, NFL, NBA, and NHL absorbing or merging with competing leagues. Today, sports is *the* content upon which the continued relevance of broadcast television is staked. As Susan Crawford's history of US telecommunication policy states, "the real value in American television entertainment lies in controlling rights to football, basketball, and baseball games."[5]

In 2020, media rights for sports were valued at $21.7 billion. According to Price Waterhouse Coopers statistics, the North American sports market is projected to grow to a value of $83.1 billion in 2023.[6] With new rights deals struck by NBC, CBS, FOX, ESPN, and DirecTV through 2022, the National Football League alone will soon earn almost $6 billion a year in television rights fees. Such costs and profits correlate to audience investment: in 2020, "around 27 percent of respondents from the United States stated that they were watching live sport at least once a week on television."[7] But why should *sports* content be more valuable to television than any other genre? As noted in the Introduction, sports is "television that matters in ways that no other entertainment can."[8] It involves "passions" and "emotional entanglements"[9] that are rooted in regional and local identifications and the sports audience's sense of *self*. As the owner of the NBA's Atlanta Hawks, Tony Ressler recently stated, "it's not a traditional business. You're buying a community asset."[10]

As a beloved local institution, sports teams or franchises are imagined to be a public good, with their continued success considered to be in the best interest of the public they "serve." Sports law scholars Arthur T. Johnson and James H. Frey observe that "sport has acquired the status of a public trust, which must be protected. As a result, public policy in the form of law or regulatory action has been implemented to guarantee the public equitable access."[11] From the inception of modern US sports and broadcasting to the present, "the belief—or perhaps the hope—that sport and the public interest are one lingers"[12] in large part because of sports' uniqueness. Sports' "difference" in terms of commerce, business practices, geography, and public access has been codified into law and upheld as such when periodically challenged. From the classic network era (1950s–1980s) through the multichannel era (1980s–2000s) and the connected viewing or streaming "post-network" era (2010s–present),[13] media law and policy and TV industry negotiations with sports leagues have defined sports as a public good and viewers' access to sports as a necessity and a right. As historian and

TV policy scholar Allison Perlman has argued, "The public interest is not a singular, knowable thing. It is a device that reflects the interests of the person or community who invokes it."[14] What follows examines the intertwined historical, institutional, and commercial interests of professional sports and television in the US. Specifically, it examines key legal and policy documents that established the framework that continues to define sports TV as a public good, serving the public interest, with sports leagues and media rights holders affirmed as public "trustees." It offers an overview of the impact of sports rights on specific networks across television history and a similar overview of the transformative power of TV upon a sports league's growth and prosperity. Finally, it considers the increasingly untenable tension between sports' appeals to local community service in relation to its leagues' and teams' conglomerate media interests.

In the Public Interest? Core Concepts in Sports Law and Media Policy

Prior to the broadcast era, the late 1800s in the US saw the growth of new media outlets and sports institutions alongside "growing concentrations of economic power in the hands of large corporations and big trusts such as oil, railroads, steel, meat packing, and tobacco."[15] Concerns over such concentrated, increasingly monopolistic power led to passage of the Sherman Antitrust Act of 1890 "to regulate unreasonable anticompetitive methods that may be used to obtain or maintain market power,"[16] including unlawful restraint of trade and exertion of monopoly power within a defined geographic market. As professional sports leagues grew, they, too, became the focus of antitrust inquiries. And yet, the Sherman Antitrust Act has also provided the legal foundation to maintain the idea that sports is not a "traditional business" and cannot be regulated as such. In 1922, writing for a unanimous Supreme Court, in *Federal Baseball Club of Baltimore, Inc. v. National League of Professional Baseball Clubs, et al.*, Chief Justice Oliver Wendell Holmes ruled that professional baseball was not commerce. According to Holmes's decision, even though its teams "play against one another in public exhibitions for money,"[17] baseball games do not produce a tangible good in exchange for the ticket. Player "effort, not related to production, is not a subject of commerce,"[18] and, therefore, team travel between states does not constitute interstate commerce. Notably, here, baseball players' labor was considered synonymous with performance, theater, and the arts rather than with commercial production and trade. *Federal Baseball* thus determined that the sport transcended conventional modes of labor, production, and market exchange. This difference established what legal scholar Mitchell Nathanson has referred to as the "cultural fiction of the baseball creed," assuring that "America's game" was in a legally separate sphere, above the mundane.[19] "To hold otherwise would be to hold that America's game was no different than a shirt factory, and this simply would not do."[20]

Baseball's special status was not legally extended to other sports leagues. However, from the *Federal Baseball* case to the present, core elements of this "cultural fiction" and "difference" of sports have been integral to understandings of the relationship between sports and television in law and policy. Across court cases, Congressional hearings, public laws, and FCC reports and policy statements, professional sports have routinely been interpreted as a business that remains "above" crass market pursuits. This premise is, largely, based on appeals to localism: the teams that make up professional leagues are not conceived as for-profit franchises but, rather, as civic institutions representing specific publics (e.g., Cardinals fans are different from Cubs fans in distinctive ways involving "St. Louis-ness" rather than "Chicago-ness"). This idealistic concept may seem hard to sustain in a highly mobile, contemporary era, but whenever the profit-motive of sports has appeared to supersede such civic myths is when, historically, legislators and regulators have intervened in sports' business practices. Simultaneously, leagues and their television partners have also routinely invoked their role as "public servants" in order to assure continued, preferential *market* access. Whenever legally challenged, leagues and networks rhetorically have aligned sports TV with the FCC's expressed commitment to television's service in "the public interest, convenience and necessity."

The Radio Act of 1927 correlated wireless transmission of radio signals to transportation of goods or services to the market while also defining "the airwaves themselves" as "a public resource."[21] Thus, the Act proscribed that broadcasters must serve "in the public interest, convenience and necessity" and that they would be required to obtain a license to operate, the allocation of which would be guided by this principle. The Communications Act of 1934 reinforced and extended these principles to telephone services and created the Federal Communications Commission (FCC) as broadcast and telecommunications' oversight body. These extensions later allowed the Act's provisions to be adopted for the cable industry. In 1946, the FCC reiterated the need for individual stations, or licensees, to be responsive to *local* interests. According to this report (known as the Blue Book, for the color of its binding), station license renewal would be premised on the licensee's use of local talent wherever possible, and on the station's responsiveness to the specific interest of the public it served.[22] Though the public interest standard remained vaguely defined,

> In the wake of the quiz show and "payola" scandals in the late 1950s, the FCC actually did attempt to clarify the public interest standard as a means to offer programming guidelines to an industry that seemed to be losing its way.[23]

In "The 1960 Programming Policy Statement," the FCC introduced an "ascertainment" requirement for successful licensing. Ascertainment required broadcasters to assess the specific "tastes, needs, and desires" of viewers or listeners in the licensee's broadcast range.[24] Among fourteen elements considered necessary to meet the public interest were regular offering of sports programs.[25] This priority would be directly referenced by league commissioners as the rationale for exclusive rights deals brokered with TV networks.

Prior to television's expansion across the country, the rights to broadcast games typically belonged to individual teams. As both sports' and television's markets and national, commercial viability grew, however, "professional sports leagues realized that pooling their teams' individual rights into packages to sell to national television networks would increase total league revenue and allow revenue sharing among their teams."[26] In 1953, the NFL's rights-pooling policy was judged to violate the Sherman Act. The league was ruled to have restricted outside competition within individual team markets and to have restrained trade, based on the NFL's practice of only telecasting certain games within a given market. In *United States v. National Football League*, Judge Allan Grim acknowledged the uniqueness of *sports* in several ways, but ultimately noted that *television* was, undeniably, interstate commerce. Specifically, the Judge conceded that, in sports, while teams had to compete to the best of their ability on the field of play, they would only be successful financially if they collaborated. Grim singled out the need for leagues to assure that small-market teams remained competitive in relation to large-market clubs. Using the example of the New York Yankees in baseball, Grim stated that market imbalances weakened a sport's competitive quality, turning away audiences and sponsors and threatening broader league stability. However, Grim affirmed individual team's rights to negotiate local and regional media contracts. The resulting consent decree prohibited the NFL from imposing restrictions on the territorial reach or market for team's rights.

Between the 1953 *Football* case and the 1960 football season, some NFL teams successfully struck individual television rights deals with CBS and NBC to telecast games regionally. Certain franchises, such as Pittsburgh, Baltimore, and Cleveland, had fairly lucrative contracts. However, as David Surdam notes, "NFL television games overlapped, which diluted audiences."[27] Further, smaller markets, such as Green Bay, were considered generally unworthy of network investment, proving Grim's own claims. Then, in 1960, ABC brokered a five-year, $11 million-dollar deal to be the exclusive television home of the NFL's competitor, the upstart American Football League (AFL). In response, the NFL's new commissioner, Pete Rozelle, signed a league-wide deal with CBS worth $4.65 million a year. The Justice Department interpreted the NFL-CBS deal to be in violation of the 1953 consent decree, so, in the spirit of football itself, the NFL executed an end run: instead of risking a court appeal, Rozelle went directly to Congress to lobby for a new law that would exempt sports leagues from antitrust law when entering into exclusive television contracts.

The hearings for the Sports Broadcasting Act of 1961 (SBA) focused on key themes uniting the "cultural fiction" of sports with broadcast television's public interest ethic: Sports were presumed to be a civic, public good. As such, equitable access to televised sports was allied with service to the public. It was argued that sports broadcasts should be available for free, on a national basis, giving priority to the Big Three national broadcast networks to compete for rights packages. According to Rozelle's opening statement at the SBA hearings,

> Independent stations are precluded from competing in this market because of the distances involved between league cities and the production and line expenses involved which put costs out of reach of local sponsors except when network affiliations reduce carrying costs per station.[28]

Finally, the SBA was promoted as a geographic leveler—unlike baseball, with its few, dominant dynasties—the NFL proposed that national network packages would democratize the market. Stated Rozelle:

> unless the league is permitted to exercise some control over its television programming, only a limited number of teams in the National Football League will have access to television facilities. . . . I don't think I have to tell this committee what the response of fans in Green Bay, Minneapolis–St. Paul, Dallas, St. Louis, Detroit . . . will be when they are informed they will no longer be able to follow the road games of their home teams on television. . . . Only by grouping the weaker and stronger clubs and the clubs with more and less favored geographic locations can the league hope to achieve any control over the manner in which its games are telecast.[29]

Endorsing Rozelle's position, Representative John W. Byrnes of Wisconsin's Eighth District stated, "I represent Green Bay, . . . the

Packers have a less-concentrated population area than teams which represent large metropolitan areas. TV income can mean the difference of life or death."[30] Thus, according to Byrnes, a "discriminatory situation . . . can be corrected by the passage"[31] of the SBA. Other commenters noted that economic parity would assure on-field, competitive parity, guaranteeing "the tight, closely contested battles which are now the league's trademark."[32] Finally, sponsors would not shun smaller market team appearances in national packages, whereas, independently, "If [a sponsor] has a choice between Green Bay . . . or Chicago, with an area population of over 5 million, you know which one he will take."[33]

The SBA applied not just to the NFL, but to all sports leagues, making them exempt from antitrust laws and permitting them to broker broadcasting agreements for all of their teams, as a package, to networks that successfully bid for telecast rights. Between passage of the SBA and the NFL's merger with the AFC in 1966, professional football's centrality to the profitability of TV became stunningly apparent: CBS paid $28 million in rights fees for the 1964 and 1965 NFL seasons and was immediately rewarded with sponsorships from Ford and Philip Morris of $14 million each.[34] The Green Bay Packers reinforced the expressed rationales for the SBA by winning the NFL championship in 1961, 1962, and 1965, and again after the league merger, in 1966 and 1967. As part of Rozelle's lobbying for the legislation, several supporters' districts were awarded expansion franchises in smaller markets,[35] guaranteeing that the NFL would be truly national in reach and, ideally, equitable in terms of public access and local representation.

The SBA emphasized sports' availability on "free TV," or over-air, broadcast networks. Though the SBA has not been formally amended to allow for rights pooling to be sold to non-commercial (e.g., subscription services) or non-broadcast networks (e.g., cable or satellite services), hearings regarding cable through the 1970s and 1980s, and into the 1990s, routinely emphasized the priority for sports to be available on free TV wherever possible with requirements, particularly, for each league's championship event to be on an over-air broadcast outlet. That said, particularly since the Telecommunications Act of 1996,

Figure 1.1 The NFL on CBS TV

Source: *Chicago Tribune*, September 1, 1964, B5

understanding of the "public interest" has transformed into prioritizing giving "consumers more opportunities to view sporting events" over those events, necessarily, being available at no cost.[36] Concessions have also been made by leagues to stave off antitrust action, by providing over-air simulcast of games in home markets when, nationally, those broadcasts are otherwise only available on cable. Increasingly, however, sports programming has been weaponized in marketplace struggles over its carriage.

Sports content can be so fraught because its viewership is so emotionally invested in its presence and resonance in daily and seasonal life.[37] While this phenomenon is explored further at the conclusion of this chapter and in Chapter 5, the concept of "free" TV, itself, requires some qualification, particularly given annual increases in sports rights fees since passage of the SBA. As legal scholar Ira Horowitz outlines, "insofar as consumers ultimately pay some or all of a television sponsor's advertising costs through higher prices than would otherwise obtain, conventional telecasts of sports events are by no means 'free' to the public."[38] And, further, given public tax support for stadiums—built, not coincidentally, in two big waves following passage of the SBA in the 1960s and then again following the Telecommunications Act of 1996 to the present—"the citizen may have supported a team even when he [sic] does not buy a ticket [or is even a fan]."[39] Overall, the SBA hearings established that, even though television *networks* were not held to the public interest standard that their affiliated stations were, sports content would, going forward, nonetheless rhetorically be aligned with the values of localism, service in the public interest, convenience, and, even, necessity. Though league business practices have been challenged periodically since passage of the SBA, it has remained the defining framework for all subsequent rights deals, and, perhaps just as importantly, it legally codified the mythic "sports creed"—that sports were a public good, and that pooling rights and placing them with the most profitable and powerful national, commercial networks would be the most "efficient" and qualitatively better provision of that good. Hence, from 1961 onward, cultural mythologies of sports' "transcendent" value have legally encouraged and enforced its concentration in the hands of the most powerful media interests, in the name of public service.

Sports, TV, and Institutional Transformation

Following passage of the SBA, television transformed professional sports in the US (enabling league mergers, expansions, and unprecedented profitability), but sports also became the driving force in institutional transformation of television. In each era of television's history, sports rights and content have allowed networks to surge to new prominence and profitability even as sports has gone from being a huge profit-center to, increasingly, being a loss-leader. Aniko Bodroghkozy's recent history of American broadcasting defines television through three eras that continue to overlap and coexist: the "classic network era" (1950s–1980s), the "multichannel network era" (1980s–2000s); and the "post-network" or streaming TV era (2010s–present).[40] The classic network era of over-air, broadcast TV was characterized by the commercial and cultural dominance of the Big Three networks (ABC, CBS, and NBC). The multichannel era was characterized by cable and satellite-delivered television. And the contemporary streaming era is characterized by "over-the-top" internet protocol TV providers and the promise of internet-enabled, tablet, phone, and laptop "TV everywhere." In each of these eras, we can chart the incredibly "symbiotic relationship" of sports and television and vividly illustrate Crawford's earlier statement that the "real value" in US entertainment television has been, and continues to be, controlling sports rights. Examples, here, include ABC in the classic network era, FOX in the multichannel era, and Comcast/NBCUniversal in the streaming era.[41] Each of these entities still has a classic network-era presence (with over-air broadcasting still core to the institution's identity), and a multichannel era presence, alongside their streaming-era presence. This overlap is significant: It underscores the reality that these eras are not distinct from and eclipsing of one another. They continue and coexist in their business practices, program content, technological platform extensions, and in viewer engagement across each of these categories.

From the early 1950s through the mid-1980s, the US television industry's dominant form was oligopolistic control by three over-air commercial networks: the National Broadcasting Company (NBC), the Columbia Broadcasting System (CBS), and the American Broadcasting Company (ABC).[42] Each of the Big Three networks was national in reach, featured standardized program forms and advertising practices, and exerted expansive control over affiliated stations, advertisers, and program producers. Through the 1950s, live sports telecasts were largely a local and regional endeavor, with networks focusing weeknight prime-time sports coverage on boxing (e.g., *Gillette Cavalcade of Sports* on NBC), wrestling, and roller derby, with weekend coverage of collegiate sports (e.g., Notre Dame football) and highlight shows that summarized professional events from the previous week. As networks moved away from packaged, single-sponsor programs and assumed greater production control following the quiz scandals and other inquiries into network programming, advertisers also "discovered that sports provided access to a very desirable market—not only for 'blue collar' products like beer and razor blades, but for big-ticket items like automobiles and business equipment."[43] With passage of the SBA, rights pooling created focused *national* sports audiences for sponsors who were able to place ads in a competitive but unified mass market. Though CBS benefitted immediately from the SBA with its 1960s NFL package, none of the Big Three was more instrumental to or transformed by broadcast-era sports rights and sports content than ABC.

Formed from the divestiture of RCA's/NBC's Blue radio network in 1943, ABC was at a competitive disadvantage given NBC's and CBS's deep roots in radio broadcasting and their existing TV market dominance, with stations in the top markets around the country. ABC developed a strategy to counter-program its established rivals by scheduling genres that attracted broad, multigenerational audiences that were generally more rural and smaller-market than those catered to by CBS and NBC. Through the 1950s, ABC also established partnerships with Warner Bros. and Disney Studios to provide original family-friendly and action-oriented programming that would have immediate marquee value and advertiser appeal. By the 1960s, these strategies had grown ABC's audience numbers but kept the network's profits stagnant, with one exception: sports programming.[44]

In 1960, ABC signed its five-year contract with the American Football League. With the immediate influx of ABC's cash distributed evenly to each club in the league (often located in smaller markets such as Kansas City), the AFL was suddenly competitive with the NFL for player contracts and salaries. The AFL's economic threat led the NFL to consider a league merger which, effective in 1966, created a new NFL made up of the National Football Conference (NFC, the former

NFL teams) and the American Football Conference (AFC, the former AFL teams). ABC's initial risk in signing the upstart AFL thus paid off in institutional stability, consolidation, and growth for *both* entities. In the years between its coverage of AFL games and the launch of *Monday Night Football* (1970–2005, ABC; 2006–present, ESPN), ABC became the industry leader in sports as it developed expertise in Olympics coverage, weekly anthology programs such as *Wide World of Sports* (1961–1997) and *American Sportsman* (1964–1986), as well as college football and bowl game coverage. As discussed further in Chapter 2, largely due to *Monday Night Football*, ABC became the top network of the 1970s, adding new affiliates and bolstering its other program divisions to the point that it had 14 of the top-20 rated programs in prime time. By the early 1980s, as deregulation policies relaxed restrictions on ownership within the broader telecommunications industry, encouraging conglomeration, ABC had been absorbed. The new Capital Cities/ABC negotiated for the purchase of the Entertainment and Sports Network (ESPN, originally launched in 1979). By 1984, Capital Cities/ABC was a majority owner of ESPN with the Hearst Corporation. In 1995, the Walt Disney Company purchased Capital Cities/ABC. So, though considered one of the flagships of the multichannel era, it is important to note that ESPN has, for most of its history, been in and extended the lineage of the ABC "family."

Indeed, one of the defining characteristics of the multichannel era is how interwoven its media outlets and interests are—something that becomes even more concentrated in the streaming era. Initially, cable TV was used solely as a delivery system—a technologically stable way to enhance viewer access to existing broadcast signals. Cable extended signals of over-air stations to those remote areas that could not capture such signals reliably due to distance from orientation or geographic barriers. Soon, however, cable providers offered selections of "certain broadcast signals based on their popularity with subscribers," and developed original "programming types and programming strategies."[45] Where sports are concerned, the "multichannels" of the multichannel era—whether carried to homes through Multichannel Video Program Distributors (MVPDs) that are cable providers or direct broadcast satellite services—include six categories of channels: traditional over-air networks that carry sports programming (e.g., ABC, FOX); general programming cable channels that carry sports programming (e.g., USA, TNT); cable channels dedicated 24/7 to sports programming (e.g., ESPN, FS1); Superstations, or, satellite and cable-distributed stations that create a hybrid competitive threat as *both* a local broadcaster *and* a national network competitor (e.g., WTBS, WGN);[46] regional sports networks (RSNs),[47] or, cable outlets that carry the rights to telecast local sports teams (e.g., Fox Sports Midwest; Prime Sports); and, conference- or league-specific channels dedicated to promotion and coverage of single conferences or sports (e.g., Big 10 Network, NBA TV). Each of these outlets sells advertising time in its programming (in the broadcasting model) while also receiving subscriber fees from MVPDs that carry the channel's signal. Notably, RSNs and ESPN command the highest per-subscriber fee in the MVPD market.

Perhaps no multichannel TV era entity better represents the centrality of sports rights to institutional well-being and strategy than FOX. FOX network launched in 1986 largely due to deregulatory policies that allowed parent company FOX News Corp. to "own more media systems than ever,"[48] including newspapers, broadcast stations, cable networks, and a movie studio all in one corporate family. FOX staked its identity and institutional strength on three key strategies: building up its audience by targeting typically underserved television viewers (youth and African-American audiences, in particular); scheduling new programming during the otherwise rerun-ridden summer months; and successfully outbidding CBS for a portion of NFL broadcasts each season. Indeed, much like ABC in the 1960s and 1970s before it, FOX was able to become a full-fledged network (with original prime-time programming seven nights a week and affiliated stations in every market across the country) thanks to sports rights deals including its unprecedented $1.58 billion NFL package, negotiated in 1993 to begin with the 1994 season. FOX's overwhelming offer was possible because it *was* a nontraditional network. It did not have the Big Three networks' sports or news divisions with their expensive personnel or infrastructure. It did not offer a full, seven-nights-per-week prime-time programming schedule, and, thus, its series development costs were considerably lower. And, FOX had the relatively unlimited resources of Rupert Murdoch's News Corp. Thus, as an emergent network, FOX was characteristic of the multichannel transition, but it only flourished as a serious threat to traditional networks by capitalizing upon NFL football's familiarizing, "mass" network–era appeals. A major sports broadcast rights contract, iconic of the classic network era, was thus necessary for the multichannel era transition to truly begin.[49] From the 1990s to 2019, FOX aggressively challenged the sports dominance of Disney Co.'s ESPN, particularly via its FOX Sports Network (FS1 and FS2) and its expansive array of RSNs. However, in 2019, Disney purchased approximately half of FOX Corporation's holdings. Given that Disney already owned ESPN and all of its extensions, regulators required that the company shed the twenty-one RSNs that came with the FOX portfolio. These were purchased by Sinclair Broadcast Group. FOX's "slimmed-down holdings"[50] now include FOX News, FOX Sports Networks, the FOX broadcast network, and FOX's chain of broadcast TV stations. The "New FOX" is, thus, redefining itself by returning to "old," classic broadcast emphases, focusing on live TV, "big sports programming and news content."[51]

As Amanda D. Lotz has outlined, though internet-distributed or streaming TV "existed before 2010," that "year marks a significant turning point because of developments that made internet distribution technology more usable"[52] and enabled the push for "TV everywhere" with the introduction of tablet technology and rapid refinement in video-enabled smartphones. For Lotz, the "key distinction of internet-distributed television from that of broadcast or cable distribution is that it does not require time-specific viewing."[53] Sports TV clearly challenges this distinction, given the need to engage with sports during live game action. Where sports TV *has* been transformed in the streaming era is by being ideal content for the new "norm of the fluid movement of 'television' among an array of screens, including those previously conceived as foremost for 'computing.' "[54] Regardless of the delivery platform or reception device, *content* remains crucial and, arguably, in an era of proliferation and increasing clutter, sports remains content that is uniquely familiar, dependable, and actively sought out. It is consumable in quick "snacks" of highlights that are meme-worthy and sharable across social media.[55] It can also sustain days of viewing on "traditional" TV (e.g., the annual Tour de France on NBCSN). Or, it can be binged (as in the 2020 ESPN and Netflix Michael Jordan documentary, *The Last Dance*). Sports content is, thus, exceptionally malleable and consumable across platforms. This helps to explain why, in the contemporary era, industrial control over the distribution routes through which sports content can be streamed has been a high-stakes battleground.

In 2009, when Comcast purchased a majority percentage of NBCUniversal, it became "the first cable operator to take over a major film studio, a broadcast network, and a host of successful cable channels."[56] As Susan Crawford notes, while Comcast's core business is "carrying digital communications through a wire," the "merged company would control one in five hours of all television viewing in the United States."[57] Significantly, following the Telecommunications Act of 1996, Comcast

> leveraged its majority interest in the NHL's Philadelphia Flyers, the NBA's Philadelphia 76ers, and Philadelphia's major sports arena into a twenty-four-hour regional channel called SportsNet Philadelphia. Within a few years, Comcast owned exclusive rights in broadcasts by teams and regional sports networks from coast to coast. . . . If there was a guiding ethos to Comcast's pursuit of NBCUniversal, it was to gain control over more sports programming. Live sports is the one thing that people can get almost nowhere else.[58]

As a content producer and distribution service, Comcast's power is immense, particularly in negotiations for channel carriage. As more sports programming has moved to sports-specific RSNs or league-owned networks, distributors "hold the upper hand."[59] Former sports producer Dennis Deninger points to the example of the

MLB Network, here. Prior to its 2009 launch, MLB offered Comcast, DirecTV, Time Warner Cable, and Cox Communications a one-third share (combined) of the network, which "guaranteed that the MLB Network would be seen in more homes on its first day . . . than the NFL Network, which had been on the air for five years."[60] Fundamentally, as Crawford observes, "If the twentieth-century paradigm was sports driving television—people buying televisions in order to watch sports for free—the twenty-first century paradigm is sports working with pay television to charge subscribers."[61]

From the Provinces to Center Ice

Within the US, television rights and media conglomeration have transformed the National Hockey League from a "provincial" minor sport to a major sports *and* media institution.[62] The NHL in the US continues to depend on the local television market for its broadcast bread-and-butter. However, the league's multichannel-era growth and streaming extensions are a model example of a *sport's* transformation by television and through television rights. Though in existence since 1917, the "modern" NHL era began in 1942 with the "Original Six" teams of Boston, Chicago, Detroit, New York, Montreal, and Toronto. The League kept this configuration until 1967, when it undertook an ambitious expansion that doubled its size and located teams in the Midwest and West as well as the Northeast. A series of regular expansions took place throughout the 1970s, including the absorption of four teams from the World Hockey Association. In the 1990s, the League expanded into "nontraditional" hockey markets in the US South and West, including Nashville, Tampa Bay, and Arizona. Currently, the League consists of 32 teams, with the most recent additions of the Las Vegas Golden Knights (2017) and the Seattle Kraken (2021).

Though NBC and CBS had sporadically telecast hockey prior to the late 1960s, US networks were generally reluctant to enter into league-wide deals with the NHL prior to the 1967–1968 season, when it grew to 12 teams and included markets across the country. Beginning with that expansion season, CBS agreed to a three-year package of weekend afternoon games with sponsors including United Airlines, Hamm's Brewing, and All State Insurance. NHL coverage moved to NBC from 1970–1975 in a package that also focused on weekend afternoon games. Though league teams did well with local over-air broadcaster telecasts, national networks complained that hockey appealed to a small audience and that the game itself was difficult to watch and understand on TV.[63]

The multichannel era brought new life to the NHL on TV. ESPN and USA engaged in bidding wars over the sport through the early 1980s. For both, securing exclusive NHL rights was perceived to be more symbolically important than economically sound: Having a national major-league sports broadcast franchise in house was understood to be a loss-leader, paving the way to larger events and other league deals. USA network also offered the NHL prime-time game exposure with Monday and Thursday regular-season games and a commitment to telecast the league's All-Star game. In 1988, the NHL broke away from broadcast network and basic cable deals to instead sign with regional sports network SportsChannel. In this same season, Wayne Gretzky became perhaps the first widely known hockey household name in the US, after he was traded from the Edmonton Oilers to the Los Angeles Kings. Between Gretzky's stardom and the league's rapid 1990s expansion into far-flung new markets, ESPN returned to the bidding fray. But, just one year after its shocking NFL coup, FOX offered a staggering five-year, $150 million deal for NHL games. According to *Variety*,

> Murdoch's acquisition of hockey is further evidence the FOX supremo is determined to be a player in the bidding rights for every major sport. But whether FOX affils. will be willing to give up three hours on weekend for a sport that gets lousy ratings is another matter.[64]

Indeed, FOX neglected to renew its deal with the NHL when the term concluded. However, professional hockey's TV fortunes were transformed once again in the streaming era.

Figure 1.2   NBC Sports' Regional Sports Network "Family"

As *New York Times* media business reporter Richard Sandomir observed in 2005, Comcast's "widening sports ambitions" included both the acquisition of NHL game telecasts and an ownership share in NHL Network (which first went on air in October of 2007). With NBC as its partner, Comcast's Versus (formerly Outdoor Life, then OLN, and now NBC Sports) secured a 10-year, $1.90 billion NHL deal in 2011. According to reports, the price "reflected the league's attractiveness to young males" and "an 84 percent increase in national ratings"[65] over the past four seasons, which had seen big boosts in viewership for the All-Star game and the New Year's Day outdoor Winter Classic matchup. As owner of the Philadelphia Flyers since 1996 (assuming full, 100% ownership in 2016), Comcast thus clearly has a stake in the success of the NHL from the bottom up. Media company ownership of sports teams is certainly nothing new. Just a few examples include CBS's controlling interest in the New York Yankees from 1964–1973; FOX Corp.'s ownership of the Los Angeles Dodgers from 1997–2004; Time Warner's ownership of the Atlanta Braves and Atlanta Hawks from 1996–2007; and, perhaps most notoriously, "Disney decided to pay $50 million for the NHL expansion [Anaheim] team after its first Mighty Ducks movie made $49.7 million in theaters. 'That was really all the marketing research we needed to know,' said a Disney sports executive."[66] In the current TV context, however, the blurring of league, team, and media-conglomerate interests has visibly challenged the foundational myths that historically had burnished sports' civic profile and, at least rhetorically, prioritized equitable public access, for free.

"Deprived of That Cohesive Force"

As early as 1974, television scholar Horace Newcomb suggested that TV had dislodged the connections between sports teams and their geographic homes:

> With television the regional or local identity of teams is destroyed. The man sitting in Arlington, Texas can watch and enjoy the success of the Los Angeles Dodgers with the same degree of interest as the man sitting in Brooklyn.[67]

Indeed, though *within* local markets access to local teams on "free TV" outlets was historically prioritized, national network contracts for league-wide telecasts have always allowed sports fans to "migrate" their emotional investments. Ted Turner's Superstation WTBS delivered Atlanta Braves games across the country through the 1980s and much of the 1990s, creating fans of the team far from the Southeast. Jerry Jones, owner of the Dallas Cowboys, has ritually insisted that his club—frequently featured in NFL game-of-the-week telecasts—is "America's Team." Premium digital sports bundles from cable providers and out-of-market league subscription packages like MLB Extra

Innings or NHL Center Ice allow access to regional coverage far from the viewer's actual location. As discussed further in Chapter 5, it is important to note that while such outlets may cultivate new fans with no connection to the place and teams featured, they also meaningfully allow fans who are *displaced* from home to remain connected to that community.

In the last several years, however, there has been an increase in rights deals made by individual teams directly with cable providers that effectively eliminate hometown access to local club games *within* their own market. Los Angeles, Chicago, and New York have each recently seen swaths of their cities and broader market areas unable to view Dodgers, Cubs, and Yankees games, respectively. According to a *Los Angeles Times* report:

> To some executives no company offers a more egregious example of how the value of sports has spiraled out of control than Time Warner Cable. In 2013 the cable company now owned by Charter Communications, Inc. agreed to pay an average of $334 million a year to broadcast Dodger games on its cable channel, SportsNet LA. . . . To cover the cost, Time Warner Cable initially charged almost $5 a month per subscriber, making it one of the most expensive in the bundle. Five years later, no other major TV provider in Los Angeles carries the Dodgers channel because of the steep price.[68]

Charter—now Spectrum—is available to roughly 40% of Los Angeles TV homes, leaving the majority of local Dodger fans with no way to watch the team in their own backyard. This was particularly offensive to Dodger fans when iconic announcer, Vin Scully, entered his final season without any additional providers agreeing to carry SportsNet LA. Said Congressman Brad Sherman, "Hearing Scully's soothing play-by-play announcing 'is important and it helps to pull our community together. . . . We as a community are deprived of that cohesive force.' "[69]

Indeed, sports is not a "traditional business." Writing in 2012, Brett Hutchins and David Rowe presciently proposed that "citizen access to popular sport is set to become a political issue over the next decade."[70] As sports rights costs escalate at the same time that TV depends on subscription and retransmission fees for such rights, *public* access to the civic "good" and source of cohesion provided through sports has increasingly migrated behind paywalls. Though freighted with myth, the ideal of sports as a site of local identification and shared, democratic community, accessed for free, offers an emotionally resonant everyday example of the continued, felt value of free TV as a public good. It is fair to ask, if sports become increasingly inaccessible, "what *are* the networked media services, content, and standards that citizens rightfully can expect to access and experience free of charge?"[71] Though recent battles over access to local teams have been particularly fraught, from the inception of radio through television's historical transformations, it is clear that conceiving sports to be a public good has effectively conferred "trusteeship" powers to its leagues and media rights holders. Though sports rights constitute the largest profit-stream in media culture, the perception that sports are civic assets, *separate* from the market, remains powerful and has real economic and social impact. Chapters 4 and 5 more closely examine the ways in which sports TV is a site of both contested and cohesive community. First, however, Chapters 2 and 3 analyze the texts and formal properties of sports TV that construct its distinctive voice and cultural resonance.

Notes

1. Robert W. McChesney, "Media Made Sport," in *Media, Sports & Society*, ed. Lawrence A. Wenner (Newbury Park, CA: Sage Publications, 1989), 49.
2. Robert W. McChesney, *The Political Economy of Media: Enduring Issues, Emerging Dilemmas* (New York: Monthly Review Press, 2008), 219.
3. Christopher Anderson and Michael Curtin, "Mapping the Ethereal City: Chicago Television, the FCC, and the Politics of Place," *Quarterly Review of Film and Video* 16, nos. 3–4 (1997): 289.
4. Mark Williams, "Issue Introduction: US Regional and Non-Network Television History," *Quarterly Review of Film and Video* 16, nos. 3–4 (1997): 222.
5. Susan Crawford, *Captive Audience: The Telecom Industry and Monopoly Power in the New Gilded Age* (New Haven, CT: Yale University Press, 2013), 141.

6. "North American Sports Market Outlook," *Sports Business Journal*, November 4–10, 2019, 7.

7. Christina Gough, "Sports on US TV-Statistics & Facts," *Statista*, July 28, 2020, www.statista.com

8. Dennis Deninger, *Sports on Television: The How and Why Behind What You See* (New York: Routledge, 2012), 2.

9. Sut Jhally, "Cultural Studies and the Sports/Media Complex," in *Media, Sports & Society*, ed. Lawrence A. Wenner (Newbury Park, CA: Sage Publications, 1989), 73.

10. Abraham Madkour, "The Education of Hawks Owner Tony Ressler," *Sports Business Journal*, October 7–13, 2019, 4.

11. Arthur T. Johnson and James H. Frey, "Introduction," in *Government and Sport: The Public Policy Issues*, eds. Arthur T. Johnson and James H. Frey (Totowa, NJ: Rowan & Allanheld, 1985), 2.

12. Arthur T. Johnson and James H. Frey, "Conclusion: Sports, Regulation, and the Public Interest," in *Government and Sport: The Public Policy Issues*, eds. Arthur T. Johnson and James H. Frey (Totowa, NJ: Rowan & Allanheld, 1985), 262.

13. *Sports TV* follows the understanding of historical "eras" of US broadcast history outlined in Aniko Bodroghkozy, ed., *A Companion to the History of American Broadcasting* (Hoboken, NJ: John Wiley & Sons, 2018).

14. Allison Perlman, *Public Interests: Media Advocacy and Struggles Over US Television* (New Brunswick, NJ: Rutgers University Press, 2016), 7.

15. David G. Surdam, *The Big Leagues Go to Washington: Congress and Sports Antitrust, 1951–1989* (Urbana, IL: University of Illinois Press, 2015), 1.

16. Lacie L. Kaiser, "Revisiting the Sports Broadcasting Act of 1961: A Call for Equitable Antitrust Immunity from Section One of the Sherman Act for All Professional Sports Leagues," *DePaul Law Review* 54 (2005): 1240.

17. *Federal Baseball Club of Baltimore, Inc. v. National League of Professional Baseball Clubs, et al.* 259 US 200 (1922).

18. *Federal Baseball Club.*

19. Surdam, *The Big Leagues Go to Washington*, 13.

20. Surdam, 13.

21. Perlman, *Public Interests*, 3.

22. Victoria E. Johnson, "Historicizing TV Networking: Broadcasting, Cable, and the Case of ESPN," in *Media Industries: History, Theory, and Method*, eds. Jennifer Holt and Alisa Perren (Malden, MA: John Wiley & Sons, Ltd., 2009), 58.

23. Jennifer Holt, "A History of Broadcast Regulations and Perspectives," in *A Companion to the History of American Broadcasting*, ed. Aniko Bodroghkozy (Hoboken, NJ: John Wiley & Sons, Inc., 2018), 176.

24. The ascertainment requirement was eliminated for radio in 1981 and for television in 1984.

25. Federal Communications Commission, "The 1960 Programming Policy Statement," in *Documents of American Broadcasting*, ed. Frank J. Kahn (Englewood Cliffs, NJ: Prentice-Hall, 1984), 191–204.

26. Kaiser, "Revisiting the Sports Broadcasting Act of 1961," 1243. Significantly, here, while Major League Baseball, the National Basketball Association, and the

National Hockey League franchises receive a share of league-wide proprietary rights deals with national networks, each of these league's teams still control their own local and regional television rights. The NFL is the only league to control all team broadcast rights and to do so only on national network platforms (with Sunday day-game telecasts on a regional basis; Thursday night, Sunday night, and Monday night games on a national basis). For detailed overviews of the history of professional basketball TV rights deals and professional baseball's TV rights history, see, respectively: Timothy Piper, "Transition Game: Television and the National Basketball Association During the Multichannel Shift, 1970–1974." (Ph.D. dissertation, University of Texas, Austin, 2020); and Stuart Shea, *Calling the Game: Baseball Broadcasting from 1920 to the Present* (Phoenix, AZ: Society for American Baseball Research, Inc., 2015). And, for a clear description of the NFL's remarkably byzantine rules for its telecasts, see Jon Kraszewski, "Pittsburgh in Fort Worth: Football Bars, Sports Television, Sports Fandom, and the Management of Home," *Journal of Sport and Social Issues* 32, no. 2 (May 2008): 125.

27. Surdam, *The Big Leagues Go to Washington*, 179.

28. "Telecasting of Professional Sports Contests," *Hearing on H.R. 8757 Before the Committee on The Judiciary*, 87th Cong. (1961) (statement of Pete Rozelle, Commissioner of the National Football League).

29. "Telecasting of Professional Sports Contests" (statement of Pete Rozelle).

30. "Telecasting of Professional Sports Contests" (statement submitted by Representative John W. Byrnes).

31. "Telecasting of Professional Sports Contests" (statement submitted by Representative John W. Byrnes).

32. "Telecasting of Professional Sports Contests" (remarks of Honorable Edward V. Long, Missouri).

33. "Telecasting of Professional Sports Contests" (remarks of Honorable Edward V. Long, Missouri).

34. Victoria E. Johnson, "'Monday Night Football': Brand Identity," in *How to Watch Television*, eds. Ethan Thompson and Jason Mittell (New York: New York University Press, 2013), 262–270.

35. These included the New Orleans Saints and the Cincinnati Bengals.

36. Kaiser, "Revisiting the Sports Broadcasting Act of 1961," 1255.

37. Notably, as a broadcast and cable-era precursor to this and a challenge to the image of the league and its network partners as public trustees: From the NFL's inception until 2015, the league had restrictive "blackout" rules that kept many local fans unable to view home team games (at least, within a 75-mile radius of the home stadium). Under pressure from President Nixon, legislators, and countless fans, the league instated a sellout rule in the 1970s that allowed for any game sold out 72 hours in advance of kickoff to air on TV. The league maintained that this encouraged stadium attendance and protected gate receipts but, in practice, local sponsors and businesses tended to buy out unsold seats to guarantee local TV coverage of home as well as away games. Effectively, by the 1990s, almost no team's games were ever blacked out. Beginning in 2014, league owners vote on an annual basis to keep the blackout suspension in place.

38. Surdam, *The Big Leagues Go to Washington*, 188.
39. Surdam, quoting Thomas Kauper, Assistant Attorney General for the Antitrust Division of the Justice Department, 189.
40. Bodroghkozy, *A Companion to the History of American Broadcasting*.
41. For exceptional histories of the multichannel era phenomena of ESPN and of the Superstation, see Travis Vogan, *ESPN: The Making of a Sports Media Empire* (Urbana, IL: University of Illinois Press, 2015); and, Jennifer Holt, *Empires of Entertainment: Media Industries and the Politics of Deregulation, 1980–1996* (New Brunswick, NJ: Rutgers University Press, 2011).
42. "Networking" describes the transmission of programs from a single distribution point to multiple points of reception. "Broadcasting" describes the process by which this method of transmission occurs over the air.
43. McChesney, "Media Made Sport," 62.
44. See my extended discussion of ABC history and the network's sports programming in, Johnson, "'Monday Night Football': Brand Identity."
45. Megan Mullen, *The Rise of Cable Programming in the United States: Revolution or Evolution?* (Austin: University of Texas Press, 2003), 35.
46. By the beginning of the streaming era, the Superstations no longer provided local programming and had migrated to fully national content.
47. Notably, major RSNs predate the multichannel era, with providers such as MSG Network having launched in 1969 on cable providers in the "urban canyons" of the New York and greater New York City market.
48. Bambi Haggins and Julia Himberg, "The Multi-Channel Transition Period: 1980s–1990s," in *A Companion to the History of American Broadcasting*, ed. Aniko Bodroghkozy (Hoboken, NJ: John Wiley & Sons, Inc., 2018), 116.
49. Victoria E. Johnson, "Everything New Is Old Again: Sport Television, Innovation, and Tradition for a Multi-Platform Era," in *Beyond Prime Time: Television Programming in the Post-Network Era*, ed. Amanda D. Lotz (New York: Routledge, 2009), 114–137.
50. Meg James, "Sinclair to Buy Disney Sports Outlets," *The Los Angeles Times*, May 4, 2019, C3.
51. Wayne Friedman, "New Fox Bets Big on Sports Programming," *Television News Daily*, January 9, 2019, www.mediapost.com
52. Amanda D. Lotz, *Portals: A Treatise on Internet-Distributed Television* (Ann Arbor: Michigan Publishing, 2017), http://dx.doi.org/ID.3998/mpub.9699689
53. Lotz, *Portals*.
54. Lotz.
55. On "snackable" media and sports content, see Ethan Tussey, *The Procrastination Economy: The Big Business of Downtime* (New York: New York University Press, 2018).
56. The merger was officially finalized in January 2011. Holt, *Empires of Entertainment*, 171.
57. Crawford, *Captive Audience*, 3, 5.
58. Crawford, 82, 141.
59. Deninger, *Sports on Television*, 180.
60. Deninger, 180.

61. Crawford, *Captive Audience*, 150.
62. Always the dominant national sport of Canada and made up of teams from both Canada and the US, the NHL was, for decades, the only truly international team sport in the US.
63. This visibility dilemma is addressed in Chapter 2's history and analysis of FOX's 1990s "glow puck" graphic technology.
64. Jim Benson, "FOX Strikes Again With Purchase of Hockey Rights," *Variety*, September 12, 1994, 25.
65. Richard Sandomir, "Networks Secure Deal with N.H.L.," *The New York Times*, April 20, 2011, B14.
66. Mike Jensen, "Disney's Mighty Bucks," *The Philadelphia Inquirer*, April 29, 1997, D1. Disney also owned the Anaheim Angels baseball team from 1996–2003. Disney sold the Ducks in 2005.
67. Horace Newcomb, *TV: The Most Popular Art* (New York: Anchor Books, 1974), 195.
68. Gerry Smith, "A Cable Bundle Whodunit: Blame Netflix, Disney, and the Dodgers for Creating a Perfect Climate for Cutting the Cord," *The Los Angeles Times*, August 20, 2018, A8.
69. Matt Krupnick, "How TV Rights Have Made the Dodgers the Greatest Team Never Seen," *The Guardian*, January 19, 2016.
70. Brett Hutchins and David Rowe, *Sport Beyond Television: The Internet, Digital Media and the Rise of Networked Media Sport* (New York: Routledge, 2012), 182.
71. Emphasis by author. Hutchins and Rowe, *Sport Beyond Television*, 182.

2

SPORTVISION

The Texts and Tech of Sports TV

In the earliest years of television sports coverage, baseball Commissioner Ford Frick proclaimed, "The view a fan gets at home should be worse than that of the fan in the worst seat in the stadium."[1] Through the 1950s, most TV coverage of any sport was generally static, as if watching from a center seat, mid-way between the field, track, floor, rink, or ring and the top of any given grandstand or arena. It was not until the late 1960s and early 1970s that TV coverage of live sporting events adopted the conventions with which viewers are still familiar today. These conventions coalesced in the work of Roone Arledge, creator of ABC's *Wide World of Sports* (1961–1998) and *Monday Night Football* (ABC, 1970–2005; ESPN, 2005–present).[2] Diametrically opposed to Frick, Arledge believed that "what television ought to be striving for was to give the fan the best seat in the house."[3] "What if I could have *any* seat," Arledge asked, "What would I want to see?"[4] In a memo pitching ABC's approach to NCAA football coverage, Arledge thus outlined a newly immersive approach to sports TV: "Heretofore, television has done a remarkable job of bringing the game to the viewer—now we are going to take the viewer to the game!"[5]

Arledge believed sports telecasts should be a successful hybrid of popular entertainment genres and news programming. Also central to Arledge's concept was that game coverage would purposefully "gain and hold the interest of women and others who are not fanatic followers of the sport we happen to be televising."[6] His key insight was that, unlike any other TV genre, sports programming defied "television's favored binary split between entertainment and information"[7] by explicitly combining the best elements of both drama and history, intimacy and newsworthiness. Indeed, Arledge envisioned game coverage to be both larger than life, in cinematic terms, *and* to be the ideal subject matter for television's ability to reach people in the most intimate ways, literally where they *lived*. Writes Arledge, "Sports were life condensed, all its drama, struggle, heartbreak, and triumph embodied in artificial

Figure 2.1 Roone Arledge, creator of the "Arledge aesthetic"
Source: ABC TV / Photofest © ABC

contests. . . . I wanted to make the game more intimate, and a lot more human."[8] Sports TV's uniqueness and power as a genre is largely based on its balance of "scientific," statistical, and technological appeals to "truth" *with* "up close and personal" stories and ineffable images of grace in motion. The most advanced technological view illuminates the action within the rules of the game while dramatic storylines connect with mythologies beyond the arena of play.[9]

What follows analyzes sports TV's ongoing attempt to balance these competing ideals in formal terms by focusing on live sports coverage. When sports TV is criticized for "failing," it is generally because coverage "erred" too much on one side of this balance. Such criticism often occurs when a visual technology is perceived as too interventionist, detracting from the game itself. While the formal properties or aesthetics of sports TV are too vast to analyze comprehensively, this chapter focuses on a few critical building blocks of sports TV's formal grammar that forged the conventions of sports coverage and remain foundational in the present. First, in the example of the classic broadcast network era's *Monday Night Football*, are slow motion, instant replay, and split-screen, with continuity and narrative conventions familiar from classical Hollywood cinema. Next is an analysis of FOX network's FOX Trax "glow puck" and 1st & Ten Line video overlay technologies, characteristic of the multichannel network era and integral to the contemporary development of "videogamegraphic" aesthetics that share conventions common to EA Sports gaming—exemplified here by the Professional Golfers' Association (PGA's) use of TopTracer ball-tracking graphics.

Aesthetic transformations in television do not happen in isolation. They are part of a larger historical, industrial, and social dialogue and context. Shifts in the look and address of sports TV often take place in periods of industrial and economic transition that involve new audience cultivation strategies. The most successful aesthetic transitions generally demonstrate innovation *within* tradition, enabling a "better view" and enhanced viewer knowledge while maintaining emotional engagement with sports' "human element." In the examples that follow, ABC went from having always been the last place network of the Big Three to holding first place through the 1970s by premiering Monday night, prime-time football coverage that created an enhanced experience for traditional football fans while also cultivating entirely new audiences through Arledge's hybrid appeals. FOX network's emergence at the vanguard of the multichannel era was staked largely on sports rights and the development of new youth audiences at the same moment that onscreen graphics exploded in a "self-conscious performance of style"[10] definitive of 1980s and 1990s TV. As the new rights' holder for the NHL, contemporaneous with the league's expansion into nontraditional hockey markets in the South and West, FOX startled purists with its "glow puck" graphic technology. That same "failure," however, helped establish the network's risk-taking, edgy brand template that continues to this day (and established the technology for successes such as the 1st & Ten Line). Finally, in the 2010s, the streaming era's advanced graphic overlay and volumetric video aesthetics, familiar from videogaming, have led some of the most traditional sports in US culture to generate new energy and buzz by gamifying onscreen action across TV, tablet, computer, and phone alike.

Beyond formal innovations, the examples here allow analysis of the ways in which sports TV aesthetics encourage particular "ways of seeing." What follows incorporates rare examples of TV studies scholarship that closely analyze the *texts* of sports TV. As addressed at some length in the Introduction, such work is rare given that the emerging, humanities-based TV studies of the 1980s largely turned its attention away from nonfiction programming and even analysis of programming itself. Featured, here, are Meghan Morse's early, foundational "Sport on Television: Replay and Display" (1983), which examines the "gaze" of sports TV within the broader "social imaginary"; John Caldwell's *Televisuality: Style, Crisis, and Authority in American Television* (1995), which theorizes "televisuality" as an industrial, programming, and audience phenomenon of the multichannel era; and recent scholarship on digital sports media, including Thomas Oates's work on videogamegraphic aesthetics. Such scholarship considers TV studies methodology to include critical analysis of the formal properties of TV texts (ads, programming, promotional discourses, and TV's "flow" across these texts) as they are created and work in *dialogue* with industrial practices, within particular contexts of reception.

Replay and Display: The Arledge Aesthetic of the Classic Network Era

Because the conventions Arledge and his production staff created for prime-time sports coverage remain so deeply ingrained as *the* way to watch games on TV, it is hard to understand the excitement that greeted *Monday Night Football* (hereafter, *MNF*) at its September 21, 1970 premiere, which featured a matchup between the New York Jets and the Cleveland Browns, at Cleveland Municipal Stadium.[11] Reviews of the premiere praise the series' high production values and striking visuals, its heightened intimacy and humanness in coverage of players' stories, its "honesty," accuracy, and expertise as regards commentary and play-by-play, and its overall "maturity" while delivering "a solid three hours of pleasure."[12] Indeed, reviewers associate *MNF*'s success with journalistic ideals of objectivity and accuracy *and* with entertainment value typically associated with popular, fictional TV series programs or Hollywood movies. *MNF*'s expert balance between news and "Hollywood" each week informed its status as a genuine cultural phenomenon.[13] *MNF* benefited, of course, by being the "only game in town" on Monday nights during football season, with NBC programming a movie of the week and CBS offering variety, comedy, and drama programming during most of these same years.[14] However, the program's success was due to its transformation of in-game sports TV coverage, combining new "truth"-telling technology with classical Hollywood film conventions. "Scientific" techniques such as slow motion and instant replay allowed viewers to see previously unseen elements of game play in an analytical, even juridical way. Principles of continuity framing, editing, and narrative elements focusing on individual "protagonists" kept viewers oriented within the action while creating relatable story arcs to follow. These "scientific" and "human" discourses were smoothly and often humorously integrated through the savvy play-by-play and color commentary of the carefully cast announcing crew.

MNF's observation of continuity practice and clear orientation of the viewer in space begins with each week's location. Although it was not until the mid-1970s that more American households had color TV than black-and-white receivers, sports broadcasts had long been shot in color, and *MNF* exploited the visual pop and glamour of nighttime stadium photography's heightened contrasts and what Susan Murray has identified as, rhetorically, "a consistent assertion made about" color TV's "dimensionality and the way that it invited viewers to completely immerse themselves in the image," promising an "intimate level of visual proximity."[15] In the Jets-Browns matchup, announcer Howard Cosell notes "the real grass" of Municipal Stadium which is a deep green, in contrast to the Jets' road green-and-white jerseys and the Browns' home white-and-brown uniforms. In the first season of *MNF*, only seventeen of the league's then-26 teams had stadiums equipped for night photography, which led most of the prime-time games to feature coastal teams. Pregame photography took advantage of this, allowing the sport's fans from all over the country to "travel" to major markets and visit cities such as Los Angeles, San Diego, and New York, among others, reveling in exterior, aerial footage of the stadium and its surrounding neighborhoods as well as getting up-close views of unique interior features and fans in the stands.

From establishing location with an overview of the stadium exterior, *MNF* observes the 180-degree rule when exploring the stadium's interior, the view from the sidelines, on-field, and from the booth. If switching from one side of the field to the other, the viewer maintains directional continuity—e.g., the Jets' bench is shot from right facing left toward the field while the Browns' bench is shot from left facing right toward the field. The viewer's eyes remain on the same 180-degree line, facing the field, with game action moving from side to side, left to right, and right to left. On kickoffs, the camera is placed behind the kicker, but quickly moves back to the "correct" side of the field as the ball is received and run back. This clear orientation in space is maintained when slow motion and/or instant replay are used.

Though instant replay is shot from multiple perspectives and the angle of replay analysis changes slightly, player direction remains stable, so that viewers are not disoriented regarding progression of the action and movement of the ball. When framing the on-field action, between plays, the frame widens out to include both huddles on either side of the line of scrimmage. During plays, overhead and medium long shots capture the game action by focusing on the travel of the ball. Medium close-ups are used on the sidelines to bring the viewer into the team's circle.

For in-game action, *MNF* distinguished itself by having two production units. The first unit featured five cameras located around the field to be focused on game coverage. The second unit featured additional cameras dedicated to slow motion, instant replay, and graphics. In all, director Chet Forte had nine cameras to coordinate, increasing coverage from the five or six that had typically been used for game production.[16] Arledge's strategy was to meld the capabilities of each unit together to create a coherent "story" for each game. Pregame interviews on the sideline would feature a particular player or players who would be identified as that game's "star" in accessible terms, introducing a narrative for viewers to follow across the game. As the game progressed, the technological "gizmos" would be used to amplify the "human" story. As Arledge explained:

> We also set out to make our stars familiar to our viewers. When, say, wide receiver Don Maynard of the New York Titans caught a pass, his name, position, and stats would appear immediately on the screen, followed, later on, by replays of other catches he'd made, either earlier in the game or the previous week—all of which became standard practice in football coverage.[17]

With mobile cameras, Arledge sought to "get the impact shots that we cannot get from fixed camera" such as "a coach's face as a man drops a pass in the clear,"[18] contributing additional depth to larger player narrative arcs through reaction shots.

The premiere of *MNF* opens with a sideline interview by Cosell with Jets' quarterback Joe Namath, who was, by that time, a household name beyond the game of football with a brash, if endearing, star persona. However, as the game became somewhat lopsided in the Browns' favor, the "protagonist" focus nimbly shifts to feature Browns players, wide receiver Gary Collins and tight end Milt Morin. Other "up close and personal" interludes throughout the game include mobile cameras roving on each team's respective sideline, with live microphones picking up snippets of player conversations and cheers for their teammates. Shots of the crowd contribute an added dimension of space and energy for the audience viewing from home and enhance the specificity of the game's setting, with the Cleveland fight song played in the stadium after each score and ambient sounds from the stands underscoring homefield advantage, throughout.

MNF thus revels in its technological capabilities while keeping viewer orientation and story at the center of the coverage. When introducing the night's game to the TV audience, Cosell stands on-field while play-by-play announcer Keith Jackson is above the field in the booth. These spaces are brought together, however, as Cosell and Jackson occupy a split-screen with Cosell on the left looking to his left, in profile, while Jackson looks to his right from the right side of the screen, in profile, in conversation with one another. A wipe from left to right returns Cosell to full-screen to introduce color-commentator Don Meredith's highlight reel from his playing days with the Dallas Cowboys. Following the clip, Cosell and Meredith now occupy the split-screen, with Cosell still framed on the left as Meredith now occupies the right, each directly addressing the camera and home viewer, while conversing with one another. Throughout the game, instant replay is used judiciously to enable visibility of close calls on penalties, pass completions, or scoring plays. Each replay is narrated by Meredith, the former player, whose expertise gives additional weight to what the viewer is, now, able to see. Meredith comments on the aesthetics of the game revealed in slow motion, noting, for example, that an offensive maneuver is a "beautifully moved, beautifully executed play" or singling out a particularly tough effort by noting the player is a "hard-nosed young fella," or, excitedly, "ain't nobody gonna catch Homer now!" Meredith's "down home" folksiness and colloquialisms intentionally contrasted with Cosell's loquaciousness and acerbic wit as commentators and interviewers, with Jackson remaining the straight-forward play-by-play announcer.

Cosell, Jackson, and Meredith in the premiere and, later, Cosell, Meredith, and Frank Gifford[19] also brought a novel, national, prime-time perspective to each week's calls. While many audiences were used to regional or home-market announcers who were often loathe to critique what they saw on the field, reviewers praised "ABC's radical idea . . . to call the game as the announcers see it, with no sugar-coating—just plain, honest, objective reporting."[20] Judicious utilization of technology supported this endeavor. According to Max Nichols of the *Minneapolis Star*, for example:

> A major step toward maturity has developed with the American Broadcasting Company's style and technical work on Monday night pro football games. . . . I like it when telecasters Don Meredith, Howard Cosell and Keith Jackson point out mistakes as well as wondrous deeds. . . . Slow motion, stop action and split screen techniques give telecasters a better chance to be accurate in criticizing or pointing out errors.[21]

During halftime, Cosell narrated highlights from the top games of the previous day, as provided by NFL Films, the league's production subsidiary. Arledge's storytelling technique—established with NCAA football coverage and *Wide World of Sports* prior to *MNF*—created a framework for storytelling in sports documentary and highlight films that are visible in NFL Films' early work. *MNF* and its successors benefited, however, from other formal strategies developed by NFL Films (such as its iconic "tight on the spiral" technique for capturing a pass, floating in the air or its use of low angles to emphasize player heroism and its "mic'd up" sideline glimpses of player interactions).[22] While the weekly highlights fit with the "journalistic," "news" elements of the telecast, the narrative and anecdotal elements added by Cosell also allied them with a romanticized vision of the game that "transform[ed] pro football games into artful and immersive cinematic experiences."[23]

A critical element of this transformation of football for ABC and the NFL was *MNF*'s ability to draw new viewers to the sport—particularly female audiences. Cosell promoted *MNF*'s appeal to women by pitching its enlightened approach to the sport, implying that female viewers would have more discriminating tastes and expectations than the typical male sports fan. In an interview with the *Washington Post*, Cosell states:

> We're going to make certain that our telecasts appeal to women. . . . First, we're adding something new. It's called humor. . . . We'll treat the game as a game. Second, we're going to have journalism rather than shill-ism. . . . And, finally, we'll bring some literacy and erudition to football. . . . We have to be good. We're competing in prime time, against movies and Carol Burnett and Doris Day.[24]

Taking a lower road, the *Los Angeles Herald Examiner* reported on league Commissioner Pete Rozelle's stated investment in drawing female audiences by acknowledging male objectification to be a compelling appeal:

> Rozelle analyzes the Sunday TV football audience as predominantly male and automatically booked. He thinks of Monday as an opportunity for family penetration and the recruitment of new fans, mainly the female of the species. Rozelle is strong for women's liberation. He wants to liberate the girls to appreciate the beauties of pro football.[25]

Indeed, sports TV coverage at-large, but particularly football coverage, encourages a gaze that is both analytic and contemplative. As Thomas Oates observes, "football sanctions kinds of behaviors between men that, in other spaces, would likely be coded as erotic"[26] and is perhaps US culture's most prominent site wherein the male body is featured as an *object* of the gaze. As addressed further in Chapters 3 and 4, theories of the gaze—or the look of the viewer upon the onscreen action, the look of the camera(s) photographing that action, and the look of the participants in the onscreen action towards one another—have been further complicated in the multichannel and streaming eras. In 1983, Margaret Morse conducted the first and only TV studies–based close, formal analysis of this unique characteristic of televised sports—that "the discourse of sport takes the male body as the object of the gaze in a society which has a strong cultural inhibition against the look at the male body."[27]

In "Sport On Television: Replay and Display," Morse proposes that, in a heterosexist, male-dominant culture, there is a prohibition of male viewers' open contemplation of the male form in erotic terms. Given this prohibition, the gaze upon the objectified male body—as an object of grace and beauty—is allowable only by allying this look with *scientific* discourses. Doing so assures that the gaze upon the male form conforms to and actually reinforces conventional cultural associations of reason, logical inquiry, distance, and objectivity with cis-gendered, heteronormative masculine ideals. Slow motion, instant replay, close-up analysis of a player receiving or bobbling a pass, or achieving or falling short of a first down, are thus allied with analytical or juridical inquiry in gendered terms, answering a question about activity that is goal-oriented. Morse thus argues that, while sports—especially through the early 1980s—remain a "masculine preserve," they are also a unique forum that centers the male body as "an *image* of fascination," with the athlete photographed, frozen, slowed down, sped up, repeatedly, presenting "the perfect machine of a body-in-motion choreographed with others as a vision of grace and power."[28]

While the violence of the game appeals to realism and authenticity (as these express sincere commitment, undeniable pain, etc.), jarring collisions are transformed into *grace*. Key to this process are slow motion and the repetition of instant replay. For Morse, "the technological-scientific cachet of slow motion"[29] rescues it from pure *display* or aestheticization of the male body, to instead align it with the "hermeneutic" gaze. The look upon sports action is repositioned from *passive* contemplation to *active* inquiry. This is the "scientific-investigative look of the will to know, the hermeneutic process which serves the contest even when the narrative has stopped."[30] This assures that appreciation of male display still supports and rewards existing structures of power rather than catering to the "liberated woman's" gaze, imagined earlier. That is, though they are, atypically, the *objects* of the gaze, *MNF*'s football players are still active subjects and protagonist-heroes who drive the narrative's action. Concludes Morse, "Perhaps players of spectator sports are safe objects of the gaze, be it male or female, because they are surrogates of power."[31] The objectified male body is, in this way, not a body in *repose*—in its active, goal-oriented movement, it remains allied with *social* power, beyond the field of play. Further, Morse proposes that techniques such as slow-motion tap into a "long-term cultural fantasy of the body as a perfect machine,"[32] disconnecting athletes from the everyday, *human* realm and investing them, instead, with "the attribute of perfect machines, automatons and robots" which exude "an aura of the divine."[33]

Morse identifies the rich contradictions and productive ambiguities inherent in sports as *both* the central cultural forum for the reproduction of masculine ideals *and* as the shared site for interrogating vulnerabilities in those same constructs. While the "scientificity" of game coverage allows a disavowal and deflection of the erotics of the gaze, still, the "perfect" images are crucial to the broader cultural construction and consistent reinforcement of hegemonic, masculine ideals.[34] Here, Morse notes the productive overlap between the image of athletes and the *advertising* images that are integral to the game's broadcast flow. Football and advertising are corresponding markets, affirming the same gender ideals. In the *MNF* premiere, for example, national sponsors include cigarette, automotive, and alcohol producers. Marlboro's cigarette advertisements use conventions of the classical Hollywood western, featuring lush orchestration and a dramatic frontier setting focused on cowboys settled around a campfire with the lone, rugged Marlboro Man, beckoning viewers to "Come to Marlboro country." Goodyear's Custom Polyglas Tread tires' advertisements are shot as cinematic thrillers (one by day, one by night) featuring "your wife" in peril without the right tire: "When a woman's at the wheel, Polyglas means more than mileage," states the narrator, ominously. Strong silence, the ability to provide as the presumed breadwinner, and the innate drive to protect the female of the species here combine with the viewer's attention to on-field inquiries and outcomes to buttress "the masculine image" that "itself becomes a commodity which can be acquired through a series of exchanges between sport and advertising images, the linked product and the consumer."[35]

For Morse, this dialogic relationship between game coverage and market address shuts down any potentially *radical* possibilities of a "sports gaze" by affirming its function in the market. Television has "enriched sport as the prime means of aesthetic and emotional gratification for millions of Americans, and has provided an image of the male body-in-motion as beautiful, graceful and powerful."[36] However, while

> that image could function as a goal and critique of the actual situation of the powerlessness of viewing . . . identification with a team and with the male image of beauty and power can be supported only in that the spectator overlooks the distance between screen and armchair and the unbridgeable difference between himself and the phantasmic image of male perfection in slow motion.[37]

Rather than breaking with cultural conventions, for Morse, sports viewing is—for male viewers—a compensatory realm, covering over lack in one's daily and work life that is momentarily salved by hermeneutic inquiry, fantastic narcissistic identification, and through commodity consumption that promises to momentarily close the circuit between the text, the viewer, and lived experience in the social world off the edges of the TV screen.

Morse wrote her essay in the context of TV studies' emergence as a field that was beginning to define itself largely in "negative" terms—by examining the ways in which television was *not* like film, given film studies' prevailing psychoanalytic and literary, textual analytical frameworks at the time.[38] "Sport on Television" was originally published in E. Ann Kaplan's edited collection, *Regarding Television*, which examined genres that were prominent within and definitive of television by comparison to film (including news, soap opera, sports). Morse's work was thus part of a particular moment of development in TV studies that took up prevailing concepts from the study of film and asked how those frameworks had to be altered to understand television. Given that film studies of the late 1970s and early 1980s was often focused on questions of the gendered "gaze" in cinema and the broader social power of the pleasure of looking, scholars such as John Hartley, John Fiske, Tania Modleski, and Morse focused on whether TV genres were "gendered" in both their address to their audience and the pleasures that they held for viewers.[39] Morse's work is also clearly contextualized within the Big Three classical network era, which focused prime-time programming and sponsor address on the male "breadwinner" or "prime" salary-earner, who was imagined to be recuperating for the workforce by watching television after the day's 9-to-5 grind.

Given this context, Morse's identification of a significant perceptual transformation via sports TV seems particularly prescient. Even though, overall, she concludes that sports affirm traditional ideals of masculinity, she asks whether there has

> been a shift in the sexual division of labor in looking since the advent of televised sport? Other areas of culture besides sport (such as fashion and politics) show an increasing tolerance of male display for an ambiguously sexed gaze, part of the growth of commodity culture in which images function as currency.[40]

Has televised sport itself—its formal conventions and techniques—reframed and challenged traditional "ways of seeing"? Chapter 3 explores this question through a focus on female voice and authorship in sports documentary, while Chapter 4 addresses this shift by reading sports controversies as "male melodrama." Here, however, it is important to emphasize Morse's awareness that, generically, textually, and in its address to its viewers, sports television has historically complicated and even confounded conventional understandings of genre, gender, and the "gaze." Further, her essay encourages us to think deeply about the ways in which the technologies of sports TV encourage us to *objectify* athletes so as to ally them with the mechanical and, therefore, "controllable" and interchangeable—as bodies that can be "managed," "owned," and traded. The remainder of this chapter more closely examines transformations in the television industry, in production technology, and in audience demography that have ushered changes in sports TV aesthetics while maintaining prior conventions and struggles for balance between the scientific and the "human."

Tweaking the Purists: The Foxification of the Multichannel Era

In his *Televisuality: Style, Crisis, and Authority in American Television*, John Thornton Caldwell proposes that from the mid-1980s through the mid-1990s, US television was increasingly characterized by an "aesthetic based on an extreme self-consciousness of style."[41] For a medium that had historically "approached broadcasting primarily as a form of word-based rhetoric and transmission," by the 1990s, "with increasing frequency, style itself became the subject, the signified, if you will, of television."[42] Caldwell describes this aesthetic transformation as the result of an economic crisis in the television industry, as cable and other new network players challenged the Big Three and the multichannel era began. "Televisuality" is Caldwell's term for the resulting aesthetic performance of style and knowing exhibitionism that sought to captivate new audiences and to break through increasing competition clutter by distinguishing programming and network brand identity through swagger and heightened presentational attitude. Technologies like video production switchers allowed for an entirely new visual syntax to enter television production, emphasizing picture flips, freezes, squeezes, and repositioning with glossy and metallic surface flourishes. New nonlinear editing tools and digital effects encouraged experimentation and play with temporality and sequencing. And, technologies like Steadicam and Skycam (or its competitor Cablecam) created new photographic points of view, physically taking "the camera away from the operator's eyes and mov[ing] it through space in very fluid ways" automating "an inherently omniscient," rather than a subjective or authored point of view, "around a technological rather than a human center."[43] It was in this era that FOX network launched and became the institutional embodiment of the economic and industrial ethos of televisuality, embracing "audaciousness and excessiveness as central elements of its brand."[44]

Brought to the network by Rupert Murdoch from Australia's Sky Sports, David Hill led FOX's sports production division. Hill might be called "Arledge 2.0" for conceiving sports TV as entertainment first and foremost. FOX Sports' motto at its inception was "Same Game. New Attitude." For baseball coverage, Hill "instituted a 'no dead guys rule' to on-air MLB announcers, complaining that broadcasters spent all their time romanticizing early players like Babe Ruth."[45] Attempting to strike a balance "between the new stuff they hoped would blow football fans' minds and comfort food that would seem reassuring and familiar," FOX used video overlay technology and televisual effects to appeal to a youthful "irreverent" audience and spirit.[46] One of Hill's now-conventional developments was the "FOX Box," which premiered in 1994. The FOX Box placed a graphic of the game score and game clock onscreen during all in-game action. With the relative compression allowed by HDTV, the FOX Box has been able to both shrink and add data to its onscreen information (e.g., in baseball, the box now notes balls, strikes, outs, and baserunner position with inning and score). The Box has alternated screen location across its history (from top of the screen to bottom, alternating corners, etc.). While now a relatively indispensable visual in all sports TV, at the time of its introduction, Hill received death threats from "purist" fans outraged by the "gizmo" "clutter." Such intense rage at a graphic intervention points to an ongoing dilemma in sports TV aesthetic development: How does a network distinguish itself from its competitors and attract new viewers with original developments that enhance knowledge of the game without detracting from the sport itself or disrespecting die-hard fans?

How do enhanced modes of visibility balance competing knowledge communities? What is the line between something enhancing a sport or being "an assault on your eyes"?[47] FOX Sports navigated this tension when its 1996–1998 National Hockey League (NHL) coverage featured "FOX Trax"—commonly referred to as "the glow puck."

FOX obtained the rights to telecast NHL games in the US TV market in 1994. In this same moment (particularly from 1992 through 1998), the NHL was rapidly expanding into new, nontraditional regions for hockey, focusing on relocations of teams from the northeast to the south and west (including the Arizona Coyotes and Carolina Hurricanes) and with new franchises in the South, the Sunbelt, and California (including the San Jose Sharks, Tampa Bay Lightning, Florida Panthers, Anaheim Ducks, and Nashville Predators). Capitalizing upon the league's growth and need to cultivate audiences that were not necessarily familiar with hockey, its rules, and its pace of play, Hill sought to develop a way to make the puck easier to track during gameplay. FOX electrical engineer Stan Honey developed electronic sensors and a circuit-board, placed inside the puck, that would send real-time coordinates to generate computer graphics onscreen resulting in a blue glow under the puck. Since shots on goal in hockey often travel over 100 miles per hour, speed tracking technology allowed that, when the puck reached speeds of 70 miles per hour and above, a red "comet-tail" would trail behind it, identifying its flight-path.

Introduced at the NHL All-Star Game of 1996, the glow puck was despised by players who argued that, because the technology inside the puck could not be frozen, the pucks themselves were uncharacteristically bouncy and acted more like rubber balls on the ice than standard pucks. Thus, FOX Trax risked intervening in normal gameplay and altering player statistics and achievements across the season. Sportswriters and TV critics called the glow puck an "unnecessary irritant" and interference with the game.[48] But, the real issue—and ultimate death of the glow puck—lay with audience reception. Were "newbie," casual fans and young audiences going to stick with the sport because of an aesthetic that was kid-friendly, commercially novel, and had a cartoony feel? Or, was the risk of losing serious hockey fans

Figure 2.2 The FOX Trax or "glow puck" at the NHL All-Star Game

who felt patronized and disrespected by the technology too high? The glow puck might best be considered an exceptionally worthy failure: As one of the earliest computerized viewer-enhancement technologies in post-1980s sports TV, it was a huge technological success and advance. The speed tracking, data-gathering, and imaging technology inside the puck became the foundation of much data-gathering and imaging technology in sports today. And yet, FOX Trax arguably revealed the limits of "putting the show business" in sports. With its much smaller percentage of casual fans than other major league sports in the US, hockey die-hards were so strongly put off by the glow puck's "instructional" impetus that FOX's entire sports division's reputation was threatened. The glow puck ultimately highlighted the delicate balance required in addressing the breadth of sports TV's audience. Game coverage has to reward existing knowledge while also enhancing the insights of a sport's core audience. Coverage must also welcome but not privilege new fans, unfamiliar with the sport. Overall, aesthetic interventions in sports TV thrive when they enrich and innovate *within* traditional conventions. The glow puck's developer would exemplify such an approach in one of his next endeavors.

"The Wondrous Banana Stripe": The EA Sports Aesthetic of the Streaming Era

Stan Honey left FOX to create SportVision with Bill Squadron in 1998 to focus on graphic overlay and digital insertion technologies for sports TV. Building on experience from FOX Trax, the company developed technologies including the K-Zone and PITCH f/x, which map pitches and the strike zone in baseball; NASCAR's car-tracking and pointer system, RACE f/x; AIR f/x, which measures vertical leap and other NBA in-game statistics; the Virtual Playbook for NFL telecasts; and the premium telestrator system which allows broadcasters the ability to "draw" on the playing surface, mapping out plays and engaging with action on the screen. While these are a few of the technologies developed by SportVision that continue to thrive today, the company's most famous invention by far is the yellow "1st & Ten Line" developed in cooperation with ESPN in 1998. Premiering on September 27, 1998 with ESPN's *Sunday Night Football* coverage of a game between the Baltimore Ravens and Cincinnati Bengals in Baltimore, the 1st & Ten Line placed a computer-generated yellow line on the field of play in football presenting a clear view indicating what yard marker the offense had to reach in order to gain a first down. In stark contrast to the glow puck, the 1st & Ten Line was, at its inception, uniformly hailed as a savvy enhancement in game coverage: "the wondrous banana stripe that graces our little screens and shows us the distance to a first down . . . the greatest thing for football since instant replay. And color TV. And bottled hops and barley products."[49]

The success of the 1st & Ten Line was due in large part to its appeal to both loyal, knowledgeable football fans *and* its ability to draw in more casual viewers. Unlike the glow puck, the 1st & Ten Line was perceived to enhance the game rather than distract from it. And, rather than patronizing knowing fans, the line was perceived to actually amplify those fans' ability to focus on the game at hand. As 50-plus-year NFL fan Robert Glasspiegel explains,

> You had to do it all in your head before. You knew roughly where they had to get to, but you had to do it all in your head or be dependent on the announcers saying "I think they got it" or "I don't think they got it."[50]

Notably, however, the 1st & Ten Line also seamlessly appealed to "unknowing" fans. In a Harris Interactive Poll commissioned by SportVision in 1999, "64% of 'casual' viewers said that '1st & Ten' increased their understanding of the game with almost half of them saying the '1st & Ten' line would increase their likelihood of watching football games." Further, "92% believe it will increase the understanding for kids."

SportVision was acquired by SportsMEDIA Technology (SMT) in 2016. SMT has continued to develop and refine video enhancement and virtual insertion for sporting events, including the swimming world record line and visual insertion of lane flags (marking swimmers' national identities). Digital advertising insertion technology has allowed for virtual signage in MLB and NHL coverage. And, the company's work with NASCAR has created increasingly refined tracking with easily identifiable digital "flags" over cars during races, showing miles per hour and race placement. In the streaming-TV era, such digital integrations and graphic overlays have not only become more integral to all sports television, but they have contributed to a growing visual interrelationship between sports *videogames* and televised sports through the growth of augmented reality integrations. This might be referred to as an "EA Sports aesthetic" after the gaming behemoth, EA Sports, founded by Trip Hawkins in 1982. In the 1980s and 1990s, EA launched sports videogames that focused on the "show" in sports by featuring actual player/stars as the featured avatars in its games (e.g., the 1980s *Doctor J and Larry Bird Go One on One*, *Jordan vs. Bird: One on One*, and *Richard Petty's Talladega*). As Thomas Oates has carefully outlined, EA Sports' innovation to include "digital renderings of active star

Figure 2.3 NHL.TV's GoPro POV

players" brought "recognizable sporting stars under the virtual control of gamers" and made "it possible for fans to embody not merely generic athletes but stars."[51]

Such videogamegraphic "embodiment" has deeply influenced television sports aesthetics. While the 180-degree line is still observed in all sports—maintaining directional continuity and orientation in space for viewers whether at a court, rink, field, ring, track, or poolside—technologies such as Skycam have, since the mid-1980s, have allowed for a view from behind the athlete, moving the game in a vertical as well as horizontal fashion. Jacob Dittmer has called this "the *Madden* effect" from EA Sports' *Madden NFL*, whereby "the NFL and broadcast networks took cues from these progressions in football video games."[52] The goal is to align the point of view of the TV viewer with the embodied point of view of the athlete in ways that are "immersive" but, also, place the viewer in the same perceptual position they would be in were they holding a game controller. A relatively "extreme" example of this phenomenon is the partnership the NHL Players' Association established with GoPro in 2015 to provide live-action, first-person subjective point-of-view streaming through helmet-mounted cameras, putting viewers "in the game," in ways envisioned by EA Sports' company motto. While only judiciously used to this point—in brief segments of the NHL All-Star Game and online in video shorts at NHL.TV—the "GoPro gaze" recalls Thomas Oates's and Robert Allen Brookey's urging to consider the ways in which "[t]he relentless pursuit of 'authentic' simulations in" sports videogames and sports TV "work to craft sophisticated acquisitive fantasies, where material goods, brands, bodies, organizations, and even national identities are presented for consumption."[53]

Between 2005 and 2010, EA Sports and ESPN entered into a collaborative agreement that led to a more formal aesthetic integration between sports TV (for both studio programs and in live game coverage) and sports videogames, "each building on the advances of the other."[54] As gaming scholar Abe Stein notes, ESPN commentators now regularly "interact with virtual characters on a digital playing field" with digital models "taken directly from EA videogame franchises such as *Madden* [NFL]" while established conventions of videogame graphics are also integrated into live game coverage and onscreen telestration (e.g., "the use of a star or circle underneath the feet of a character").[55] Of course, just as television incorporates gaming aesthetics and conventions, so games themselves—such as the iconic *Madden NFL*—look increasingly like telecasts.

The Professional Golfers' Association (PGA) might seem a surprising venue to thoroughly integrate and visualize the gamification of sports TV. However, the PGA has been activist in its attempts to "digitize golf," broadening its audience through the use of videogame graphic aesthetics with the help of TopTracer. Founded in 2006, TopTracer provides digital video overlay graphics that track the flight of a golf ball with a visible line complete with arcing trajectory, speed, apex, curve, and carry tracing. TopTracer's shot tracker technology has been favorably described as "golf's version of the yellow 1st & Ten line. It's at that level of importance to the viewing experience."[56] CBS's PGA tour coverage now also integrates drone footage and 4D replay, offering a 180-degree view around each player on the tee in order to create a

Figure 2.4 TopTracer's "videogamegraphic" aesthetic in PGA coverage on CBS

thorough breakdown of their swing. As sportsvideo.org recently noted, PGA viewers "may feel that they're watching a new videogame more than an old sepia-toned film. Turner and CBS are rolling out a slew of technologies—live ball tracking, green mapping, even 360-degree camera rigs."[57] While TopTracer and other technologies may be bringing the PGA into a new era and energizing a new demographic, it is also significant that TopTracer is invested in a broader immersive gamification of golf *outside* of sports television, in the form of its Topgolf driving range/dining/drinking/recreation complexes which also include esports lounges. Here, TV and videogame images of golf encourage fluency in a larger "experience economy" focused on the gamification of, historically, an exceptionally traditional, change-resistant sport. TopGolf proposes to reimagine a sport that has historically been overwhelmingly white, wealthy, suburban, and unwelcoming (if not overtly restrictive) to diversification through brick-and-mortar complexes removed from country-club environments, gamifying golf for a digital generation.[58]

Revenge of the Glow Puck?

The technology essential to the glow puck has not only survived but has become the basis for an exceptionally refined system of puck- and player-tracking technology, data integration, and graphics generation. SMT has installed its "OASIS" system in every NHL arena to "track the movements of the puck and each on-ice player during every game."[59] Such tracking data has also extended into athlete biometrics, including alliances with wearable technology companies like Whoop, Zebra Technologies, and Athos. These wearables generate a quantification of the *self* through digital datafication which is visualizable. These tech/media alliances thus gamify player physiology and monetize athlete "biometric data through agreements with various third parties in media, video games, health and wellness and the collectibles industries."[60]

From streaming video overlay technology and omniscient point of view (via volumetric-360-degree video and drone photography) to immersion in game action through first-person point of view (via GoPro photography and, increasingly, biometric feedback), videogame aesthetics and sports TV are clearly mutually informing and impacting. Such interdependence is particularly invested in and responsive to a generation of sports viewers (with certain technological and economic privileges) who have always only known and engaged with multiple mobile HD screens and realistic 3D gaming—often while multitasking across platforms and applications—and who expect personalization and individuation with TV engagement. "Videogame graphics" with HD resolution travel fluidly across viewing devices in an era in which the device upon which you watch TV is increasingly irrelevant.[61] Streaming media offer broadband speeds and digital video compression that enable HD mobile TV and, increasingly, volumetric video, capturing "plays from all angles" and recreating "360-degree highlights and player perspective video."[62] Such immersion technologies are designed to encourage sports TV viewers to use their second (or third, or fourth) screens to interact directly with video overlay technology in response to onscreen action.

Beyond personalization, sports television is entering the next phase of computational aesthetics in what might be called the "artificial intelligence" era—one that conjoins onscreen space with lived space, generating, organizing, manipulating, and disseminating data, "recording and revealing our interactions with"[63] our favorite stadiums, teams, and athletes. While such data-mining leads to greater individualization of the viewing experience and promises exciting interactive developments—allowing streaming video viewers to "interact with content, from social media to merchandise to in-game wagering"[64]—these trends also encourage sports viewers to further objectify and commodify the on-field athletes and action while themselves serving as "free labor."[65] As ESPN Digital executive Josh Kosner states, to enhance sports broadcasting going forward (especially after the COVID-19 pandemic forced rethinking regarding what attendance at sports venues might look like in the future)

> envisions the potential of live video shots of fans and influencers watching the game at home being interspersed into the live game broadcast. . . . "We are moving to a model where the audience makes content for the game."[66]

Though sports and media organizations benefit from cultivating "prosumers" (fan/viewers who produce as well as consume content), it is worthwhile to consider how streaming-era television connects its viewer both figuratively *and* literally "to larger flows of labor, culture and power."[67]

Tiziana Terranova describes "free labor" as a defining characteristic of the contemporary cultural economy which is marked by the "increasingly blurred territory between production and consumption, work and cultural expression."[68] Sports TV is an ideal venue for such labor, as fans are

> repeatedly addressed as active consumers of meaningful commodities. Free labor is the moment where this knowledgeable consumption of culture is translated into productive

activities that are pleasurably embraced and at the same time often shamelessly exploited.[69]

SportsTV can engage fans as knowledgeable and joyful laborers because of the deep emotional and narrative resonance of sports as a broader media and cultural ecosystem. The next chapters thus examine more closely what *kind* of narrative world sportsTV is, as expressed through athlete "voice" and documentary, narratives of "contention" and melo-drama, and narratives of "consensus" and civic identity.

Notes

1. Thomas J. Fleming, "Fond Farewell?" *Baltimore Sun Magazine*, May 29, 1966, 12. Frick was Major League Baseball Commissioner from 1951–1965.
2. Arledge began his career at DuMont network in 1950 before entering Army ser-vice until 1955, when he joined NBC as a studio TV producer. He moved to ABC in 1960, producing NCAA sports before developing *WideWorld of Sports* and becoming Vice President and later President of ABC Sports (1968–1986), ABC News (1977, 1980–1998), and ABC News and Sports (1985–1990).
3. Roone Arledge, *Roone: A Memoir* (New York: Harper Collins, 2003), 27.
4. Arledge, *Roone: A Memoir*, 27.
5. Arledge, 30.
6. Arledge, 30.
7. John Thornton Caldwell, *Televisuality: Style, Crisis, and Authority in American Televi-sion* (New Brunswick, NJ: Rutgers University Press, 1995), 331.
8. Arledge, *Roone: A Memoir*, 28.
9. As Markus Stauff has proposed, "the entire history of sports can thus be writ-ten as a history of competing forms of visibility" between data-centric, juridi-cal knowledge that supersedes human vision, alongside "the ideological desire to preserve" and celebrate "the so-called 'human element' of the game." Markus Stauff, "Smartphone Referees: Social Media and Sports' Politics of Visibility." (Paper presented at the annual meeting of the Society for Cinema and Media Studies, Seattle, WA, March 2014).
10. Caldwell, *Televisuality*, vii.
11. At the time of this book's submission, the full premiere episode of *Monday Night Football* (including national commercial advertisements) was available at www.youtube.com/watch?v=0zPj6lFuzL4.
12. Tom Riste, "Sugar-Coated Commentary Debunked by ABC Football," *The Arizona Daily Star (Tucson)*, August 31, 1970. Notably, the only criticism of the premiere in major papers and trade-industry press was the unpredict-ability of the game's running time, having gone 30 minutes over schedule by the final gun.

13. In Travis Vogan's study of NFL Films, he quotes the company's former editor-in-chief, Bob Ryan who identifies NFL Films' highlights as "more movies than news," unlike run-of-the-mill highlights which he allies with reportage. This tension of sports coverage seeming to be more news than movies or more movies than news, and, generally, an attempt to balance the two is often (if implicitly) what is at stake in critical reception of new aesthetic conventions in each of the eras discussed in this chapter. See Travis Vogan, *Keepers of the Flame: NFL Films and the Rise of Sports Media* (Urbana, IL: University of Illinois Press, 2014), 61.

14. For further discussion of the classic network era and of *Monday Night Football*, please see Victoria E. Johnson, "The Classic Network Era in Television: 1950s–1970s," in *A Companion to the History of American Broadcasting*, ed. Aniko Bodroghkozy (Hoboken, NJ: John Wiley & Sons, 2018), 93–109. And, Victoria E. Johnson, "'Monday Night Football': Brand Identity," in *How to Watch Television*, eds. Ethan Thompson and Jason Mittell (New York: New York University Press, 2013), 262–270.

15. Susan Murray, *Bright Signals: A History of Color Television* (Durham, NC: Duke University Press, 2018), 3.

16. "ABC Giving Deluxe Coverage to Primetime Grid With 9-Camera Setup," *Variety*, August 19, 1970, 32.

17. Arledge, *Roone: A Memoir*, 65.

18. Vogan, *Keepers of the Flame*, 133.

19. Keith Jackson was play-by-play announcer for *Monday Night Football* in only its first season. The trio of Cosell, Meredith, and Frank Gifford was together with some additions in various seasons, from 1971–1973 and 1977–1983. "Dandy" Don Meredith was part of the commentary crew from 1970–1974 and then returned from 1977–1984. Cosell left the show after the 1983 season. Frank Gifford remained with *Monday Night Football* from 1971–1997.

20. Riste, "Sugar-Coated Commentary."

21. Max Nichols, "TV Sport Coverage Growing Up," *The Minneapolis Star*, November 14, 1970.

22. Travis Vogan outlines NFL Films' distinct aesthetic practices and its significance in creating broader mythologies of football and of the NFL as a cultural institution, in *Keepers of the Flame*.

23. Vogan, *Keepers of the Flame*, 61.

24. Lawrence Laurent, "Pepping Up TV Football," *The Washington Post*, July 2, 1970.

25. Morton Moss, "Games and Dames," *Los Angeles Herald Examiner*, May 12, 1970.

26. Thomas P. Oates, *Football and Manliness: An Unauthorized Feminist Account of the NFL* (Urbana, IL: University of Illinois Press, 2017), 80.

27. E. Ann Kaplan, "Introduction," in *Regarding Television: Critical Approaches—An Anthology*, ed. E. Ann Kaplan (Los Angeles: The American Film Institute, 1983), xvi.

28. Margaret Morse, "Sport on Television: Replay and Display," *Regarding Television: Critical Approaches—An Anthology*, ed. E. Ann Kaplan (Los Angeles: The American Film Institute, 1983), 44.

29. Morse, "Sport on Television," 51.

30. Morse, 57.
31. Morse, 58.
32. Morse, 56.
33. Morse, 56.
34. Morse, 45.
35. Morse, 61.
36. Morse, 61.
37. Morse, 62.
38. Particularly as evidenced in Laura Mulvey, "Visual Pleasure and Narrative Cinema," *Screen* 16, no. 3 (1975): 6–18.
39. See, for example: John Fiske and John Hartley, *Reading Television* (New York: Routledge, 1978); John Fiske, *Television Culture* (New York: Routledge, 1987); Tania Modleski, "The Rhythms of Reception: Daytime Television and Women's Work," in *Regarding Television: Critical Approaches—An Anthology*, ed. E. Ann Kaplan (Los Angeles: The American Film Institute, 1983).
40. Morse, "Sport on Television," 58. Joe Namath (featured in the premiere episode of MNF), and Muhammad Ali (whose star persona was developed, in part, through interviews with Howard Cosell) are two figures in the 1970s who are overdue for analysis in these terms.
41. Caldwell, *Televisuality*, 4.
42. Caldwell, 4.
43. Caldwell, 80, 81. Skycam was invented by Garrett Brown who had previously developed Steadicam. Skycam suspends a remotely controlled camera on cables over the game venue and was first demonstrated in 1983.
44. Bambi Haggins and Julia Himberg, "The Multi-Channel Transition Period: 1980s–1990s," in *A Companion to the History of American Broadcasting*, ed. Aniko Bodroghkozy (Hoboken, NJ: John Wiley & Sons, 2018), 120.
45. Mark Wilson, "The Secret History of Cleatus, Fox Sports's Bizarre Football Robot," *Fast Company*, March 27, 2019.
46. Curtis, "The Great NFL Heist," quoting Tracy Dolgin, FOX Sports Executive Vice President on FOX's NFL coverage appeal.
47. Chuck Finder, "Hold On! Here Come the Gizmos," *Pittsburgh Post-Gazette*, January 16, 1997, E6.
48. See, for example, Finder, "Hold On!" E6; Barry Jackson, "Glowing Puck, Skycam, NHL, NBA Plan Reprises of Their Technical Innovations," *Miami Herald*, January 17, 1997, 9D; and "Bowman: NHL Should Bounce Fox's Glow Puck," *San Diego Union-Tribune*, June 1, 1998, D3.
49. "Yellow Line Now Viewing Necessity," *Pittsburgh Post-Gazette*, November 20, 2000. Beyond football fans, others agreed that the invention was an historic development. In 2018 Stan Honey was inducted into the National Inventors Hall of Fame for the 1st & Ten Line.
50. Quoted in Sam Laird, "The Yellow First-Down Line: An Oral History of a Game Changer," *Mashable*, September 25, 2013, www.mashable.com/2013/09/25/yellow-first-down-line/.

51. Thomas P. Oates, "'Madden' Men: Masculinity, Race, and the Marketing of a Video Game Franchise," in *Playing to Win: Sports, Video Games, and the Culture of Play*, eds. Robert Allen Brookey and Thomas P. Oates (Bloomington: Indiana University Press, 2015), 50–51.

52. Jacob Dittmer, "Football's New Forms," *Flow*, October 16, 2009, www.flowjournal. org/2009/10/footballs-new-forms-how-new-media-is-changing-football-fandom-jacob-dittmer-university-of-oregon/.

53. Thomas P. Oates and Robert Allen Brookey, "Introduction," in *Playing to Win: Sports, Video Games, and the Culture of Play*, eds. Thomas P. Oates and Robert Allen Brookey (Bloomington: Indiana University Press, 2015), 15–16.

54. Abe Stein, "Playing the Game on Television," in *Sports Videogames*, eds. Mia Consalvo, Konstantin Mitgutsch, and Abe Stein (New York: Routledge, 2013), 118.

55. Stein, "Playing the Game on Television," 130, 131.

56. Brandon Costa, "PGA Championship Spotlight, Part 1: Video-Gamification of Golf's Final Major Changes How Viewers See the Sport," *www.sportsvideo.org/>* August 10, 2018.

57. Costa, "PGA Championship Spotlight."

58. The increasing importance and overt pursuit of such "experience economy" extensions of sports TV are examined in detail in Chapter 5.

59. *SMT*, "National Hockey League and SportsMEDIA Technology Expand Partnership," October 10, 2019, www.smt.com.

60. Eric Fisher, "Data in Motion," *Sports Business Journal*, October 22–28, 2018, 26.

61. Amanda D. Lotz, *Portals: A Treatise on Internet-Distributed Television* (Ann Arbor: Michigan Publishing, 2017).

62. Sarah Redohl, "Volumetric Video Is So Much More Than VR," *Immersive Shooter*, January 10, 2019, www.immersiveshooter.com/2019/01/10/ volumetric-video-means-so-much-more-than-vr.

63. Eric Freedman, "Software," in *The Craft of Criticism: Critical Media Studies in Practice*, eds. Michael Kackman and Mary Celeste Kearney (New York: Routledge, 2018), 320.

64. Eric Prisbell, "A New Reality Powered by AI," *Sports Business Journal*, April 13–19, 2020, 21. Sports betting looks to be a primary revenue growth area for all major league sports in the US particularly as supported by in-stadium statistical data via AWS and other providers, allowing bets on any aspect of games that can be tracked.

65. Tiziana Terranova, "Free Labor: Producing Culture for the Digital Economy," in *The Media Studies Reader*, ed. Laurie Ouellette (New York: Routledge, 2013), 331–349.

66. Prisbell, "A New Reality Powered by AI," 21.

67. Terranova, "Free Labor," 332.

68. Terranova, 333.

69. Terranova, 333.

3

GENERATION IX

Sports TV, Gender, and Voice

In *Let Me Play: The Story of Title IX, The Law That Changed the Future of Girls in America*, author Karen Blumenthal recounts an early-1970s encounter between tennis champion Billie Jean King and Gloria Steinem, the feminist icon and editor of *Ms.* magazine. King believed that sports and its potential as a venue for equal rights activism remained underappreciated and untapped. "'You should use us more,' Ms. King urged Ms. Steinem. Ms. Steinem replied, 'Billie, this is about politics.' 'Gloria,' Ms. King replied, 'we *are* politics.'"[1] This chapter and the next interrogate competing understandings of sports as a diversion *from* or an ideal forum *for* engagement with potentially contentious social issues and political expression. Televised sports consistently negotiate these competing ideals: the conviction that sports is a realm for education and intervention in the status quo alongside the belief that sports is an inherently integrative cultural realm, separate from potentially divisive concerns. Sports' richness and relevance is largely due to this both/and quality whereby sports both *preserve* cultural conventions and provide a space that persistently challenges them.

Many of our shared popular images of historical progress—particularly as regards race and gender rights struggles—are iconic images of sports events as they were seen on TV. We think here, for example, of defining moments such as John Carlos's and Tommie Smith's silent protest in recognition of the international struggle for Black liberation atop the 1968 Mexico City Olympic medal podium. Or, of the spectacle of Billie Jean King's own "Battle of the Sexes" match with Bobby

Riggs at the Houston Astrodome in 1973. Or, of the United States Women's National Soccer Team's summer 2019 World Cup victory whose final whistle was accompanied by chants from the Stade de Lyon crowd calling for "Equal pay! Equal pay!"While Chapter 4 underscores the continued historical *unevenness* of social change in and beyond the sporting realm, this chapter focuses on the significant legislative, cultural, textual, and technological transformations that—particularly since the late 1990s—have challenged and shifted, if not entirely destabilized, historically conventional practices of gender representation in sports TV. I should note, here, that in referencing gender and race in this chapter, I follow Thomas P. Oates's and Sharon Patricia Holland's examples to argue that, in sports TV, "*binaries*—white/black, men/ women" continue to play a crucial role. As Oates notes, "though many scholars have justifiably pressed critical inquiry to move past binaries as a means of understanding social relations," contemporary sports offer a particularly prominent and insistent "opportunity to examine the persistent power of binary thinking,"[2] its tenacity and social power in everyday life.

Following passage of Title IX and, by now, a second full generation's access to the educational and athletic opportunities that followed, the female athlete has been invigorated as an icon, literally embodying sports participation and its benefits as liberating and "empowering." Simultaneously, the explosion of new modes of media expression—particularly, the rise of first-person media—has enabled athletes to assert their voice as creators of media content and managers of its distribution.[3] This post–Title IX era of "networked media sport"[4] has encouraged scholars to consider whether the hegemonic masculinity thesis should be reconsidered as the primary framework for understanding sports' cultural relevance and power. Certainly, recent developments in sporting culture have troubled conventional portrayals of female athletes as inherently subordinate. Consider, for example, that the ultra-violent, male-dominated MMA's highest ratings in 2017 were for female bouts, expanding both understandings of femininity as performance *and* the receptivity of audiences to female athletes in traditionally "masculine" roles. The WNBA's 2018 season was themed "Take a Seat to Take a Stand" in support of six female and LGBTQ-supporting political organizations, embracing sports as a venue for activism and recognizing sexual identity in all of its fluidity and diversity. Major League Baseball and National Basketball Association prime-time TV coverage now feature Jessica Mendoza and Doris Burke, respectively, calling games, breaking down historical myths of audience resistance to female expertise in predominantly male sports. Given these examples and, as a second and third generation of post–Title IX female athletes now engages with fans (and, also, haters) across connected media, *has* there been a transition in voice, questions of authorship, and corresponding complexities in the construction and reception of the female athlete for a broad audience? Further, does sports TV offer opportunities to intervene in commonsense "Contemporary power arrangements" that "project white, male, middle-class, heterosexual identity as central norms in relation to which all other identities must be understood"?[5] Or, do such examples merely throw into relief the dishearteningly "deepening quantitative dearth of coverage of women's sports and . . . the tendency to present most of the few women's sports stories in a matter-of-fact, uninspiring, and lackluster manner."[6] While today's youngest viewers have *only* known women to be sports heroes, action series stars, gaming heroines, and social media influencers, does such inclusion and commercial success actually translate into revision of conventional gender "norms" and foster equality?

This chapter focuses specifically on televised sports documentary as a site of productive ambivalence. The series in focus here each struggle with questions of voice, authorship, and gender identity. They expose tensions between popular feminism, postfeminism, and differing understandings of "empowerment" as a route to social change. Examining ESPN's espnW-branded[7] documentary series *Nine for IX* (2013), and HBO's documentary series *Being Serena* (2018), this chapter takes up key debates in feminist studies of sports media that foreground the question of voice: Whose commentary underscores and guides coverage of female athletes? How is female athletic achievement often either undermined through conventional objectification and fetishization *or* qualified and made "safe" through reference to maternity and heteronormative coupling? How do ESPN's "women's" extension and Serena Williams's "authorship" challenge or re-inscribe these tensions, particularly as they brand these networks as prestigious homes to "quality" discourses and discerning audiences? What challenge do female athlete icons pose to the hegemonic masculinity thesis as they invoke feminist politics to cultivate and appeal to new audiences?

Title IX, Feminism(s), and the "New" Female Athlete

Though Title IX of the Education Amendment of 1972, in its entirety, is only 37 words long, it has been hailed as "the most important step for gender equality since the 19th Amendment gave [women] the right to vote."[8] Title IX provides that "no person in the United States shall, on the basis of sex, be excluded from participation in, be denied the benefits of, or be subjected to discrimination under any education program or activity receiving Federal financial assistance."[9] Signed into law by President Richard M. Nixon on June 23, 1972, Title IX's regulations did not take effect until 1975, and its "three-part test" for compliance was not instituted until 1979.[10] Though Title IX did not explicitly mention sports, one of its most visible legacies has been the marked increase in female participation in organized school sports which, in turn, has led to an expansion of women's competitive amateur sports and to the development of professional team sports leagues. According to reporter Betsey Butler, "Between the year Title IX was passed (1972) and the first Women's World Cup (1991), the sport saw a 17,000% increase in US girls playing on high school soccer teams."[11] In other arenas, significant outcomes of Title IX include the increase in degrees awarded to women in fields including Business (11,578 degrees awarded in 1972 versus 110,096 degrees awarded in 1997), Law (1,498 versus 17,531), and Medicine (830 versus 6,450).[12] By the mid-1990s, one generation of women had grown up with the protections and expectations of Title IX. The 1996 Olympic games were dubbed "The Year of the Woman." But perhaps most emblematic of a generation of women who had always been able to participate in sports was the famed "'99er" US National Women's Soccer

Team, whose 1999 World Cup victory in Pasadena, California was accompanied by massive audiences—including thousands of men and boys—and generated unprecedented mainstream embrace of sports as a route for female "empowerment," self-esteem, self-expression, sense of community, and achievement.

Though straightforward and seemingly commonsense, however, Title IX remains controversial. While the law was bolstered with passage of the 1988 Civil Rights Restoration Act, its provisions have been under threat following a series of post-2011 mandates, and additional state-enacted protections.[13] Such ongoing struggles point to the fact that laws are not enacted in a vacuum, at a remove from their broader social and cultural context. Indeed, though Title IX was taken to be a victory for a broader women's rights movement of the 1970s, subsequent decades saw explicit political and cultural backlash in the face of these gains. Paradoxically, it is within this context of antagonism toward collective gains that a *new* image of the "female athlete as cultural icon" emerged in the 1990s, becoming "utterly mainstream" by the 2000s.[14] Historically, the period from the 1980s through the present has been theorized as a legislative, cultural, and economic turn to *neoliberalism* as the dominant "commonsense." As Julie Wilson notes, "neoliberalism is a set of social, cultural, and political-economic forces that puts competition at the center of social life."[15] According to neoliberal logics, "public social infrastructures (such as social security, unemployment benefits, public education) are believed to squash entrepreneurialism and individualism and breed dependency and bureaucracy. Competition, on the other hand, is heralded to ensure efficiency and incite creativity."[16]

The "'liberalism' in neoliberalism"[17] is not aligned with our colloquial understanding of "liberal" to be on the "left," politically. Instead, we can understand "liberal" here to refer "to a belief in individual liberties, property rights," and, above all, "free markets."[18] The broad impact of such philosophy and the real policies that follow from it has been an active encouragement of individual competition and discouragement of collective action. Neoliberal ideals have thus encouraged positive values "like personal agency, autonomy, and self-determination"[19] that squarely meld with athletic ideals as seen in expressions such as Nike's "Just Do It!" or the urging to "Livestrong." Indeed, in this broader political and rhetorical climate a new, largely white, middle- and upper-middle-class "fitness boom"[20] cast the disciplined, "self-made," toned athletic body as "a new ideal of accomplishment and grace, a standard for women's achievement."[21] While on the one hand, such self-fashioning opened up gender ideals to a broader continuum that now incorporated both "female masculinity" and the development of a male beauty culture, by the 1990s, female athleticism became newly iconic of individual fulfillment *as* rights discourse.

Transformations in consumer markets in the 1990s through the present have encouraged and supported the promotion of this new athlete icon. By the mid-1990s, professional women—that boom of degree-earners of the post–Title IX generation—"were a demographic waiting to be tapped."[22] As seen in sports apparel–makers such as Nike (particularly in its iconic 1995 "If You Let Me Play" campaign) or Title 9 Sports (1989–present), or magazines such as *Women's Sports and Fitness* (Condé Nast, 1997–2000), or even corporate charity endeavors such as the Komen Race for the Cure (1983–present), a new ideal image for women (focused on middle- and upper-class white women in urban and suburban markets)

> relied on a clever mixture of liberal feminist and American individualist ideals: the trained, self-reliant female athlete, the chick who can "do it for herself," who gets beyond all the old gender stereotypes and limitations and does whatever she pleases.[23]

Concurrently, the television industry was undergoing a transition from the broadcast era's focus on attracting mass-audiences to the new 1990s landscape of cable and satellite provider competition. In this context, an "invigorated attention to market research, demographic targeting, and narrowcast practices . . . encouraged networks to focus their attention . . . toward newly reconfigured 'quality' audiences, 'niche' programming, and sponsorship appeals."[24] Thus, both the "self-made" weekend warrior and the superstar professional athlete are prominent popularly circulating icons of female "power" articulating political discourses (expressive of post–Title IX rights), social discourses (expressive of publicly visible gendered achievement), economic discourses (exerting market value), and personal discourses (self-expression, as inscribed on the body) into the "new" athlete ideal.

"Empowerment" is idealized in the new female athlete and, as such, she is claimed as a contemporary icon of both postfeminism and popular feminism. While some scholars conflate postfeminism and popular feminism, others have drawn important distinctions between the two. The documentaries examined in this chapter emerge within the ongoing ethos and sensibility of postfeminism but are arguably expressions of popular feminist ideals. Postfeminism insists that "feminism is no longer needed as a politics" because it has "done the political work needed to eradicate gender asymmetry"[25] *or* because it is an outmoded, "spent-force,"[26] and, after all, "women are empowered."[27] Popular feminism, on the other hand, "explicitly *embraces* feminist values and ideologies and is dedicated to recognizing that gender inequality still exists."[28] And yet, popular feminism is "popular" because its political awareness and commitments are *market*-oriented and, in that sense, remain allied with the status quo.[29] An example here might be the Go Fund Me phenomenon by which private fundraising via personal networks may support women's needs or explicitly feminist causes (e.g., support for medical care for a breast cancer patient) but does so through individuated market engagement as opposed to collective intervention for systemic change that would eliminate the root problem and achieve a broad, community or public good (e.g., structural transformation of the US healthcare system and for-profit pharmaceutical corporations). Because the new female athlete-as-icon does challenge conventional understandings of the female form, public expression, and physical prowess, reactions to this figure have inspired backlash.[30] To prevent such backlash, athletes have distanced themselves from political expression and, particularly, explicit embrace of feminism.[31] In sports media, this strategy is known as the "feminine apologetic" by which "women's physical power and capabilities" are deemphasized by always coupling "female athleticism with female sex appeal,"[32] or by underscoring the female athlete's ability to balance her public, physical, athletic achievements with her roles as a wife and mother in the private realm.

Thus, in the 21st century,

> sport continues to operate as a form of "stealth feminism" . . . an arena where feminist questions emerge, where feminist principles and goals can be articulated, and where feminist strategies for change achieved all without an explicit declaration of those questions, principles, goals, or achievements as feminist.[33]

To illustrate how sport's transformative social potential is balanced with the preservation of individuated, status quo "norms," we can turn to espnW's *Nine for IX* and HBO's *Being Serena*.

Documentary, Prestige, and Sport Content Economy

Documentary historically has been hailed as a "prestige" television genre. It has flourished on the TV schedule particularly in moments of broader industrial transition. In such moments, documentary has helped to burnish network brand identity, has served to cultivate new audiences and, increasingly, has represented a cost-efficient and easily recyclable source of content across a media outlet's multiple extensions. Historically allied with "high" cultural capital as a serious, educational, and potentially challenging, thought-provoking program form, television networks—from the broadcasting and cable eras to the streaming present—have invested in documentary to promote their association with "quality" TV and, perhaps, even more so, their *distance* from "typical" TV of a given era.[34] In the 1960s, for instance, documentary series were produced by the "Big Three" broadcast networks (ABC, CBS, NBC) in part to counter increasing critical attacks on the industry for a perceived focus on profit to the exclusion of service to the public.[35] At that moment, with television finally available in a majority of US homes, a broader national conversation regarding the medium's *purpose* had become part of a larger debate over the US's postwar priorities. Documentary and its presumed appeal to a new generation of college-educated, middle- and upper-middle class TV viewers—often imagined by producers and advertisers to be white suburbanites—promised to associate television with "official" culture and its attendant educational, social, and economic capital. In other words, long before HBO used it as a marketing slogan, documentary was promoted as TV that was "not" TV—TV that was associated with the literary or novelistic, the theatrical or "legitimate" stage, and with *cinematic* qualities.

Though sports TV has, by contrast, always been associated with the quintessentially *televisual*, "mass" audience appeal and inclusiveness, it has also, through documentary, embraced conventions historically associated with film and with socially relevant, educational discourses. As seen in Chapter 2, ABC's Roone Arledge has been singled out for establishing a grammar of sports TV conventions, featuring "up close and personal" attention to human interest stories regarding athletes and programs that explored sport's broader importance in social, historical, and geographic context. As evidenced particularly in *Wide World of Sports* (ABC, 1961–1998) and in Olympics coverage, but also in *Monday Night Football* (ABC and ESPN, 1970–present), Arledge sought to attract and engage audiences for whom the appeal of sports coverage was not necessarily *about* sports.

Arledge may be credited with having developed a highly conventionalized approach to such sports content—particularly in the interest of cultivating new audiences and markets for sports TV—but he did so in a broader context in which both sports' "cinematic" and potentially educational promise was increasingly recognized and exploited.[36] Also significant to the development of a "grammar" of socially relevant television documentary in the 1960s and 1970s were two ostensibly unrelated phenomena: the development of children's educational TV that used conventions of advertising and the sounds of popular music to *teach*; and the emergence of the made-for-TV movie as a weekly staple that used melodrama to probe "serious issues from a socially critical and informed perspective."[37] Phenomena such as Children's Television Workshop's *Sesame Street* (1969–present), Marlo Thomas's *Free to Be You and Me* (ABC, 1974), and *Schoolhouse Rock* (ABC, 1973–1996) used advertising conventions and contemporary popular music to engage an explicitly multi-racial, geographically diverse youth audience for educational purposes. TV movies such as the sports-focused melodrama *Brian's Song* (ABC, 1971) used the context of pro football as a forum to examine struggles over racism and, ultimately, to portray sports as a shared venue for racial harmony. I raise these examples to suggest that televised sports documentaries' content, aesthetics, and address are indebted both to cinematic documentary traditions as well as to television genres that historically merge entertainment with education, the popular with the pedagogical, in order to engage audiences in socially relevant ways.

Though often lost in more recent critical and awards acclaim of HBO for its original fiction series, the premium cable network has always been dependent on sports programming for its institutional health and its broader self-promotion as a home for discerning audiences. HBO's first telecast in 1972 was of an NHL hockey game. In 1975, it used satellite technology to telecast the "Thrilla in Manila" World Heavyweight title bout between Muhammad Ali and Joe Frazier. With increasing competition from additional programming outlets and the home video market in the 1980s, however, HBO turned to original film production and series programming to expand its subscriber base. HBO's first made-for-TV movie was about cancer research activist and long-distance runner Terry Fox, in *The Terry Fox Story* (1983).[38] Though HBO's newsmagazine program *Real Sports* (1995–present) has long been the channel's flagship sports documentary series, in the early 2000s, HBO doubled its documentary production output.[39] As discussed later, *Being Serena's* hybridity—blending reality TV and social media conventions with first-person documentary pedagogical address—allows HBO to reach both its traditional subscriber base and its more app-engaged, mobile demographic in the era of networked media sport.

Though launched in 1979 as an "Entertainment and Sports Programming Network," ESPN began its initial Original Entertainment

Figure 3.1 Real Sports with Bryant Gumbel features HBO Sports' "quality" aesthetic

Source: HBO/Photofest © HBO

Program Division in 2001 largely to expand its viewer base by developing programming that might "attract 'casual fans,' or those who enjoy sports but are not voracious devotees."[40] The Original Programming Division was restructured in 2005 and re-emerged in 2008 as "ESPN Films." ESPN thus explicitly aligns the network's production arm with *cinematic* values, "calling attention to their use of the film medium; the involvement of well-known filmmakers in their production, and their inclusion in film festivals prior to their appearance on TV."[41] "ESPN Films" signals ESPN's investment in branding itself—particularly through its prestige documentary series—as "the public historian of record for twentieth-century sports."[42] The following specifically examines *Nine for IX*'s role in ESPN's claims to capital through the series' appeals to its status and relevance as an educator. These claims must be understood as industrial discourses that are also textual and social, reflecting presumptions about *whose* stories count and which audiences are worth cultivating in a multiplatform era in which sport content drives much of the media economy.

Nine for IX: ESPN as Educator

Even though ESPN had been the self-proclaimed "Worldwide Leader in Sports" since 1979, it was slow to include women's sports coverage or to acknowledge the new female athlete of the late 1990s. By 2010, however, as television irrevocably extended beyond (or, more accurately, alongside) the living room set to mobile devices, networks were compelled to cultivate new audiences that would intuitively and actively follow stories across multiple platforms. In addition to "traditional," scheduled programming viewed on a TV set, networks had to produce content that was amenable to viral distribution and sharing and to quickly consumable, "snackable" bits.[43] In this context, ESPN launched its "women's extension," espnW. Begun as a blog in 2010, in 2011 espnW was a website accessible from its own homepage or via ESPN.com's site. The "espnW" label also accompanied branded content and events across ESPN's platforms and at public venues such as the Tribeca Film Festival and industry or charitable events. According to then-ESPN vice president Laura Gentile, espnW-branded content would be designed with the expectation that "women consume media differently than men," with women presumed to be focused on the importance of narrative and a communal and holistic experience of actively "connecting to other women."[44] Addressing such holistic interests, links on the espnW website include threads emphasizing self-esteem and broader health and fitness resources, as the "Life/Style" section links to "Food & Nutrition," "Music & Motivation," "Style & Gear," "Training," "Women Going Places," and "How They Got That Body."

ESPN's imagination of its audience and desired content drew early critical fire for its apparent focus on casual fans less interested in sports than in widely available health and fitness blogs and marketing. As

Kristi Dosh reported in *Forbes* magazine, "Females who were already frequenters of ESPN.com and viewers of ESPN television were outraged."[45] In fact, ESPN launched espnW specifically to target the *new* female athlete (and athlete-aspirant) audience that had not previously engaged with the network. According to Dosh,

> what they've found through their research is that . . . there is an entire generation of women out there who grew up pre–Title IX who may not have had the same opportunities to participate . . . but they are athletes and sports fans (albeit of a different sort), too.[46]

Dosh quotes an "informant" who

> pointed out that they'd heard from women who watched their child's little league game from the car because they were afraid they would clap at the wrong time. . . . These women—the ones who aren't part of ESPN's existing 25% female audience—deserve to be engaged. . . . They are lost in a world of sports and no one is catering to their needs.[47]

For this audience, espnW ostensibly represents a safe space to become educated about all aspects of sports culture while also finding shared community.

Executives at ESPN also imagined a second audience to be targeted by espnW: those who *had* grown up with Title IX's protections and had been involved with sports but were admittedly oblivious to the ongoing struggles required for such opportunity and the continued *unevenness* of such equality. According to Libby Geist, associate director of development at ESPN Films:

> Growing up in North Jersey, Geist, 33, didn't think much about the issue of gender equality. "I played sports although terribly," she said. "I was never told no, whether it be a school, a class, a sport, any activity. My generation and I have

never been told no. I think inadvertently I was a beneficiary of Title IX and I had no idea of the fight and [what] all the struggle had offered me."[48]

Thus, espnW welcomed and served a community that had benefitted most from the gains of Title IX and best fit the market profile of predominantly white, middle-class professionals who had not encountered systemic, institutional impediments to educational or sports participation and had achieved goals of access and equality *within* existing structures, seeking and securing equity within the system rather than seeking to change the fundamental values upon which gender norms (or raced or classed ones) are, themselves, based.[49] Given that ESPN presumed the audience for its women's extensions, while not necessarily naïve, was also not necessarily knowledgeable about sports, or about "being told no" when it came to questions of equal access, espnW's branded content was promoted as more allied with ESPN's philanthropic and educational service ventures than with day-to-day profit imperatives. As such, espnW's inaugural branded documentary series, *Nine for IX*, was positioned to bolster ESPN's value in the 21st century's "rising ethic of corporate social responsibility (CSR) among television networks and sponsors."[50]

The *Nine for IX* series was the culmination of a three-month, multi-platform initiative for the espnW brand. "The Power of IX" celebrated the legislation's 40th anniversary with weekday morning editions of *SportsCenter* highlighting the top-40 female athletes of the prior 40 years (though the top 10 were revealed over 10 days in June, 2013, on the most-watched daily episode of *SportsCenter*, at 11:00 p.m.). *ESPN The Magazine* devoted a special issue to Title IX and its legacies. On the June 23, 2013 anniversary of the law's enactment, US soccer star and ESPN correspondent Julie Foudy hosted a celebration aired live on ABC and across the ESPN networks (including ESPN, ESPN2, ESPNU, ESPN Classic, and online at the precursor to ESPN+, ESPN3). A social media program encouraged users to upload photos to create a collage of female athletes in action. From July 2, 2013 to August 27, 2013, the ESPN Films–produced *Nine for IX* documentaries aired in prime time on ESPN. Accompanying the series' airing, espnW, in collaboration with the Tucker Center for Research on Girls & Women in Sport at the University of Minnesota, hosted the "*Nine for IX* Knowledge Center," a dossier including discussion guides, bibliographies of additional readings, and suggested activities.[51]

Nine for IX consisted of nine hour-long programs airing in the prime-time series and seven shorts, available online at the *Nine for IX* portal of espnW (where they are still available). At present, six of the full-length episodes remain available on the ESPN+ subscription app. A "complete collection" DVD box set was produced for the holiday gift market in 2013. Identifying the series as a library-worthy keepsake, this set includes the original nine hour-long programs with an additional episode on soccer star Abby Wambach, *Abby, Head On*. Executive produced by former ESPN anchor and current *Good Morning America* (ABC) host Robin Roberts, with Tribeca Film Festival co-founder and film producer Jane Rosenthal, as with *30 for 30* before it, *Nine for IX* "emphasizes its cinematic pedigree by positioning its directors," including Ava Duvernay, "as visionaries with license to explore their inspiration, integrating filmmakers' perspectives on subject matter into the films' presentation and on the *Nine for IX* website, and packaging its documentaries with movie-ticket and filmstrip graphics."[52] Screenings of *Nine for IX* episodes took place at film festivals including Tribeca, at which Bess Kargman's *Coach*—executive produced by Academy Award–winning actress and host of *The View* (ABC, 1997–present) Whoopi Goldberg—was awarded Best Documentary Short. Screenings also took place at educational venues and libraries around the country, followed by panel discussions. Critics embraced *Nine for IX* in these terms—as award-worthy, discussion-provoking, cinematic narratives—describing them as "engrossing film(s),"[53] and noting that "the episodes are so well crafted that even if you're not a sports fan, you'll find them extremely interesting and informative, and many are downright moving in their exploration of the characters involved."[54]

Nine for IX's tagline is "About Women. By Women. For Us All." Though each episode is directed "By Women" secured by ESPN for their distinct cinematic bonafides, the *Nine for IX* series at large is still

Figure 3.2   espnW's website's *Nine for IX* portal emphasizes "balance" between
athletic achievement and maternity

characterized by striking similarities in theme, content, and tone. The
overwhelming majority of the series' hour-long episodes and shorts
are "About Women" who are portrayed as exceptional individuals who
have thrived in pursuit of communal goals. The series particularly ide-
alizes imagined balance between public/career achievements and pri-
vate/familial success. The struggles for gender equality at stake in most
of the episodes are resolved through figures of singular genius that help
to secure female equality without challenging status quo, feminine ideals.[55] Specifically, the success stories of *Nine for IX* are one of two types:
icons of "the feminine apologetic" who help "viewers forget the incred-
ible amount of strength that is necessary"[56] to excel at their sport,
thereby deemphasizing "women's physical power and capabilities" by
linking "female athleticism with female sex appeal"[57] (*The Diplomat* and
the shorts *Play A Round With Me*, and *Rowdy Ronda Rousey*); or, second,
icons whose undeniable athletic achievements are couched as, ultimately, only valuable as they parallel or are balanced alongside familial
success within conventional understandings of femininity, heterosexu-
ality, and maternity (*Pat XO, Runner, The '99ers*, and the short *Coach*).
Arguably, the strongest entries of the hour-long *Nine for IX* episodes
avoid focusing on either of these two types for broader examinations

of collective actions (*Let Them Wear Towels*), permanent transformations in a sport (*VenusVS.*), and the ongoing dilemma of this very striving for balance between salability and achievement, in "nonthreatening" terms (*Branded*). Finally, a group of *Nine for IX* episodes deal with figures that are somehow "unbalanced" according to the previously given ideals and values. Focusing on athletes or family members who are unable to be categorized as either conventional sex symbols or as "appropriately" maternal (i.e., out of balance through overinvestment or focused on a partner to the exclusion of family and community), these episodes appear to address the audience as cautionary tales about isolation and to those who would challenge normative ideals (*No Limits*, *Swoopes*, and the shorts *Think Normal*, *Love & Payne*, and *Uncharted Waters*). In the following, I examine two *Nine for IX* episodes—*Pat XO* and *Branded*—to consider how the series "For Us All" positions sports as transformative in the struggle for gender equality while also upholding status quo norms as idealized. Sports are portrayed as a forum for securing market-based rights as an integrative space that activates for progress *within* preservation of traditional cultural conventions.

In the film discussion guides at the online *Nine for IX* Knowledge Center, one of the "key concepts" alongside terms such as "role model," "gender equality," "sexism," and "gender and leadership" is "Elite Mother-Coaches." The figure of the mother-coach is embodied in the hour-long *Pat XO* by Pat Summitt, Hall of Fame University of Tennessee's women's basketball coach.[58] The very title of *Pat XO* is a doubled reference to both the "x's and o's" of a coach's play diagram and to sentimental shorthand for "kisses and hugs." Pat Summitt's public persona has often seemed daunting—famous for her withering stare often directed at her own players. To instead show "a side of Pat you very, very rarely get to see," the filmmakers sent "$50.00 cameras" to "those who were coached, taught, transformed, and elevated by Pat Summitt" and asked that they record their stories. The resulting "home movie" aesthetic (conveyed both through the low-tech cameras and the fact that most contributors shot their segments in home settings) and differing production values across the episode convey an intimate, "authentic" aesthetic and appeal. Summitt's son Tyler's voice-overs, and his one-on-one segments with his mother, form the spine of the film, as he and she sit with photo albums between contributor segments and archival footage documenting Summitt's biography prior to coaching as well as her storied career.

Pat XO was produced and directed by Lisa Lax and Nancy Stern Winters, identical twin sisters whose Lookalike Productions has focused on documentary filmmaking and biography. Independently, Lax's and Winters's careers were honed as segment producers and directors for up-close-and-personal segments on *Wide World of Sports* (Winters) and NBC's Olympics coverage (Lax). Winters also had experience directing soap operas for ABC. The "Arledge aesthetic" and family drama are, thus, key conventions throughout *Pat XO*. Contributors focus, particularly, on the guiding phrases or mottos that Summitt as mother-coach imparted which still guide their actions in the present: "Left foot, right foot, breathe," to take things one step at a time; and "don't play the victim, ever."

Though several segments in *Pat XO* paint a potentially unflattering portrait of Summitt's controlling and demanding ways (including a coaching colleague's revelation that, while in labor, Summitt insisted her plane return to Tennessee rather than going to a local hospital in order to abide by her proclamation that "I will not have a baby in the state of Virginia"), the overall tone of the film instead remains glowing, if melancholic, due to Summitt's revelation of her "early-onset dementia, Alzheimer's type" and subsequent retirement at the age of 59. Further, Summitt's tendency to severity is, here, contextualized with friend and family anecdotes that cast her father in an even more rigid light. Summitt herself recounts that the first time her father hugged her was when she won her first national championship at the age of 43.

While clearly outlining the staggering accomplishments and unwavering expectations marking Summitt's elite coaching career, *Pat XO* emphasizes "up close and personal" history that ultimately foregrounds her role as a *mother* first. Family members are courtside for every game, and the coach's teams are portrayed as successful only when they embrace familial unity and maternal guidance. The film uses the home video segments interspersed with conventional, static, talking-head interviews, archival game, practice, and news footage. Here, successful coaching is great *teaching* and guidance in life skills beyond the court. But the film strays from straightforward recounting of professional achievements to focus on questions of maternity. *Pat XO* uses "amateur" production techniques and medicalized drama to humanize Summitt's formidable persona and to position her *primary* role as being a Mom to son, Tyler, and his "161 sisters" who played for Summitt in his lifetime.

Of the handful of *Nine for IX* productions that do not couch women's sports in familial, maternal, or (heterosexual) romantic terms are episodes dealing with women's athletics as a potential site for collective progress and transformation in the struggle for gender equality. Notably, these programs take sport's integrative capacity as a commonsense given. This stance honors the tradition of Title IX as a law of inclusion and access, while it also preserves sports as an inherently *consensual* realm, rather than a revolutionary one. *Branded* specifically interrogates the feminine apologetic to address the ongoing struggle for parity between women's athletic achievements and broader, commercial, market rewards. Directed jointly by documentarians Rachel Grady and Heidi Ewing, *Branded* examines two dilemmas facing female athletes who hope to make a career from their sport. On the one hand, there is not typically enough money in a given sport to succeed and be paid on merit alone. On the other hand, success in the market beyond sport often depends upon downplaying athletic skill for "sex-appeal." Succeeding as an athlete alone is noble but under-resourced. But succeeding in the endorsement market risks diminishing one's sporting reputation and criticism for "selling out." Rather than necessarily being a sports world problem, *Branded* suggests more pointedly that this is a broader socioeconomic, structural dilemma. As Sandra Rosenbush, former editor of (the now defunct) *Sports Illustrated for Women* states, "It's a white male world. We're just living in it." As if to prove Rosenbush's point, the next interviewee, (white, male) sports marketer Leonard Armato, responds, "What makes a woman valuable? Her currency is how attractive she is."

Branded is thoroughly conventional in its construction and address. All interviewees are shot in a black box studio with exposed lights.

Commentary alternates between athletes, sports journalists, marketing experts, and sports agents. The episode makes it overwhelmingly clear that traditional ideals of "femininity" and "sex appeal" *or* "the girl next door" translate into commercial success because, as then-ESPN reporter Darren Rovell acknowledges, "In order for women's sports to survive, you need men to be into it." Voices from tennis star Chris Evert to sports agent Jill Smoller to volleyball icon Gabrielle Reece wearily affirm this stance. Multiple WNBA MVP Lisa Leslie states:

> At the end of the day, it's about business . . . having enough money to be able to pay players, to be able to raise salaries. . . . We *are* a product. We're selling something. We're selling our sport. And how we look is just as important as how we play.

Branded thus returns us to Sarah Banet-Weiser and Laura Portwood-Stacer's proposal that the popular feminist text "explicitly *embraces* feminist values and ideologies and is dedicated to recognizing that gender inequality still exists" and yet, market-based marks of achievement, while requisite to achieving equality, also must necessarily "stop short of recognizing, naming, or disrupting the political economic conditions that allow inequality to be profitable."[59] On this point we are confronted with a fundamental paradox that haunts *Nine for IX* in spite of its educational project and archive of online resources. As Travis Vogan has noted, while on the one hand, *Nine for IX* "composed an unprecedented platform for sports documentaries about women and for women filmmakers,"[60] ESPN aired the series "across July and August—the sports calendar's slowest season,"[61] and, presently, accessing espnW content on ESPN+ or at ESPN.com requires an investment in rooting through layers of submenus by the user. All of this suggests that while espnW established a distinctive brand and new audience for its flagship network, "The Worldwide Leader in Sports" itself has not yet carved out a level playing field for women's sports. Several years beyond *Nine for IX*, how might a subscription, premium cable network, and its app extensions offer a different sense of voice and exposure?

Figure 3.3 Being Serena emphasizes Serena Williams's authorship and labor

HBO's *Being Serena* (2018) positions Serena Williams as the author of her own story, simultaneously challenging the previously given conventions while, strategically, re-inscribing them.

HBO's *Being Serena* and the Athlete Auteur

While *Being Serena* contributes to HBO Sports' tradition of using documentary to burnish the network's industrial and broader critical capital it also utilizes different aesthetic practices and modes of address than prior HBO Sports documentaries. The mini-series combines HBO's traditional reliance upon Arledge-era conventions of "up-close-and-personal" humanizing of otherwise superhuman athletes and their feats with what David P. Marshall has theorized to be "presentational media"—a hybrid "expression of the self that . . . is not entirely interpersonal in nature nor is it entirely highly mediated or representational."[62] Specifically, *Being Serena* combines conventional sports documentary appeals with an Instagram aesthetic characterized by modes of direct address to a presumptively female audience that evokes social media modes of self-presentation.

Julia Eckel has described the selfie as "a photo that documents and at the same time exhibits an act of authorship."[63] The selfie is "a visual gesture of 'see me showing you me.'"[64] While direct address, medium close-up sequences in *Being Serena* do not include other familiar indicators of the selfie—such as the outstretched hand or the selfie stick—Serena Williams's huge social media following[65] and the striking narrative and aesthetic overlap between her social media feed and the mini-series' aesthetics and address positions the documentary series as an *articulating* text, simultaneously grounding Williams's star text while acting as an "*agent* of media convergence that functions through *connection*."[66] *Being Serena* thus functions as a "star text of connection," potentially pulling "audiences from one site"—Williams's Instagram feed, in particular—"to another," here, the relatively more staid and old-school HBO or its mobile and streaming app HBO Max, "which can then serve to bolster the star image even further."[67]

Being Serena foregrounds shifts in sports media discourse both as it emphasizes female voice and as it exemplifies "contemporary changes to the concept of 'the author' in times of media ubiquity."[68] A screen capture from Williams's Instagram feed indicates her account's general aesthetic: Absent any indicators of a traditional selfie, the feed alternates between direct address of Serena's gaze and "candid" shots, taken as if unobserved. Similarly, throughout *Being Serena*, sequences are punctuated by direct address, medium close-ups, and shots of Serena "unaware" of the camera in tableaux that evoke her social media stream.

Here, however, we should interrogate HBO's promotional claim that *Being Serena* is "Her Story. Her Words." *Being Serena* was created and produced for HBO Sports' division by IMG Original Content. According to IMG's own promotional materials, the company is a global concern specializing in sports, fashion, events, and "branded entertainment experiences" as well as sports training complexes and league development, "marketing, media and licensing for brands, sports organizations and collegiate institutions." As part of the William Morris/Endeavor group, IMG runs Fashion Weeks in New York, Milan, and London and holds the merchandising licenses to over 200 US sports

Figure 3.4   Serena Williams's Instagram feed: direct address, labor, the intimate and familial

teams, Wimbledon, and the Australian and US Opens. IMG represents sports stars and models and—with WME as its partner—actors and other entertainers as well. Serena Williams's IMG agent, Jill Smoller, is a recurring interviewee in *Being Serena*. IMG Original Content thus represents a full-circle return to early broadcasting's practice of agency packaging of programming, content, talent, and all elements of production.[69] Through this partnership, *Being Serena* clearly fits with Richard Dyer's conception of a star text of *promotion*. As Dyer notes, while "promotion is probably the most straightforward of all the texts which construct a star image, in that it is the most deliberate, direct, intentional and self-conscious" that, however "(is not to say that it is by any means *entirely* any of those things)."[70] Indeed, in spite of *Being Serena's* "packaged" nature, Williams uses voice and embodiment to cut through display, in order to critique and comment in explicitly Black, feminist terms. *Being Serena* is, in this way, a space for Serena Williams's visible performance of code-switching.

On the one hand, throughout the mini-series and its promotion, Williams performs "strategic ambiguity" that, as argued by Ralina Joseph, "entails foregrounding crossover appeal, courting multiple publics, speaking in coded language, and smoothing and soothing fears of difference as simply an incidental side note."[71] On the other hand, throughout *Being Serena*—and in her tennis activism outside the text—Williams overtly engages what Samantha N. Sheppard identifies as "an embodied history represented on screen that goes *beyond* the film's diegesis, that engages *social* issues, conditions, and changes specific to Black lived and imagined experience."[72] One of the most striking features of *Being Serena* in this respect is its focus on work and *labor* as constants across each defining element of Williams's persona: to excel as the world's greatest athlete requires grueling, constant, physical labor; to survive childbirth requires constant surveillance of one's body and oversight of one's medical care; to forge a relationship and marriage requires cross-country and global management and coordination as well as new vulnerability and intimacy; to be a Mom requires decisions about labor, the body, and childbirth as well as management of breastfeeding, sleep, and diet all while training. This emphasis on work and labor was read by some of the series' reviewers as creating a cold, stylized, managerial tone,[73] while others praised the series' raw, vulnerable, intimate, and candid revelations.[74]

What *Being Serena* allows—particularly in dialogue with Instagram—is for Serena Williams to revel in and reveal a home life featuring her role as a wife and mother in ways that revise Williams's star athlete persona, intersecting instead with what Suzanne Leonard's *Wife, Inc.* acknowledges to be "postfeminist media culture's most favored icon, . . . depictions of wives are the foremost way in which American culture currently negotiates norms of femininity."[75] Featuring heart-rending scenes of Williams as Olympia's mom, as Alexis Ohanian's partner, and in daily life with her sisters, Mom and Dad, and friends, *Being Serena* quite literally re-inscribes Serena's body within the logics of maternity and family, ameliorating historic discourses of perceived "threat" of her physical prowess and expertise, coded as female masculinity.[76]

In promotional interviews for the series, Williams emphasized this image as the core of *Being Serena* and, further, as a more "honest" image than her better-known tennis persona. For example, in an interview with the *Toronto Star*'s Christopher Clarey, Williams states:

> That's not me, actually, to be honest, on the court. As much a part of my life as it is, I become a different person when I play tennis. The second I step onto the facilities, the grounds, I become a different person, and the second I step off I'm back to being Serena, no pun intended.[77]

Similarly, on *Good Morning America* (ABC, April 26, 2018) she said:

> When I'm on court, that's not necessarily me. That's just my tennis, two hours of the day. There's the mom, I can say now. There's the wife, I can say now. There's, and it's just me. It's just Serena. I'm just being myself. Being Serena.

Here, Williams appears to be extending her "brand" through embracing a "new domesticity" that is aligned with popular and neoliberal modes of feminism, epitomized by "mom-lebrities" such as Reece Witherspoon and corporate figures such as Facebook COO Sheryl Sandberg and her *Lean In* movement. This is feminism as a sensibility which, while ostensibly about community-building, has historically been associated with explicitly affluent, corporate, white, mainstream, non-activist allegiances.

And yet, throughout the text of *Being Serena*, Williams is also clearly visibly and vocally allied with Black, activist feminism. In a somewhat jarring sequence in episode 4, titled "Change," Serena's voice takes on particular resonance following an awkward good luck call from Sheryl Sandberg herself, as Williams prepares to return to Indian Wells. As Serena is eating and pumping breastmilk for Olympia, Sandberg calls to wish her luck. Serena says she is nervous, and Sandberg asks if she's ever felt nervous before. Serena responds, "Always—I'm nervous before every match." "Well," Sandberg replies, "then that's probably what's making you *you*, and nervous must be good." Sandberg notes the "profound" nature of Serena's return to a venue where she was once "booed for being Black," then concludes the call by telling Serena, "I cannot wait to see you show everyone what a Mom can do." While acknowledging the gutting racism that forever marks Indian Wells as a public space in Serena's career, Sandberg quickly "restores" the over-arching value of the private sphere, arguably, the lens through which Serena will *now* be received by Indian Wells' attendees. After Serena hangs up to finish dinner, the scene cuts to an empty, stormy, over-cast Indian Wells tennis stadium, and Serena's voice-over explains the venue's racist past. Referencing her sister, Venus, and her dad, Richard, she says,

> We were always outsiders. I don't think anyone knew what to do with these two Black sisters and their daddy, a strong, proud, Black man. I swore I'd *never* return to Indian Wells. But . . . it was important to forgive. To start again. To make *that* part of the story.

Here, Sandberg seems to stand in for a politically naïve but admiring white female fan, who Serena is then able to educate to a history of systemic racism.

This sequence and two others in particular point to Samantha N. Sheppard's proposal that African American sports documentary indexes "Black athletes' embodied passions," to "show how 'black bodies carry within themselves a history, a memory' (Young, 2010, p. 20) and, in turn, are repositories of these histories and memories."[78] For Sheppard, such documentaries "are expressive, communicative bodies of work that highlight, document, investigate and historicize Black sporting bodies *doin' work*."[79] In the first of these sequences, Serena meets with her coach, Patrick Mouratoglou, about her post-pregnancy training and preparation for the Grand Slam season ahead. In the second, Serena concludes a training session by explicitly invoking a "Black girl attitude." Both of these scenes take place in the final episode of the series, titled "Resolve," which focuses on Serena's intense commitment to isolate herself in order to focus on regaining her championship form, post-partum. Williams meets with Mouratoglou in a medical examination room at his training center in France. With a hand-held camera peering over his shoulder as the viewer looks at Serena's nervous expression while facing him, the coach raises his voice to implore her to "stop breastfeeding! You are too heavy. You are stocking a lot of fat." Tearfully, Serena responds, "I'm doing everything. . . . It seems like you guys think I'm being lazy." But, she also admits, in voice-over, that "I miss my body; being able to do amazing things. I miss winning." A training montage follows which concludes with Mouratoglou looking up at the newly "resolved" Serena powering through an elliptical session. She throws him side-eye and notes, "I mean, I didn't get here by giving very little effort. Twenty-three Grand Slams later, not including doubles and other things. And gold medals and titles. . . . I've never, never not given a full effort." As Mouratoglou speaks inaudibly beneath her, Serena steps down and, just above under-her-breath, says, "And, here comes the 'Black girl attitude.'" These scenes, together, visualize Claudia Rankine's observation that:

> Serena's grace comes because she won't be forced into stillness; she won't accept those racist projections onto her body without speaking back; she won't go gently into the white light of victory. Her excellence doesn't mask the struggle it takes to achieve each win.[80]

Being Serena is itself a strategically ambivalent text. It is a public relations electronic press-kit for IMG and Serena Williams. It is a bid by HBO to attract a younger Instagram-follower viewing population to an aging premium outlet. But, it is also a Black, feminist meditation on medical advocacy and self-care, the labor of mothering (and its resource demands), and the constancy of work required to seamlessly yet vigilantly code-switch to sustain both self-hood and a multi-faceted career that underwrites the livelihood of its extended community.

Sports stars are high-profile cultural influencers and content-creators with a notable ability to both provoke broad public discussion and, further, to effect real, tangible policy change (as in Serena Williams's influence on professional tennis's rule change regarding player ranking following pregnancy leave). And yet in spite of inspiring and even empowering images that frame race, gender, and sexual identity in seemingly new, progressive ways as they "circulate in an 'economy of visibility' . . . gaining ever more eyeballs and 'fans,'" still, overall, power relations "don't seem to change very much."[81] Indeed, perhaps more visibly than in other fields, and on a more quotidian basis, sports events, athletes, and their actions make it clear that history does not move in a smooth, teleological manner, advancing towards consistent progress. Instead, as Sheppard has noted, the sporting/society intertext is characterized by what Stuart Hall calls "the double movement of containment and resistance,"[82] or progress *within* tradition, and challenge that creates rupture but also provokes backlash and is, often—if not always—re-inscribed into conventional, institutional frameworks as the consensual common-sense. Chapter 4 takes up this tension between the potentially resistant and even revolutionary power of sports events and icons and the broader institutional, corporate, and commercial concerns that consistently contain, claw back, or, even *punish* such ruptures in the name of broader "community" and "shared" national ideals. Chapter 4 further explores Fleetwood's paradox "between racial iconicity and racial precarity"[83] whereby Black athletes and celebrities in particular simultaneously drive viewer engagement and profits to white-owned leagues, media interests, and their advertisers, while they remain threats to those same interests.

Notes

1. Karen Blumenthal, *Let Me Play: The Story of Title IX, The Law That Changed the Future of Girls in America* (New York: Atheneum, 2005), 51.
2. Thomas P. Oates, *Football and Manliness: An Unauthorized Feminist Account of the NFL* (Urbana, IL: University of Illinois Press, 2017), 21. And, see Sharon Patricia Holland, *The Erotic Life of Racism* (Durham, NC: Duke University Press, 2012).
3. First-person media forms, here, particularly include reality TV, streaming-era documentary TV, and social media outlets.
4. Brett Hutchins and David Rowe, *Sport Beyond Television: The Internet, Digital Media and the Rise of Networked Media Sport* (New York: Routledge, 2012), 5.

5. Oates, *Football and Manliness*, 20.

6. Cheryl Cooky, Michael A. Messner, and Michael Musto, "'It's Dude Time!' A Quarter Century of Excluding Women's Sports in Televised News and Highlight Shows," in *No Slam Dunk: Gender, Sport and the Unevenness of Social Change*, eds. Cheryl Cooky and Michael Messner (New Brunswick, NJ: Rutgers University Press, 2018), 211.

7. As discussed in detail later in the chapter, espnW was launched as ESPN's "women's extension," initially via an online blog in 2010. It remains an online presence as a submenu within ESPN's website and as a content area within ESPN's subscription service, ESPN+.

8. Quoting Bernice "Bunny" Sandler, whose research and complaints regarding discrimination in higher education in the 1960s encouraged the drafting of Title IX. Steve Wulf, "Title IX: 37 Words That Changed Everything," *espn.com*, April 29, 2012, www.espn.com/espnw/title-ix/article/772632/37-words-changed-everything. Notably, while the 19th Amendment was ratified in August 1920, universal women's enfranchisement was not extended in the US to most Native Americans (1957), Asian Americans (1952), and African Americans (1965) until much closer to Title IX's own passage.

9. "Title IX of the Education Amendments of 1972, 20 U.S.C. A § 1681 Et. SEQ," 1972, www.epa.gov/ocr/title-ix-education-amendments-act-1972

10. Blumenthal, *Let Me Play*, 88. The three-part test requires an educational institution receiving federal funding to "offer its males and females roughly equal opportunities to play sports" proportionate to enrollments; to "show a history of improving opportunities for girls and women" and to "show it was meeting the demands and interests of its female students."

11. Betsey Butler, "How Title IX Transformed US Sports," *Los Angeles Times*, July 10, 2019, A11.

12. Blumenthal, *Let Me Play*, 111.

13. Nancy Hogshead-Makar and Andrew Zimbalist, eds., *Equal Play: Title IX and Social Change* (Philadelphia, PA: Temple University Press, 2007), 104.

14. Leslie Heywood and Shari L. Dworkin, *Built to Win: The Female Athlete as Cultural Icon* (Minneapolis: University of Minnesota Press, 2003), xv.

15. Julie A. Wilson, *Neoliberalism* (New York: Routledge, 2018), 2.

16. Wilson, *Neoliberalism*, 2.

17. Wilson, 2.

18. Wilson, 2.

19. Wilson, 3.

20. Samantha King, *Pink Ribbons, Inc: Breast Cancer and the Politics of Philanthropy* (Minneapolis: University of Minnesota Press, 2006), 48.

21. Judith Butler, "Athletic Genders: Hyperbolic Instances and/or the Overcoming of Sexual Binarism," *Stanford Humanities Review* 6, no. 2 (1998), https://web.stanford.edu/group/SHR/6-2/html/butler.html.

22. Heywood and Dworkin, *Built to Win*, 3.

23. Heywood and Dworkin, 3.

24. Ron Becker, *Gay TV and Straight America* (New Brunswick, NJ: Rutgers University Press, 2006), 80–81.

25. Sarah Banet-Weiser, *Empowered: Popular Feminism and Popular Misogyny* (Durham, NC: Duke University Press, 2018), 19.

26. Angela McRobbie, "Post-Feminism and Popular Culture," *Feminist Media Studies* 4, no. 3 (2004): 255.

27. Banet-Weiser, *Empowered*, 19.

28. Banet-Weiser, 20.

29. Sarah Banet-Weiser and Laura Portwood-Stacer, "The Traffic in Feminism: An Introduction to the Commentary and Criticism on Popular Feminism," *Feminist Media Studies* 17, no. 5 (2017): 886.

30. King, *Pink Ribbons, Inc.*, x.

31. King, xi.

32. Amanda Roth and Susan A. Basow, "Femininity, Sports, and Feminism: Developing a Theory of Physical Liberation," *Journal of Sports & Social Issues* 28, no. 3 (August 2004): 252.

33. Cheryl Cooky, "Women, Sports, and Activism," in *No Slam Dunk: Gender, Sport and the Unevenness of Social Change*, eds. Cheryl Cooky and Michael Messner (New Brunswick, NJ: Rutgers University Press, 2018), 86.

34. The term "quality TV" is most often associated with Jane Feuer's definition as applied to the "socially relevant" sitcoms produced by MTM Enterprises in the 1970s, including *The Mary Tyler Moore Show* (CBS, 1970–1977). This term has, since, become commonplace in popular TV criticism, especially in reference to original series produced by cable and premium channels such as AMC's *Mad Men* (2007–2015) or *Breaking Bad* (2008–2013) or HBO's *The Sopranos* (1999–2007) or *Game of Thrones* (2011–2019). See Jane Feuer, Paul Kerr, and Tise Vahimagi, eds., *MTM: Quality Television* (London: BFI Publishing, 1984). And: Jane Feuer, "HBO and the Concept of Quality TV," in *Quality TV: Contemporary American Television and Beyond*, eds. Janet McCabe and Kim Akass (New York: I.B. Tauris & Co., Ltd., 2007), 147–157.

35. Michael Curtin, *Redeeming the Wasteland: Television Documentary and Cold War Politics* (New Brunswick, NJ: Rutgers University Press, 1995), 7, 3.

36. Travis Vogan, *Keepers of the Flame: NFL Films and the Rise of Sports Media* (Urbana, IL: University of Illinois Press, 2014).

37. Elayne Rapping, *The Movie of the Week: Private Stories, Public Events* (Minneapolis: University of Minnesota Press, 1992), ix.

38. Notably, two of HBO's early original series both focused on the world of professional sports. The oft-forgotten (and, therefore, pointedly absent from HBO's self-styled history of its qualitative "difference" from the rest of TV) *1st and 10* (1984–1991) was a sitcom that featured Delta Burke as the owner of a pro football franchise. *Arli$$* (1996–2002) featured creator Robert Wuhl as a sports agent.

39. Catherine Johnson, "Tele-Branding in TVIII," *New Review of Film and Television Studies* 5, no. 1 (2007): 8–9.

40. Travis Vogan, *ESPN: The Making of a Sports Media Empire* (Urbana, IL: University of Illinois Press, 2015), 96.

41. Vogan, *Keepers of the Flame*, 126.

42. Travis Vogan, "ESPN: Live Sports, Documentary Prestige, and On-Demand Culture," in *From Networks to Netflix: A Guide to Changing Channels*, ed. Derek Johnson (New York: Routledge, 2018), 52.

43. See, here, Ethan Tussey's discussion of "snackable media," the workplace audience, and conglomerate commercialization of online behavior in his *The Procrastination Economy: The Big Business of Downtime* (New York: New York University Press, 2013).

44. Gentile, quoted in "ESPN Aims for Female Audience With espnW," *USA Today*, September 30, 2010.

45. Kristi Dosh, "espnW: A Marketing Message Gone Wrong," *Forbes*, December 13, 2010.

46. Dosh, "espnW."

47. Dosh.

48. Quoted in Kara Yorio, "Bergen Native Heads Series on Women's Sports," *Herald News*, July 9, 2013, D1.

49. See also: Pamela J. Creedon, "Women, Media and Sport: Creating and Reflecting Gender Values," in *Women, Media and Sport: Challenging Gender Values*, ed. Pamela J. Creedon (Thousand Oaks, CA: Sage Publications, 1994), 2–27.

50. Laurie Ouellette, *Lifestyle TV* (New York: Routledge, 2016), 76.

51. Though no longer available online, the Knowledge Center is discussed in: Tara Chozet, "espnW Uses *Nine for IX* Films to Drop Some Knowledge," *ESPN Front Row*, July 31, 2014, espnfrontrow.com/2014/07/espnw-uses-nine-for-ix-films-drop-knowledge/.

52. Vogan, "ESPN: Live Sports," 142.

53. "'Nine for IX' Gets Off to Terrific Start with 'Venus VS.'," *Examiner*, July 3, 2013.

54. A.K. Easton, "ESPN's 'Nine for IX' Features Katarina Witt in 'The Diplomat'," *Entertainment Examiner*, August 6, 2013.

55. See here, also, Chris Holmlund's discussion of film documentaries about female body builders that assure viewers that reimagining feminine ideals does not "entail loss of love, power, and privilege." Chris Holmlund, *Impossible Bodies: Femininity and Masculinity at the Movies* (New York: Routledge, 2002), 22.

56. Roth and Basow, "Femininity, Sports, and Feminism."

57. Heywood and Dworkin, *Built to Win*, 9.

58. The *Nine for IX* short, *Coach*, features Rutgers University coaching legend C. Vivian Stringer as an "Elite Mother-Coach." For detailed analysis of feature documentary *This Is a Game, Ladies* (2004) about Stringer, see Samantha N. Sheppard, *Sporting Blackness: Race, Embodiment, and Critical Muscle Memory on Screen* (Berkeley: University of California Press, 2020).

59. Sarah Banet-Weiser and Laura Portwood Stacer, "The Traffic in Feminism: An Introduction to the Commentary and Criticism on Popular Feminism," *Feminist Media Studies* 17, no. 5 (2017): 886.

60. Vogan, *ESPN: The Making of a Sports Media Empire*, 143.

61. Vogan, 144.

62. David P. Marshall, "The Promotion and Presentation of the Self: Celebrity as Marker of Presentational Media," *Celebrity Studies* 1, no. 1 (2010): 35.

63. Julia Eckel, "Selfies and Authorship: On the Displayed Authorship and the Author Function of the Selfie," in *Exploring The Selfie: Historical, Theoretical and Analytical Approaches to Digital Self-Photography*, eds. Julia Eckel, Jens Ruchatz, and Sabine Wirth (London: Palgrave Macmillan, 2018), 131.

64. Eckel, "Selfies and Authorship," 132.

65. Serena Williams has 1.7 million Instagram followers and 6.1 million Twitter followers.

66. Elizabeth Ellcessor, "Tweeting @feliciaday: Online Social Media, Convergence, and Subcultural Stardom," *Cinema Journal* 51, no. 2 (2012): 52.

67. Ellcessor, "Tweeting @feliciaday," 48.

68. Eckel, "Selfies and Authorship," 132.

69. IMG also partnered with HBO on the production of *March to Madness* (2017) about UConn's women's basketball team.

70. Richard Dyer, *Stars* (London: British Film Institute, 1998), 60.

71. Ralina Joseph, *Postracial Resistance: Black Women, Media, and the Uses of Strategic Ambiguity* (New York: New York University Press, 2018), 3.

72. Samantha N. Sheppard, "Historical Contestants: African American Documentary Traditions in 'On the Shoulders of Giants'," *Journal of Sport & Social Issues* 4, no. 6 (2017): 475.

73. See, for example Christina Cauterucci, "Show Everything, Reveal Nothing: HBO's 'Being Serena' Is an All-Access Pass to the Tennis Star's Life That Provides No Access to Her Heart or Brain," *Slate*, May 2, 2018.

74. See, for example: Ira Madison, III, "In 'Being Serena' Serena Williams Bares Her Soul," *The Daily Beast*, May 2, 2018.

75. Suzanne Leonard, *Wife, Inc.: The Business of Marriage in the Twenty-First Century* (New York: New York University Press, 2018), 4–5.

76. See, for example Jamie Schultz, "Reading the Catsuit: Serena Williams and the Production of Blackness at the 2002 US Open," *Journal of Sport & Social Issues* 29 (2005): 338–357.

77. Christopher Clarey, "No Strings Attached," *The Toronto Star*, April 29, 2018, 81.

78. Sheppard, "Historical Contestants," 475. Sheppard is here quoting Harvey Young, *Embodying Black Experience: Stillness, Critical Memory, and the Black Body* (Ann Arbor: University of Michigan Press, 2010), 20.

79. Sheppard, 475.

80. Claudia Rankine, "The Meaning of Serena Williams: On Tennis and Black Excellence," *The New York Times Magazine*, August 25, 2015, www.nytimes.com/2015/08/30/magazine/the-meaning-of-serena-williams.html.

81. Banet-Weiser and Portwood Stacer, "The Traffic in Feminism," 885.

82. Samantha N. Sheppard, "Give and Go: The Double Movement of 'Shut Up and Dribble'," *Los Angeles Review of Books*, February 12, 2019, https://lareviewofbooks.org/article/give-go-double-movement-shut-dribble/.

83. Nicole Fleetwood, *On Racial Icons: Blackness and the Public Imagination* (New Brunswick, NJ: Rutgers University Press, 2015), 111.

4

THE LEVEL PLAYING FIELD?

Sports TV and Cultural Debate

This book's cover photo was taken by Mitchell Leff on November 26, 2017, when the Philadelphia Eagles defeated the Chicago Bears in Chicago, 31–3. In an image that was widely telecast, Eagles defensive back Rodney McCleod, Jr., defensive back Malcolm Jenkins, and defensive end Chris Long stand on the sidelines during the national anthem. McCleod and Jenkins hold their fists in the air while Long puts a supportive hand on Jenkins's back. The shot immediately conveys two competing yet definitive mythologies of US sports culture. In one reading, this photo conveys the dominant cultural imagination of sports as a masculine realm of equality and collectivity representing a "colorblind" level playing field. Together, this bonded and "woke" Eagles team forged a community both epitomizing *and* transcending everyday life, leading to a Super Bowl victory at the conclusion of the season.[1] The raised fists of African American athletes, McCleod and Jenkins, however, immediately call to mind iconic protests of Black athletes from John Carlos's and Tommie Smith's awards podium protest at the 1968 Mexico City Olympics, to Muhammad Ali's criticisms of US imperialism abroad and racism at home in the 1970s, to Colin Kaepernick's anthem action in 2016.[2] In this reading, the teammates connect with and reenergize a rich history of Black activism and of sports' importance as a stage from which to make a "mainstream," broad public aware of systemic *in*equality and the importance of color *consciousness* or awareness of, and response to, the fact that the systemic biases (and privileges) that structure US society are premised on race.

Here, sports are not separate from or transcendent of the everyday, but are an intensified realm confronting the same issues that are present in any community or family. The image thus powerfully communicates paradoxical ideals—often held at the same time—that define major, male-dominated, US sports culture: sports remains the most prominent weekly and seasonal space for the idealization of homosocial bonds and the conservation of consensus, while also, increasingly, serving as the primary social institution at the forefront of civil discourse, calling for systemic transformation.

The photo also symbolizes the fact that sports TV's defining narrative and aesthetic mode is *melodramatic*. Though melodrama is often associated with "feminized" cultural discourses, sports represent mainstream commercial culture's domain of masculine melodrama. As Pro Bowl NFL defensive end Michael Bennett has stated, "I know people love this league, and I think above all else it's because the NFL is a soap opera for men."[3] Linda Williams has proposed that "melodrama is a peculiarly democratic and American form that seeks dramatic revelation of moral and emotional truths through a dialectic of pathos and action."[4] Sports consistently exemplify this dialectic and, further, are characterized by strong emotionalism, extreme situations and actions, narratives of good and evil, the reward of virtue, and preservation of the (usually male) group against external threat.[5] Melodrama is marked by anxiety about transformations, particularly as these may challenge received race and gender hierarchies and "norms." In the climactic scene of *Brian's Song* (ABC, 1971)—perhaps the most renowned "male weepie" of all time—Gale Sayers (Billy Dee Williams) begins his acceptance speech for the NFL's George S. Halas Courage Award by focusing on his teammate, who lies in a hospital bed, dying of cancer. Says Sayers, "I *love* Brian Piccolo—and I'd like all of you to love him, too." Male-dominated sports are the only mainstream cultural venue of publicly acceptable male *tears* and vocal expression of same-sex, homosocial love.

The fact that sports are firmly located within the cultural "mainstream" consistently reinforcing the hegemonic dominance of cis-gender, heterosexual, white men against perceived threats to that dominance informs its melodramatic expression. Sports narratives address their audiences in "populist" terms. Reece Peck has theorized a "populist aesthetic" in news television. These characteristics are evident in sports coverage as they align with melodrama: Sports TV invokes personalized modes of social analysis; it arrives at unambiguous (moral) conclusions; and it is marked by visceral language, graphic images, colorful presentation, and embodied performance.[6] Though there is no innate correlation between populist aesthetics and political disposition, historically, sports discourse has been associated with conservative cultural orientations. As one of the largest commercial markets in media culture, sports TV prioritizes consistency and stasis over rupture and transformation. Overall, sports is characterized by progress *within* tradition, or "change within continuity."[7]

Arguably, the period from 2016 to the present has been the most activist and contentious period in sports' history of overtly political expression since the late 1960s and early 1970s. Though the Black Lives Matter movement began in 2012, following the killing of 17-year-old Trayvon Martin, athlete support of BLM began garnering sustained national media attention in 2016. Many commentators have suggested that Muhammad Ali's death in 2016 activated a new generation of athletes to find and express a more politically engaged voice.[8] Actions in solidarity with BLM and racial justice initiatives included the University of Missouri football team's support of student demonstrators, and WNBA and NBA player demonstrations and collective statements (as with Carmelo Anthony, Chris Paul, Dwayne Wade, and LeBron James's ESPY Award call for the end to gun violence). However, it was with San Francisco 49er quarterback Colin Kaepernick's seated and, then, kneeling protest during the national anthem in the 2016 season that such activism became a broader cultural phenomenon, topic of kitchen table and watercooler debates, and the focus—in some quarters—of a tremendous, enraged backlash.

The vitriol that was visited upon Kaepernick for his protest was, ostensibly, premised on the belief that sports "should" be a space "free" of politics, or a separate and transcendent sphere where athletes "stick to sports," do what they're "paid well" to do, and function as an escape

119

hatch "apart from the viewer's work, from bills, from family anxiet-
ies, from conflicts in the community, from national and international
politics."[9] By bringing political expression to the field, Kaepernick
ostensibly took the game out of the mainstream. And yet, the genu-
inely overwrought—or, "excessive," in melodramatic terms—nature
of the backlash suggested that it was less the entry of "politics" into
sports that was objectionable to Kaepernick's detractors than *whose*
message was being expressed and the corporeality and iconography of
its expression. For Kaepernick's critics, his protest ruptured the "invis-
ibility," interchangeability, and object-like status of athletes common
to the smooth functioning of the game. Kaepernick's call for critical
consciousness and awareness required rational apprehension and recognition of both his individual voice and larger, collective claims. It
called for recognition of the humanity of the claimant and virtue of the
cause. Such deliberative discourse directly contradicts the imagination
of athletes as objectified (and objectifiable), machine-like, and playing
by rote. The unwillingness to recognize Kaepernick's protest is thus,
also, raced. As critical race theorist kihana miraya ross notes, "in the
minds of many, the relation between humanity and blackness is an
antagonism, is irreconcilable. Anti-blackness describes the inability to
recognize black humanity."[10] Further, it might be asked who has "the
luxury of viewing sports as an escape" rather than seeing "the same
inequalities in sports we see on a daily basis"?[11] For Kaepernick's critics and those that boycotted the NFL in the season that followed, then,
it is not that "politics" has no place in sports, but that political speech
and who may voice it have highly conventionalized, "acceptable" limits.

One might consider, here, the relative lack of outcry at white New
England Patriot quarterback Tom Brady's display of a "Make America
Great Again" cap in his locker during the 2017–2018 season; or, the
widespread acceptance of the NFL's intertwined relationship with the
US armed forces, militarism, and "weaponized patriotism."[12] It is not
that sports and politics do not mix, but that

> the very pleasures involved in sports spectatorship may
> involve some degree of "taking up" the dominant position

offered by sports texts: identifying with normative masculine points of view; celebrating the utopian fantasies of integration and incorporation and engaging in a discursive practice which rationalizes ideological contradictions and disintegration with artificial oppositional structures.[13]

What follows thus examines three sites of *rupture* of the mainstream "pleasures involved in sports spectatorship" as each posed a challenge to "acceptable" discourse at the intersection of sports, community, the visibility of athlete labor, and political expression or *voice*. Each of these ruptures is, however, consistent with sports' broader melodramatic mode, as the "crisis" each represents is infused with strong emotionalism and pathos, moral judgments and polarization centered on the gendered and raced body and bodily identity as labor(er), commodity, and potential threat to sports' status quo. In each case, rupture is premised on a challenge posed to white, male, middle-class, heterosexual identities as "norm" and in control of the narratives in play. The first rupture connects back to issues at stake in Chapter 1, with a crisis in *policy* in the aftermath of the Super Bowl XXXVIII halftime show featuring Janet Jackson. The second rupture connects back to Chapters 2 and 3's analysis of sports TV's *textuality*, genre hybridity, and blurring of "news" and "entertainment," as it examines criticism of LeBron James's "Decision" to leave the Cleveland Cavaliers for the Miami Heat. The final rupture examines the *contextual* crisis of sports' negotiation of the Black Lives Matter movement, featuring the contrasting philosophical and aesthetic approaches of the NFL's "Protest to Progress" campaign and "The Justice Movement" of the WNBA.

The Wardrobe Malfunction

The NFL's annual championship, the Super Bowl, is the most-watched TV event of the year. Viewers who have no interest in sports tune in for the "mythic spectacle,"[14] including the extravagant commercials and the pyrotechnics and star-wattage of the halftime show. While the Super Bowl's status as a national holiday was forged early in its history, the halftime show has only relatively recently become must-see-TV. Prior to the 1990s, halftime performances were very traditionally "square" and consistent with football's more conservative profile, featuring marching bands, beauty queens, crooners like Andy Williams, the Up With People singing group, and the US Air Force cadet chorale. In the early 1990s, halftime began to feature family-friendly pop musicians such as Gloria Estefan and "boy" band New Kids On the Block. In 1993, the NFL partnered with Pepsi to feature Michael Jackson as the sole halftime performer. That year, viewership of the halftime show outranked the game itself. In 2001, the NFL partnered with MTV to produce halftime with CBS, its Viacom conglomerate sibling. In 2004, the game returned to CBS, and MTV again served as producer, with a halftime lineup slated to feature performers that would appeal across genres and generations of viewers while also appearing "MTV-edgy," lending CBS and the league some "hip" credibility for the newish decade. Featured acts included country-fried rock rapper Kid Rock, "country grammar" hip hop artist Nelly, hip hop icon P. Diddy, pop icon Janet Jackson, and pop star Justin Timberlake. As the final performer of the show, Jackson sang two of her hit songs before being joined by Timberlake for a duet of his "Rock Your Body." In sync with that song's lyric, "Better have you naked by the end of this song," Timberlake ripped Jackson's bustier, revealing her breast and nipple, which was covered by an ornamental shield. The exposure—which Timberlake famously referred to as a "wardrobe malfunction"—led to an unprecedented 542,000 complaints to the FCC.[15]

Public complaints cited "obscenity" and the inappropriateness of the content, given that a "family" audience was watching the game. Complaints further expressed annoyance with performer, producer, network, and league refusal to acknowledge that, rather than a random accident, the "malfunction" was likely scripted as part of the act, as a purposeful attempt to gain notoriety. Others countered that to be outraged about the performance required an enormous level of naivete and hypocrisy, given that the Super Bowl was sponsored by male sexual enhancement drug ads and "commercials featuring a crotch-biting dog, a flatulent horse and a potty-mouthed child."[16] However, the malfunction occurred in a broader context preceding the Super Bowl that led to inflamed reactions, including a fraught political election cycle and heated culture wars in an increasingly conservative climate. Additionally, the increasing availability and ease of registering online complaints with the FCC alongside watchdog groups' coordination of complaint campaigns had ushered in a new era of public engagement with the FCC. As Jennifer Holt notes,

> In 2000, there were 111 complaints about 111 programs made to the FCC. In 2002, there were almost 14,000 complaints made about 389 programs. The following year there were over 200,000 complaints about 375 programs, and in 2004 there were 1.4 million complaints about 314 programs.[17]

The "nipplegate" case became a flashpoint in broader debates over questions of obscenity and freedom of expression in the media. It had an immediate chilling effect on TV and radio content. The FCC more than doubled fines for broadcaster violations and instituted a delay on all live broadcasts. After two years of hearings and deliberations, the FCC ruled against CBS, finding its stations liable for violating rules regulating the broadcast of indecent material. This ruling was, ultimately, overturned in 2012.

Though an important case in FCC history, the malfunction is perhaps just as noteworthy for the broader cultural assumptions about the Super Bowl that it illuminated: critics of the malfunction premised much of their outrage on their understanding of the Super Bowl to be a ritual, national, family holiday—a rare annual, multigenerational, shared, communal event. Such sentiments imagine that the NFL and its broadcast partner serve in the public interest and are responsible for the public's trust. By this understanding, MTV was an interloper and "the incident a 'classless, crass and deplorable stunt.'"[18] And yet, of all the entities involved in this "betrayal" of the public, only Janet Jackson became the focus of a "big-media morality play"[19] backlash. Jackson was disinvited from the CBS Grammy telecast and was denied airplay and promotional opportunities for her new album release across Viacom-owned radio stations and talk shows, and a filmed biography she was producing on the life of Lena Horne was scuttled.

The NFL played it safe for many years following the malfunction, featuring "legacy" Hall of Fame rock artists like Paul McCartney, the Rolling Stones, and The Who at the half. Then, following the Kaepernick controversy, between 2016 and 2018, the NFL "became toxic to social-justice-minded artists and their fans—turning the once-coveted performance slot into guaranteed bad PR."[20] In this context, the NFL extended its perceived tone-deafness by inviting Justin Timberlake to perform at 2018's halftime, without making any acknowledgement of the 2004 show. However, the cultural tide had once again shifted and, with it, the public's routes for expression of outrage: "Super Sunday" social media was now flooded with calls for #JanetJacksonAppreciationDay and #JusticeforJanet.

Though in 2018 he sang, "I said no to the Super Bowl/You need me, I don't need you,"[21] in August of 2019, hip hop mogul Jay-Z's Roc Nation signed a deal to curate musical acts for the Super Bowl and Pro Bowl as well as league-branded playlists and podcasts on Spotify and Apple Music. Roc Nation client Shakira took center stage (with Jennifer Lopez) at Super Bowl LIV in 2020. As discussed later in this chapter, the NFL once again turned to a hipper music entrepreneur and major media entertainment entity to reengage the public in ways that would strive to combine continuity with change, merging its traditional, institutional identity with a newly "aware," "woke" profile.

The Decision

Michelle Alexander notes that, in the imagined "postracial" era, "it is no longer socially permissible to use race, explicitly, as a justification for discrimination, exclusion, and social contempt. So we don't."[22] LeBron James's "Decision" represents a sports TV crisis that underscores the ways, historically, sports encourage that we don't talk about race by talking, instead, about other things. In the case of James's free agency choice to leave Cleveland for Miami, coverage displaced the

"threat" of young, male Black labor power and mobility by transfer-
ring anxiety about such power onto questions of place-identity and
gendered criticisms and "confusion."[23]

On July 8, 2010, Akron, Ohio native and Cleveland Cavalier professional basketball phenomenon LeBron James collaborated with the
cable sports television outlet ESPN to announce "The Decision" to
move to Miami, Florida, to join the NBA's Miami Heat. This prompted
immediate outrage from Clevelanders and across the US sports world,
with critics interpreting the move as an act of betrayal of James's previously heralded, loyal, and even self-sacrificing commitment to his
home state. How does a local sports hero transform, literally over-
night, from "The Chosen One" to a "breathtaking narcissist"?[24] Con-
versely, given such criticism, how was James's status as "redeemer" and
"king" so smoothly restored with his July 2014 decision to return to
Cleveland, following success with the Heat?

According to Nielsen ratings, "more than 25 percent of homes with
TVs" in Cleveland watched the Decision, and "of the nation's 56 biggest cities, more than 7 percent of households with TVs were watching."[25] The Decision was presented as an hour-long prime-time special
telecast by ESPN but "wholly packaged by Team LeBron—from the
venue to the format to the ads to the hand-picked journalists to interview him."[26] Thus, even before it aired, the Decision was criticized
for abdicating any semblance of *news* standards. Given that "Entertainment" is the first word in ESPN's name, this criticism may be somewhat
curious. However, as sports journalism itself has historically fought a
reputation "as the 'toy department of the news media' "[27] it is clear why
sportswriters, in particular, felt threatened by this blurring of authorial
control and content. Further, the program's length, absent any information until the final two minutes, meant that its anti-style, impover-
ished, studio-bound look with its flat "interview" format was so out of
synch with sports TV's textual conventions and greatest strengths—as
exemplar of the most advanced audiovisual and technological aesthetics in screen culture—it was baffling. Indeed, the aesthetic poverty of
the Decision is such that even the crawl at the bottom of the screen
limps along with no information. Though the Decision betrayed the

Figure 4.1   LeBron James's "Decision" is announced on ESPN

conventions of news and sports TV, its deepest offense, however, was that its mash-up of realist genres and melodramatic storylines *did* conform to conventions of reality TV, with all of its gendered resonances and accompanying critical disdain.

Indeed, reactions to the Decision suggest that it was the gendered genre-blurring by which ESPN betrayed "its role as a *news* organization and [went] into the reality TV business with LeBron" that caused the most critical revulsion.[28] That said, the Decision's melodramatic narrative mode *was* consistent with sports TV's recurring concerns with the perceived *threat* of femininity, with protection of the community and team at all costs, with the dialectic of action and pathos, and with sports as the source and domain of public, male tears. The Decision played out like a climactic, soap-operatic reality TV finale: its telecast resisted narrative closure, involved a multiplicity of characters (Cleveland? Miami? Chicago? New Jersey? New York?); its use of time paralleled real time (rather than compressing, replaying, or offering more enlightening angles of view common to sports TV); it featured intimate conversations with an emphasis on problem solving through dialogue rather than action (as is common to soap opera); and its male hero was a sensitive man.[29]

Beyond gendered genre confusion, critics focused on ESPN's willing allowance of prepackaged content control by the program's subject, or, granting LeBron an *authorial* voice and command of his own narrative. Finally, there was widespread outrage at LeBron's "betrayal" of historically downtrodden, Rust Belt icon Cleveland for its presumed sporting and civic opposite in the vibrant, global city of Miami. Deftly combining each of these perceived "threats," Scott Stinson of the *National Post* called it a "much-anticipated Very Special Episode of LeBachelor. Who would get the final rose? Would it be loyal-but-dull Cleveland? The sultry Miami? That flashy temptress New York? Or that trashy, wealthy slut New Jersey?"[30] When James "proposed" to Miami and "dumped" northeast Ohio, his iconic Clevelanderness was swiftly rewritten. In commentators' displacement of emotional distress over the Decision from the presumptively "masculine" domain of sports to the presumptively "feminine" sphere of emotion, intimacy, and open-ended narrative, LeBron's choice was recast from being a business decision, fully consistent with the logics of a "dynamic capitalist economic rationality—utilitarian, competitive, and profit-maximizing,"[31] to being "LeBronsense."[32] Further, echoing one of *The Bachelor:After the Rose* specials, within two hours of James's announcement, Cavaliers' owner Dan Gilbert posted a scathing letter to fans of the team calling James disloyal. Wrote Mike Wise of the *Washington Post*, "It's the kind of psycho ex-girlfriend letter that certifies LeBron made the right decision. When a major municipality's identity is that wrapped up in one special athlete, what does it say about Cleveland's self-worth?"[33]

Striking here is commentators' effacement of characteristics of both sports culture and reality TV that might nuance their critiques as well as prevailing notions of gendered capital. As Laurie Ouellette and James Hay have carefully outlined, reality TV, in its contemporary iterations, is exemplary of neoliberalism's "normalizing of individual entrepreneurism and the branding" of the self whereby the "citizen is now conceived as an individual whose most pressing obligation to society is to empower her- or himself privately"[34] as, arguably, LeBron's free-agent move did. Further, here, James's charitable contribution to the Boys and Girls Club, resulting from the Decision telecast, underscored that now "the management and care of the self becomes an imperative in different and arguably more urgent ways," including "in the sense of replacing public services"[35] with privatized corporate social responsibility. James is CEO of Brand LeBron. His move to Miami, with its added endorsements, exposure, and revenues, allowed ongoing private service endowments to sustain several organizations and populations in Akron, Ohio, that are otherwise underserved or, rather, have been abandoned by traditional public sources of support.

In "taking his talents to South Beach" on his quest to finally win an NBA championship—in which he succeeded in 2012 and 2013—James exemplified an individualism essential to his free agency but inimical to residual modes of community and tradition. The Miami Heat were a relatively new franchise (having entered the NBA in 1988) that already had a roster of stars and had not only made the playoffs in most of its seasons but had already won one championship. Alternately praised and derided for being a team accessible to casual fans, with a national and international profile, the Heat were easily cast by Clevelanders as a high-profile, financially driven, self-serving choice for James to have made. Alternately, Miami fans hailed James's awareness of the city's and franchise's vibrancy as entities characterized by talent that would buttress his own and a legacy of hope rather than despair. Further, Miami represented a media capital worthy of James's transnational, transmedia celebrity and multiplatform endeavors.

For all the criticism, more people watched LeBron's Decision on ESPN than watched him play in his first NBA final with the Cavaliers. And, more than $2.5 million was raised for the Boys and Girls Clubs of America. Notably, following the Decision, media coverage finally began to disconnect Cleveland and Akron in discussing those "jilted" by the move, noting that James never gave up his Akron home or any of his ongoing charitable organizations and work there. Notes Keith Dambrot, one of James's high school coaches and current men's basketball coach at the University of Akron, "'We're a different place. It's not like Akron is a suburb. It's separate, and I think it's different in a lot of ways. I don't think anyone from Akron says, 'I'm from outside Cleveland.' We're from Akron."[36]

Nonetheless, local critics couched LeBron's Decision to leave for Miami as a betrayal of his very core identity. According to local author David Giffels, if Clevelanders are defined by doing things "the hard way on purpose," then "choosing Miami was choosing to *not* do things the hard way on purpose. If there was a betrayal, that was it."[37] Implicit in these local critiques was that LeBron was turning his back on his "debts" to the "village" and community services that helped raise and educate him. LeBron's local betrayal was thus, in large part, his "escape" from residual networks of social welfare and regional emplacement to embrace a self-made, entrepreneurial, individualistic ideal commensurate with the post–civil rights–era mobile, postracial neoliberal ideal. This is also the terrain on which LeBron's Decision was excoriated in the national media, where he was called out for, now, being a "self-centered" player. The national press focused criticism on LeBron's courting of the free-agency market and what it meant for the "integrity" of the game (implying that LeBron would be choosing to play with a stacked deck of superstars rather than "work" his way to the top). Instead of addressing head-on the apparent deeply felt threat posed by "young black stars taking full ownership of their own legacies,"[38] these critics displaced raced discourses onto gendered and "genre" critiques—misogyny and disdain for reality TV and other "women's genres" remaining, apparently, "acceptable" public discourse. LeBron's "betrayals" thus exposed the active work that is required to *not* speak of race or to cast sports crises in racialized terms.

In the end, the Decision and its aftermath exposed an unresolvable tension between continuity and change: between the residual but ongoing hope that sports is a mythic realm populated by local heroes who are transcendent of commercial concerns, and the reality of sports' market identity, global popularity, and athlete entrepreneurialism and self-possession. Arguably, one of the reasons sportswriters and other commentators invoked the perceptively "safe"—or safe-to-disdain—feminized logics of reality TV to couch their critiques was as a strategy to diffuse the raw, emotional sense of loss and mourning the Decision provoked in *public*, in the convention-ally male-dominated venues of news and sports. In recasting LeBron from "Chosen One" to "LeBachelor," critics and commentators strove to separate *themselves* from reality TV (imagined to be "insincere" and "beneath" emotional investment), while embracing and upholding sports as "true" and, therefore, worthy of public displays of male pas-sion and, even, tears.

With his July 2014 announcement that he would return to the Cleveland Cavaliers, James reactivated hopes for Cleveland's reverse-of-the-curse, economic resurgence, and community unity through the utopian possibilities of sports. Announced via "letter" in the pages of *Sports Illustrated*, the Return was greeted as "a stunning victory for maturity and perspective,"[39] indicating "elevated . . . vision and . . . love for his community first."[40] In voluntarily returning to a place that "topped Forbes's list of the most miserable cities," James was "setting the standard for the role of the athlete today."[41] LeBron's letter claims that his years with the Heat were

> almost like college for other kids. These past four years helped raise me into who I am. . . . I see myself as a mentor now. . . . I feel my calling here goes above basketball. . . . My presence can make a difference in Miami, but I think it can mean more where I'm from. . . . In Northeast Ohio, nothing is given. Everything is earned. You work for what you have. I'm ready to accept the challenge. I'm coming home.[42]

Thus, James's successful return is assured following an exile in which he "matured" to be restored not only as favored son but as *patriar-chal* figure and redeemer. Whereas the free-agent move to Miami was portrayed as *self*-centered, about market and championship bling, the Return is welcomed as about self-*actualization*, love, and social virtue. LeBron kept his promise to bring a championship to Cleveland, with the Cavaliers' dramatic game-seven victory over the Golden State Warriors in June 2016. The return to Cleveland arguably returned LeBron to a narrative about "knowing one's place" in all the ways that both restored him to public affection and, also, circumscribed his imagined mobility. Having made Cleveland a world champion, LeBron's 2018 move to the Los Angeles Lakers was greeted much differently, with recognition and gratitude that James would always be Akron's favorite son.

Indeed, James's charitable commitments in Akron have flourished and expanded with the growth of his media empire and enhanced public presence in LA's media capital. Since his move to Los Angeles, James's *activist* voice has both sharpened and come under concerted attack. In mid-February 2018, James became the target of Fox News television host Laura Ingraham, after his appearance on *Rolling with the Champion*, via his streaming channel (www.uninterrupted.com). During the inaugural episode, James noted that while, as a child, he looked up to three different entities—the President, sports heroes, and musicians—at present, "it's a bad time" under an administration that "doesn't understand the people; doesn't really give a f- about the people." Here, James notes that the best defense at this moment is to use his media outlets to "continue to alert the people who watch us, the people who listen to us" to real social issues and concerns. Ingraham used her telecast the next day to tell James to "shut up and dribble." On Twitter, James responded, "I am more than an athlete #wewillnotshutupanddribble."

James's charitable and social service activism throughout his career is perhaps the most visible and heralded example of a much broader, increasingly *expected* phenomenon: the simultaneously held but directly opposed expectations that athletes should *both* stand in for entire populations' political voice *and* should "just play the game." In a neoliberal era characterized by the "offloading of duties and services historically performed by the state onto corporations and individual consumers,"[43] athletes have become a focal point of "connected celebrity activism,"[44] urged to excel at their sport, as media professionals, *and* as CEOs and diplomats. Indeed—particularly in the case of iconic Black sports figures—there is increasingly an expectation that the athlete is *obligated* to remedy state failings through charitable endeavors while, simultaneously, being subject to excoriation for having a voice. What is the expectation for and role of sports *leagues* in relation to such social activism, outreach, and support? And, why has sports TV become the contemporary venue and resource for civic engagement?

Sports Leagues as Public Servants?

Though Chapter 1 explores ways that the NFL rhetorically claimed to be a public servant as early as the 1960s, from the 1990s onward the league's corporate philanthropy and investment in social responsibility programs has expanded significantly. The NFL's charitable and social programming endeavors have been strategic in attempting to allay crises particularly related to player welfare (focused on concussion concerns) and off-field issues (focused on domestic violence). Such initiatives are also intended to cultivate new audiences to a league whose fan demographics skew older if more affluent than other sports.[45] Indeed, by the 1990s, the league strove to rework its *Monday Night Football* franchise to have hip hop appeal; it actively courted and marketed to female fans; it initiated multiplatform appeals to youth audiences; it ambitiously launched new media extensions; and it reconceived itself, in-house, as a global entertainment business. But—as seen in Super Bowl XXXVIII— the league's voice has not been consistent, often retrenching, and always prioritizing market imperatives over service ideals.

Since entering into its partnership with Roc Nation in August 2019, the NFL has leveraged Jay-Z's cultural credibility and has featured the voices and social program commitments of its athletes to develop its "Inspire Change" and "Protest to Progress" platforms. According to the terms of the Roc Nation partnership, the NFL is to invest $100 million over the next 10 years on initiatives focused on "education and economic advancement, police and community relations, and criminal justice reform."[46] For Jay-Z, "the higher purpose is to get inside the establishment to bring representation of color and try to foster a nationwide cultural dialogue."[47] The NFL, on the other hand, "seeks to capitalize on the emergent activist power of professional players to build the league's brand as an authoritative and inclusive American institution contributing to social good."[48]

Following the 2020 spring and summer of COVID-19, marked by continued police violence and resulting heightened tensions and protest action for the Black Lives Matter movement, the NFL began its "Kickoff"Weekend by launching its "season-long campaign 'It Takes All of Us.'"[49] According to the NFL's announcement, the campaign

> leverages the scale and power of the league to unite the country during a critical time in our nation. The league is committed to integrating important causes vital to players and fans, such as social justice, among others, throughout the season.

End zones on each field during the first week were stenciled with the words, "It Takes All of Us," and "End Racism." The television premiere of the brand campaign featured the telecast of the "It Takes All of Us" video, prior to each of the league's first week's games. The video's voice-over features Hall of Fame running back LaDanian Tomlinson's 2017 induction speech, "Football is a Microcosm of America." The video's musical score features Roc Nation artist Alicia Keyes's song, "Love Looks Better." The one-and-a-half-minute film is a classic example of NFL Films' production aesthetics and emotional appeal.

As noted in Chapter 2, NFL Films' aesthetic follows classical Hollywood cinema conventions to convey a sophisticated, romantic, earnest,

Figure 4.2 The NFL's 2020 Kickoff video claims "Football is a Microcosm of America"

burnished image of football and of the NFL as mythic American institutions. "It Takes All of Us" exemplifies NFL Films' style with its slightly gauzy, soft, filtered, slow-motion images. The film opens by linking the joy of professional athletic accomplishment with the loyal commitment of everyday fans of the league. The Kansas City Chiefs' Demarcus Robinson is shown making snow angels in confetti on the field after his Super Bowl victory before Tomlinson's voice-over and superimposed onscreen text state, "Football is a microcosm of America." The film cuts to an older pickup truck on a rural two-lane highway, headed into a prairie sunset. In quick succession, three geographically and demographically diverse fans are shown in close-up, directly and somberly gazing into the camera. As Tomlinson intones, "All races, religions and creeds, living, playing, side by side," scenes transition from a 20-something, female "graffiti" artist spray-painting a wall, to a mural of civil rights activist and statesman John Lewis, to COVID-ward hospital workers, to children's hands clasping, closing with the image of Black Lives Matter marchers, and hospital workers receiving a food delivery. "When we open the doors to others to compete," says Tomlinson, "we fulfill the promise of one nation." Cross-cutting between several different players running drills and working out, Tomlinson continues, "Let's open it wide for those who believe in themselves that anything is possible." As the film alternates between images of BLM marches, NFL team meetings and workouts, and medical team huddles, Tomlinson concludes:

> I am asking you to believe in your ability to bring about change. We represent the game, our team, our community. We all have to try harder. My great, great, great, great grandfather had no choice. We have one. I pray we dedicate ourselves to be the best team we can be, working and living together.

As the speech concludes, there is an extreme close-up on a Minnesota Vikings player's helmet being affixed with a "Breonna Taylor" nameplate. The film concludes by returning to its diverse sample of individual fans, in close-up, closing with an end zone "reveal" of the stenciled

"It Takes All of Us." The screen fades to black as the iconic NFL shield takes center frame.

"It Takes All of Us" links the US geographically—from the "Heartland" prairie and Southwestern desert to John Lewis's Atlanta and George Floyd's Minneapolis, to the hospitals of New York and the Houston Texans' locker room. It underscores the demographic diversity—racially and generationally—of the league's fans as well as of BLM activists and healthcare's essential workers. It links activism with teamwork and professionalism by conjoining marchers, locker rooms, and emergency rooms. However, in spite of these images of collectivity, across each tableau, narration reinforces *individual* determination and perseverance as the American way. Through self-belief, trying harder, the right choices, and prayer, a nation/"team" succeeds.

The dilemma of corporate social responsibility is that corporations such as the NFL—no matter how socially and politically progressive—are market-based entities. The *systemic* racism being called out and seeking redress by the Black Lives Matter movement requires fundamental rethinking of the socioeconomic status quo to effect genuine social, political, and institutional change. While outreach, awareness, and discussion are crucial steps to "progress," corporate endeavors in social justice activism necessarily default to consumer solutions and continuity *within* change. Arguably, the NFL's "protest to progress" initiative as articulated in the lush lyricism of "It Takes All of Us" encourages our engagement in "communicative capitalism, an enticement to play politics without *doing* it, to delight in political speech without the work involved in organizing and forming coalitions."[50] Should crisis get incorporated into the mainstream only to reinforce and consolidate existing structures of power?

In spite of the NFL's continuity practices, the summer of 2020 arguably represented a transition in sports activism. In June, NASCAR banned the Confederate flag from any of its speedways. In July, after over 83 years of history and decades of outcry, Washington, DC's football franchise changed its offensive nickname. Twenty-two-year-old Japanese-African American tennis phenomenon, Naomi Osaka, boycotted her semi-final match in the Western & Southern Open, following the shooting of Jacob Blake in Kenosha, Wisconsin, in August. She subsequently entered each round of September's US Open wearing facemasks printed with the names of individual Black Americans who have been killed at the hands of police or by hate crimes, including Breonna Taylor, Tamir Rice, and Ahmaud Arbery.

As George Lipsitz proposes, hegemony "always runs the risk of unraveling when lived experiences conflict with legitimizing ideologies."[51] Athletes are speaking from and speaking for lived experiences that expose myths of "transcendence" and "colorblindness" to be, in actuality, systemic commitments to fixity and the entrenched privileges of whiteness. The COVID-19 and Black Lives Matter summer of sports appears—in the contemporary moment—to have licensed *new* voices or, rather, new TV attention to and amplification of voices that had *always been* engaged. As suggested in Chapter 3, *female* athletes are central to this project. As sports scholar and journalist Shira Spring emphasizes:

> The lives of female athletes *are* lives of advocacy and activism. Always. By necessity. To create opportunities in sports, women must disrupt, push against tradition, challenge conventional thinking, be difficult in the best possible way. They've effectively been preparing for this moment their entire lives. It's also why WNBA players have been leaders in social activism for years. . . . The players' activism is real, not staged, not performative, not PR-motivated. . . . By their very existence, women's sports challenge tradition and change what's considered "legitimate."[52]

Indeed, long prior to Kaepernick's widely publicized action, the WNBA had been a leader in engagement with the BLM movement. Further, as noted in the Introduction, the league dedicated its 2018 season to several different women's health and LGBTQ+ causes. Its 2020 season was marked by the WNBA league and WNBPA player association collaboration on "The Justice Movement." This initiative was designed to honor the #sayhername campaign, to intentionally

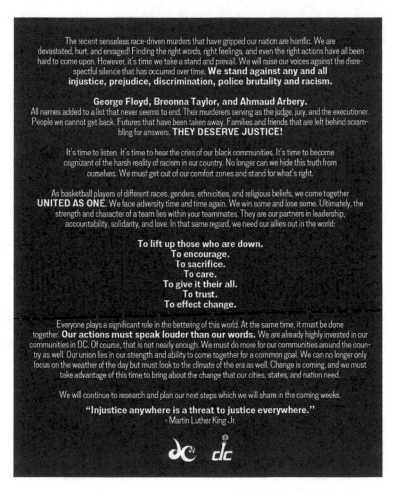

The recent senseless race-driven murders that have gripped our nation are horrific. We are devastated, hurt, and enraged! Finding the right words, right feelings, and even the right actions have all been hard to come upon. However, it's time we take a stand and prevail. We will raise our voices against the disrespectful silence that has occurred over time. **We stand against any and all injustice, prejudice, discrimination, police brutality and racism.**

George Floyd, Breonna Taylor, and Ahmaud Arbery.
All names added to a list that never seems to end. Their murderers serving as the judge, jury, and the executioner. People we cannot get back. Futures that have been taken away. Families and friends that are left behind scrambling for answers. **THEY DESERVE JUSTICE!**

It's time to listen. It's time to hear the cries of our black communities. It's time to become cognizant of the harsh reality of racism in our country. No longer can we hide this truth from ourselves. We must get out of our comfort zones and stand for what's right.

As basketball players of different races, genders, ethnicities, and religious beliefs, we come together **UNITED AS ONE.** We face adversity time and time again. We win some and lose some. Ultimately, the strength and character of a team lies within your teammates. They are our partners in leadership, accountability, solidarity, and love. In that same regard, we need our allies out in the world:

To lift up those who are down.
To encourage.
To sacrifice.
To care.
To give it their all.
To trust.
To effect change.

Everyone plays a significant role in the bettering of this world. At the same time, it must be done together. **Our actions must speak louder than our words.** We are already highly invested in our communities in DC. Of course, that is not nearly enough. We must do more for our communities around the country as well. Our union lies in our strength and ability to come together for a common goal. We can no longer only focus on the weather of the day but must look to the climate of the era as well. Change is coming, and we must take advantage of this time to bring about the change that our cities, states, and nation need.

We will continue to research and plan our next steps which we will share in the coming weeks.

"Injustice anywhere is a threat to justice everywhere."
- Martin Luther King Jr.

Figure 4.3 The WNBA's (Washington) Mystics tweet for social justice

engage with local community, and to advocate for a variety of social issues, including voting rights, gun control, implicit bias, and systemic racism. The WNBA's engagements are perhaps all the more laudable considering the players' relative economic precarity, compared with much-better-resourced men's leagues. Activism comes with a potentially higher price for female athletes, particularly when withholding labor by cancelling games or by opting out of a season to focus on social justice advocacy. Sports activism seeks to revise the myths of sports as somehow transcendent and apart from the everyday in order to realize a more equitable, just shared community. As we've seen throughout this chapter, this hope—the lure of sports as a site of shared community, progress, and face-to-face *consensus*—remains its most alluring, appealing, and potentially hopeful and promising myth. It is to this promise and examples of its potential—struggled over and momentary though it may be—that the next chapter turns.

Notes

1. Dave Zirin, "Eagles Super Bowl Win Shows That Having a Conscience Does Not Distract From Winning the Game," *The Nation*, February 5, 2018.
2. As Samantha N. Sheppard has written, Smith's and Carlos's protest remains "one of the most pivotal visual spectacles of Black resistance in sports history . . . as a potent and symbolic act of Black opposition to racist national and international scripts that attempt to project Black athletes as metonyms for the mediation of US racial harmony." Samantha N. Sheppard, *Sporting Blackness: Race, Embodiment, and Critical Muscle Memory on Screen* (Berkeley: University of California Press, 2020), 141, 146.
3. Michael Bennett and Dave Zirin, *Things That Make White People Uncomfortable* (Chicago, IL: Haymarket Books, 2018), 55.
4. Linda Williams, "Melodrama Revised," in *Refiguring American Film Genres: History and Theory*, ed. Nick Browne (Berkeley: University of California Press, 1998), 42.
5. On characteristics of melodrama: Peter Brooks, *The Melodramatic Imagination: Balzac, Henry James, Melodrama and the Mode of Excess* (New Haven, CT: Yale University Press, 1976); Thomas P. Oates, *Football and Manliness: An Unauthorized Feminist Account of the NFL* (Urbana, IL: University of Illinois Press, 2017).
6. Reece Peck, *Fox Populism: Branding Conservatism as Working Class* (New York: Cambridge University Press, 2019).
7. Michael Oriard, *King Football: Sport and Spectacle in the Golden Age of Radio and Newsreels, Movies and Magazines, the Weekly & the Daily Press* (Chapel Hill: University of North Carolina Press, 2001), 367.
8. Notably, in the years before his death, Ali's image had transformed from being a "threat" to the status quo to having been taken up as a mainstream, All-American cultural hero. Ali's majoritarian "recuperation" happened after he, literally, had lost his voice due to the ravages of Parkinson's disease.
9. Michael R. Real, "Super Bowl: Mythic Spectacle," *Journal of Communication* (Winter 1975): 42.

10. kihana miraya ross, "Call It What It Is: Anti-Blackness," *The New York Times*, June 4, 2020.

11. Julie DiCaro, "Fans at Arrowhead Can Go Kick Rocks," *Deadspin*, September 10, 2020.

12. See, for example Michael Serazio and Emily Thorson, "Weaponized Patriotism and Racial Subtext in Kaepernick's Aftermath: The Anti-Politics of American Sports Fandom," *Television & New Media* 21, no. 2 (2020): 151–168; Adam Rugg, "America's Game: The NFL's 'Salute to Service' Campaign, the Diffused Military Presence and Corporate Social Responsibility," *Popular Communication: The International Journal of Media and Culture* 14, no. 1 (2016): 21–29; and, Michael Butterworth and Stormi D. Moskal, "American Football, Flags, and 'Fun': The Bell Helicopter Armed Forces Bowl and the Rhetorical Production of Militarism," *Communication, Culture & Critique* 2 (2009): 411–433.

13. Ava Rose and James Friedman, "Television Sport as Mas(s)culine Cult of Distraction," *Screen* 35 (Spring 1994): 34.

14. Real, "Super Bowl: Mythic Spectacle."

15. George Raine, "Super Bowl Advertisers Walk on Eggshells After Backlash," *San Francisco Chronicle*, January 30, 2005, E1.

16. Frank Rich, "My Hero, Janet Jackson," *The New York Times*, February 15, 2004, AR1.

17. Jennifer Holt, "NYPD Blue: Content Regulation," in *How to Watch Television*, eds. Ethan Thompson and Jason Mittell (New York: New York University Press, 2013), 277.

18. Quoting FCC Chair at the time, Michael Powell, in Emmanuel Hapsis, "Nipplegate Revisited: Why America Owes Janet Jackson a Huge Apology," *KQED.org*, February 4, 2016.

19. C.L. Cole, "PR Malfunction?" *Journal of Sports & Social Issues* 28, no. 2 (May 2004): 91–92.

20. Maeve McDermott, "RIP to the Super Bowl Halftime Show, No Longer a Cultural Institution," *USA Today*, January 24, 2019.

21. A lyric featured in his "Apes*t," with Beyoncé.

22. Michelle Alexander, *The New Jim Crow: Mass Incarceration in the Age of Colorblindness* (New York: The New Press, 2011), 2.

23. An extended and previous version of this section appears within Victoria E. Johnson, "More Than a Game: LeBron James and the Affective Economy of Place," in *Racism Postrace*, eds. Roopali Mukherjee, Sarah Banet-Weiser, and Herman Gray (Durham, NC: Duke University Press, 2019), 154–177.

24. Grant Wahl, "The Chosen One: High School Junior LeBron James Would Be an NBA Lottery Pick Right Now," *Sports Illustrated*, February 18, 2002; Danny Groner, "The Decision: 2010's Worst Sports Moment?" *The Huffington Post*, December 27, 2010.

25. "Put Off by the LeBron Spectacle? Here's a Redeeming Virtue," *The Christian Science Monitor*, July 9, 2010.

26. Patrik Jonsson, "LeBron James Show," *The Christian Science Monitor*, July 8, 2010.

27. Brett Hutchins and David Rowe, *Sport Beyond Television: The Internet, Digital Media and the Rise of Networked Media Sport* (New York: Routledge, 2012), 125.

28. Michael Wilbon, "Exit Strategy Leaves Much to Ponder," *The Washington Post*, July 10, 2010, D1.

29. John Fiske, *Television Culture* (New York: Routledge, 1989), 179–197.

30. Scott Stinson, "Sultry Miami Gets Final Rose in LeBachelor," *National Post*, July 9, 2010, S2.

31. Zubin Meer, *Individualism: The Cultural Logic of Modernity* (New York: Lexington Books, 2011), 1.

32. Matthew Lysiak, "A Final Day of Lebronsense!" *(NY) Daily News*, July 8, 2010, 3.

33. Mike Wise, "Having His Fun But Losing His Legacy," *The Washington Post*, July 9, 2010, D1.

34. Laurie Ouellette and James Hay, *Better Living Through Reality TV: Television and Post-Welfare Citizenship* (Malden, MA: Blackwell, 2008), 3.

35. Ouellette and Hay, *Better Living Through Reality TV*, 12.

36. Christopher Maag, "Back in His Hometown, James Remains Royalty," *The New York Times*, August 8, 2010, 8.

37. David Giffels, *The Hard Way on Purpose* (New York: Scribner, 2014) Kindle Edition, 22.

38. Dave Zirin, "Kevin Durant and the Discomfort With Player Power," *The Nation*, July 5, 2016.

39. Bill Plaschke, "James Proves He Can Go Home Again," *The Los Angeles Times*, July 12, 2014, A1.

40. Leigh Steinberg, "LeBron Transcends Superstar Athletic Profile," *Daily Pilot* (Orange Coast, CA), July 12, 2014, A13.

41. David A. Love, "Return to Cleveland Spotlights Urban Problems," *Philadelphia Inquirer*, July 18, 2014.

42. LeBron James, "I'm Coming Home," *Sports Illustrated*, July 11, 2014, www.si.com/nba/2014/07/11/lebron-james-cleveland-cavaliers.

43. Laurie Ouellette, "Citizenship," in *Keywords for Media Studies*, eds. Laurie Ouellette and Jonathan Gray (New York: New York University Press, 2017), 38.

44. Elizabeth Ellcessor, "'One Tweet to Make So Much Noise': Connected Celebrity Activism in the Case of Marlee Matlin," *New Media & Society* 20, no. 1 (2018): 255.

45. According to 2017 statistics by Mintel, avid fans of the NFL were more male than female (62% to 54%) and averaged 45+ years of age with incomes between $50,000–$75,000.

46. Katherine Rossman, "Jay-Z Takes on the Super Bowl," *The New York Times*, February 1, 2020.

47. Rossman, "Jay-Z Takes on the Super Bowl."

48. Adam Rugg, "Incorporating the Protests: The NFL, Social Justice and the Constrained Activism of the 'Inspire Change' Campaign," *Communication & Sport* (2019): 1.

49. NFL Press Release, "NFL Launches Season-Long Brand Campaign 'It Takes All of Us,'" September 10, 2020, www.nfl.com.

50. Abraham Iqbal Khan, "A Rant Good for Business: Communicative Capitalism and the Capture of Anti Racist Resistance," *Popular Communication: The International Journal of Media and Culture* 14, no. 1 (2016): 41.

51. George Lipsitz, "The Struggle for Hegemony," *The Journal of American History* 75, no. 1 (June 1988): 147.

52. Shira Springer, "WNBA Has the Map, and They're Driving the Bus," *Sports Business Journal*, August 24–30, 2020, 23.

5

THE SPORTS MEDIA ECOSYSTEM

Sports TV's Out-of-Home Communities

In 2008, Senator Arlen Specter, then the senior Republican on the Senate Judiciary Committee, introduced a bill that would allow churches to show the Super Bowl on big-screen TVs. "In a time when our country is divided by war and anxious about a fluctuating economy, these type of events give people a reason to come together in the spirit of camaraderie."[1] The Senator's understanding of out-of-home TV viewing as a powerful locus of *consensus* and shared community has a history as long as the medium itself. When RCA introduced television to the public at the New York World's Fair in 1939, one of the first live telecasts featured a college baseball matchup between Princeton and Columbia. Fair telecasts of a major league baseball game and college football game soon followed. Though sports programming was a cornerstone of television's domestic introduction and standardization, most TV viewers would not have settled in to watch such events at home: in 1950 only 9 percent of the US public owned a TV; it was not until 1955 that more than half of the US public had a television set; and it was not until 1965 that over 90 percent of Americans owned a TV.[2] Perhaps more than any other genre, sports TV's out-of-home viewing history has always been almost as robust as its in-home engagement. While out-of-home viewing initially offered the only access to live coverage of sporting events outside of stadium attendance, today it thrives by offering a powerful site of shared community in a day-to-day environment that is often otherwise experienced in more individual, atomized, and even divided ways. In the contemporary context, sports

TV can take place in a wide variety of out-of-home spaces: restaurants and bars, while in transit (subways, airplanes, rideshares, etc.), in waiting rooms, hotels, and, yes, even churches. Given such diversity, Garry Whannel has asked, "where does the modern sport event now take place? Is it at the stadium, in the town centre, in all public spaces, in the living room, in the pub or sports bar?"[3] He notes that, while sports have become "de-centered" with "audiences and rituals . . . dispersed across the nation,"[4] these audiences and spaces of sports viewing are still united and linked together *by* television. While it may be "no longer easy to attribute primacy to any of these viewing contexts," sports remain "heavily television dependent."[5]

This chapter examines three sites of out-of-home sports TV viewing: the historic role of closed-circuit exhibition, particularly in movie theaters; pub and sports-bar viewing, especially as focused on displaced fans of out-of-market teams who gather to game-watch together; and the built-environment of the urban sports district as a primary contemporary strategy for civic renewal, particularly in the US Rust Belt. At each of these sites it is clear that, in spite of sports' global appeal and reach, sports teams and fandoms remain crucially representative of and emotionally foundational to specific *places*. The spaces of sports are thus heavily television-dependent in ways that rely on a renewed relevance of the *local*. This is evidenced both on a large scale—as cityscapes are reshaped through new stadiums and urban sports districts—and, also, simultaneously on an intimate plane, as enhanced mobility and travel *of* the local to elsewhere are enabled through mobile apps and subscription services that allow out-of-market access to hometown teams, commentators, and advertisements.

This chapter thus emphasizes sports' intimate, affective, *and* social, communal significance in everyday US life, to analyze how shared community is now, fundamentally, imagined and defined *through* sports, particularly in public "third-places"[6] between the home and the stadium. Though important in the past, out-of-home sports TV has arguably become an even more significant site in a contemporary context that Brett Hutchins and David Rowe have called the "new media sports order"[7]—a "media sport economy"[8] in which we must think "less in terms of the longstanding relationship between sports *and* media, and more about *sport as media*."[9] For Hutchins and Rowe, this transformation to sports *as* media happened "within a broader leisure framework"[10] that has accelerated since the mid-1990s. This transformation is part of a broader constellation of transitions in the economy, urban planning and design, and changes in television technology and the business of sports leagues and their franchises. This period witnessed the US economy's final transition to a service-based economy, which encouraged the expansion of new "experience"-based leisure concepts and venues including themed restaurant/bar and "shoppertainment" environments as well as large-scale urban renewal ventures (including new "retro" ballparks and their anchored sports districts). Simultaneously, this period saw the introduction and wide public installation of HDTV, whose aesthetic advances were largely promoted through sports broadcasts. Further, the expansion of digital broadcast, satellite TV providers, and the growth of digital tier and streaming services, saw the flourishing of out-of-market sports league subscription packages (such as DirecTV's NFL Sunday Ticket and MLB's Extra Innings). Each of these developments has worked in constellation to cultivate community through sports in otherwise increasingly transitory times. Together, these phenomena powerfully appeal to *local* identifications and a sense of "home" as sports teams are increasingly positioned as civic leaders, accruing private profit in the name of public service and the public interest.

In other words, while out-of-home sports viewing has been a part of TV history from the medium's introduction, since the late 1990s an emergent sports media *ecosystem* has transformed not just TV but broader everyday life and culture. As former TV sports producer and author Dennis Deninger stated in the Introduction, "Sports is television that matters to people in ways that no other entertainment can."[11] Eva Illouz's theorization of emotional capitalism is instructive, here. Sports *teams*—the identification, loyalty, and place-specificity they encourage—symbolize the unique emotional capital of sports in forging civic identity and individual claims to place and identification with home. The sports franchise and its fandom convert this loyal affection and allegiance to the team "into economic and social benefits."[12] The sports team is, here, a metonym for its city and region—a civic icon through which "disparate institutions are tightly linked together in a process of commodification of selfhood."[13] A city's iconic sports franchises are crucial symbolic capital, forging a civic brand identity that—energized by generations of emotional investment—also creates economic capital, particularly as realized in the brick-and-mortar urban sports district development which has, since the 2000s, been increasingly embraced as a means of urban renewal. This chapter thus traces the history of out-of-home sports TV to examine the broader sports media ecosystem whose unifying thread is the televised team / franchise, iconic of home.

"Fee TV": Closed-Circuit Television and Out-of-Home Sports

"Closed-circuit television" describes the process by which TV signals are not broadcast, but are sent over a closed loop to a fixed group of receivers. Signals are sent "either via coaxial cable or as scrambled radio waves that are unscrambled at the point of reception."[14] Prior to television's standardization in the home, indoor and outdoor demonstrations of closed-circuit TV, projected onto large screens (generally 12 feet by 15 feet) allowed the public access to both the new audio-visual technology and to attend sporting events that were otherwise distant or sold out. According to *Billboard* magazine and other industry trade press of the early-TV era, out-of-home audiences "showed a greater preference for sports than the at-home audience."[15] Sports thus became a focal point for investors in closed-circuit TV from the late 1930s through the mid-1970s, after which cable and satellite-enabled pay-per-view and subscription services became the primary routes for out-of-home and premium sports event transmission though the legacies of "theater TV," in particular, live on.

Closed-circuit TV exhibition developed in two primary phases. From the late 1930s through the early 1950s, Hollywood film interests were involved in developing TV transmission systems for installation in

Figure 5.1   Contemporary theater TV in Las Vegas
Source: Ethan Miller © Getty Images

movie theaters and other out-of-home venues such as hotels and civic
centers. From the early 1950s through the mid-1970s, "non-Hollywood"
or independent theater TV interests—largely in cooperation with
sports promoters—ushered out-of-home closed-circuit events
through their peak years of popularity.[16] Only a handful of film and
broadcast media historians have analyzed closed-circuit TV as a public
exhibition phenomenon. Michele Hilmes, Douglas Gomery, and Timothy R. White have each examined Hollywood film studios' investment
in television stations, television technology, and "theater television"
with particular focus on the years between the establishment of the
Paramount decrees in 1948 and 1954, by which time investment had
shifted primarily to the transformation of movie theaters for expressly
cinematic phenomena.[17] "Theater television" was the term used to
describe closed-circuit TV systems developed for exhibition in theaters

owned by film studios, though these systems were also adapted to be portable to convention centers, public halls, hotels, and other venues.

In *United States v. Paramount* (first filed in 1938 but concluded in 1948), eight motion picture studios were found to have engaged in a range of anti-competitive practices and "conspiracy to illegally fix motion picture prices and monopolize both the film distribution and movie theatre markets" including practices that controlled theatrical prices, guaranteed distribution of particular film releases, and discouraged competition from independent theaters and producers. Consent decrees handed down in 1948 mandated that there be a separation of production from film distribution and/or film exhibition. The five defendants who owned movie theaters were to divest of *either* their distribution operations or their exhibition venues.[18] Among the defendants, Paramount, Warner Bros., and RKO (which dissolved in 1959) each maintained ownership of theaters and had to develop new business practices for the coming decade. Paramount, in particular, had already invested deeply in television—owning TV stations and developing a trial subscription TV service. However, Paramount's TV involvement is perhaps best remembered for its development of a large-screen theater television system known as the "film intermediary method," which received broadcast signals, transferred them to film, then projected the film—all within about a minute's time.[19] RCA developed an alternative system that, instead, allowed for direct projection to a 16-foot-by-20-foot screen. Over 75 percent "of all theatres equipped for theatre TV installed RCA's system."[20]

Hollywood investors' forays into theater TV were eventually discouraged by the mismatch between the expense of outfitting theaters, navigating ongoing technical and image-quality glitches, and the relatively small size of the audiences served by events. With only 100 theaters outfitted with closed-circuit capabilities, the costs of programming could not be spread out over a large enough audience to make up for the expense of the investment. Because theater television signals traveled by closed circuit, the Federal Communications Commission did not have jurisdiction over the practice. Theater TV interests petitioned the FCC to open up broadcast spectrum space in the UHF band in order to ease transmission quality and technical issues. However, with the FCC's lifting of its licensing freeze on new TV stations in 1952 and the increasing availability of home television to a broader US public, film industry investment turned away from TV toward new cinematic technologies such as CinemaScope.

By 1954, however, "non-Hollywood" theater TV interests began to thrive, particularly as they focused on the exhibition of major sporting events. Anna McCarthy and Travis Vogan are the only TV and sports media scholars to closely study closed-circuit, out-of-home sports exhibition in this period. As McCarthy notes, "after Hollywood abandoned it" closed-circuit "established a basic income structure for licensing the rights to closed-circuit sports broadcasts, and is thus a precursor of the pay-per-view cable business."[21] By 1954, there were three prominent closed-circuit TV promoters: Theater Network Television (TNT), Box Office Television (BOT), and Dor Theatre Television. TNT focused on boxing matches, with boxer Sonny Liston eventually becoming an executive with the company. TNT also planned to offer stage-plays and symphony performances. BOT secured rights to theater-cast Notre Dame football games and Harlem Globetrotter basketball. Dor Theatre Television intended to focus on symphonic and other performing arts telecasts, having made a deal with the New York Philharmonic.[22]

Closed-circuit sports events included the Kentucky Derby, the Indianapolis 500, Big 10 conference football, and professional wrestling. Only boxing achieved overwhelming popularity over closed circuit, however. As Vogan writes, boxing's "biggest money-maker and the principal way marquee fights were consumed from the mid-1950s through the mid-1970s" was via closed circuit. The rights to the 1951 Joe Louis v. Lee Savold fight held at Madison Square Garden proved too pricey for "free TV" broadcast networks, so the International Boxing Club (IBC) "sold live exhibition rights to eight theaters in six cities."[23] The fight became a tremendous success. While 18,179 audience members attended the match in-person, over 39,000 viewers attended closed-circuit screenings "and forced participating theater operators to turn away 10,000 more they could not accommodate."[24]

McCarthy's and Vogan's studies of closed-circuit boxing restore to exhibition history the fact that closed circuit flourished particularly as it featured African American investors, fighters, and audience engagement. McCarthy writes that, in Chicago,

> After 1952, as more theaters began to host closed circuit screenings of heavyweight bouts, the demographics of Chicago theater TV shifted . . . the highest concentration of screenings in any one area was consistently in Black south side neighborhoods.[25]

Vogan notes that out-of-home boxing telecasts often had to navigate "the local politics surrounding exhibition sites" including segregation practices. Sonny Liston had to invoke his contracts' anti-segregation clauses to pull his fight with Cassius Clay (soon thereafter to become known as Muhammad Ali) from two theaters in New Orleans.[26] Vogan also highlights the ways in which closed-circuit matches became rare spaces for African American sociality and community-building at venues such as Dootsie Williams's Dooto Music Center in Compton, CA.[27] Finally, Vogan details the history of Main Bout, Inc., a group formed to handle the ancillary rights for Muhammad Ali's matches, whose ownership included Ali and football great Jim Brown among its principle shareholders. Said Jim Brown, "For the first time Negroes own stock in closed-circuit TV and will be in some of the big money."[28] Writes Vogan, "Ali and Main Bout asserted economic control and fostered cultural solidarity by ensuring black audiences could watch the fight in welcoming environments while sharing its profits" as was evidenced, particularly, by Ali's paying for fights to be exhibited on Historically Black College and University campuses and letting "those schools keep the proceeds."[29]

Though most histories of TV focus on its relatively rapid acceptance in US homes in the 1950s and beyond, the examples of theater TV and broader uses of closed circuit make it clear that out-of-home TV was not only always a part of TV history but that, for many, through the 1950s, it would have been one of the few opportunities to even see

TV and, particularly, the telecast of major sporting events. Because closed-circuit entertainment and sports-based exhibitions usually charged admission (exceptions being most bars or restaurants, as discussed next), out-of-home TV (and, later, its pay-per-view and subscription TV legacies) was labeled "fee TV" in opposition to in-home, over-air "free TV." As detailed in Chapter 1, "free TV" interests proposed that—in exchange for the cost of a TV set and viewing some advertising—its audience received local and national sports coverage as a service, in the public interest, for the good of the community. These advertising-supported, commercial broadcasters thus regularly argued that "fee TV" threatened "free TV's" telecasting of major events and, therefore, was not in the best interest of the public. In 1951, a critic from the *Kansas City Star* summarized these concerns, following the closed-circuit telecast of the Louis-Savold fight:

> the families owning 13,000,000 TV sets have a right to feel cheated at being denied the pleasure of a sports program which otherwise would have been brought into the homes of most of them. This wasn't what they expected when they bought their television sets. . . . [T]hey assumed that they would be able to see as well as hear the major sports events they were accustomed to hearing on the radio. . . . The main appeal of television is that it can be enjoyed in the home.[30]

"Fee TV" players like Nate Halpern's TNT, on the other hand, argued that closed-circuit television was explicitly designed to provide access to special events that were otherwise unavailable on home TV and, therefore, were non-competitive with home viewing. Halpern addressed these concerns in a 1955 *Broadcasting* interview in which he allied home TV with "run-of-the-mill sporting events" while casting closed-circuit as a

> "distinct and different type of medium" that so far has been limited to special sports events. "Only a heavyweight championship bout such as the Marciano-Moore fight could have,

and did, pull in a record-breaking $1,300,000 gate for a one night stand."[31]

Rather than be a threat to home TV, theater TV interests argued that they were supplemental to broadcast coverage and more in-line with the excitement and experience of the *stadium* or arena crowd than with the in-home viewing experience. Indeed, a *Variety* reviewer observed that closed-circuit telecasts would have to adapt their presentational style, as "[s]ince the public that attends the closed-circuit fights or football games reacts similarly to fans at the actual event, the broadcaster must wait for a lull in the excitement to get his words across."[32]

In the 1960s and 1970s, the free-TV-versus-fee-TV debates would escalate as cable TV's penetration expanded and in-home pay-per-view, premium channels and other subscription services developed to offer prime sporting and cultural events and theatrical films. As noted in Chapter 3, Home Box Office (HBO) staked much of its early reputation on coverage of boxing, including 1975's "Thrilla in Manila" between Ali and Joe Frazier. As Vogan notes, that "broadcast marked the beginnings of a pay-per-view model that distributed big-ticket events directly to homes via cable TV."[33] With the growth and standardization of cable, satellite, and now digital broadcast services, premium TV providers and subscription packages have become the primary domain of pay-per-view,[34] shifting the majority of fee TV into the home, with a few key exceptions. Closed-circuit theater TV still succeeds in cinemas through Fathom Events' use of a proprietary digital broadcast network to link over 1,500 screens across the country for concert events, classic film screenings, and faith-based programming.[35] In the 1990s, however, out-of-home sports viewing primarily moved to the sports bar, sports-themed restaurant, and related entertainment economy venues.

Home Away: Beer. Wings. Sports . . . Phamily

The most popular place for out-of-home TV sports viewing remains the tavern or bar/restaurant. The Nielsen ratings service first launched an out-of-home TV measurement service in 2017. According to 2019

Nielsen numbers, 66 percent of adults aged 18 and older watched sports in a restaurant or bar, with 70 percent of the 18–24 year old demographic having done so.[36] Bar viewing has historically been sports' "third space," balancing the comforts and intimacies of home viewing (including beer and food at one's command) while also featuring stadium-like energy and engagement with others. But sports viewing in bars also has a history as long as TV itself.

Prior to television's widespread availability, the bar was particularly popular with working-class male viewers—representing a masculine preserve that offered "a potent sense of collectivity" and "the thrill of the crowd."[37] Within the tavern, hierarchies among these men prevailed, with better seating for customers who paid more for top-shelf liquor. Bar owners worried that patrons might settle in for the length of a game without actually purchasing much food or drink, making TV a potentially expensive distraction. Sports viewing also led to concerns that—given TV's "usual" place within the home—the bar itself might become feminized, privatized, and domesticated, "undermining its traditional masculinist ideals of free entry and conversational democracy."[38]

At the height of the three-network broadcast era's dominance, Roone Arledge's *Monday Night Football* became a genuine social phenomenon that provoked industry and public conversations about out-of-home sports TV. With the series' premiere in 1970, bar and restaurant owners jumped on the opportunity to create traffic on what was otherwise the slowest day of the week. Offering special dinner deals or buffets and drink specials, *Monday Night Football* saw "saloon clubs" created, and usual business up as much as 50 percent on Mondays.[39] With examples such as "a posh gourmet spot in San Antonio" installing "individual color TV sets in one area of the restaurant for fans to watch the Monday night games as they dine," football TV was suddenly welcomed into spaces from which it previously had been forbidden.[40] Other restaurants used the series' popularity to create "ladies' nights out" events to capitalize upon expectations that most of *Monday Night Football*'s viewers were male, though the series was notably popular with female viewers and youth audiences as well.[41]

In the 1990s, however, the sports bar began to transform. This transformation emerges out of a dynamic mix of transitions in the economy, the restaurant industry, television hardware, and television content delivery systems. Media scholars Garry Whannel, Lawrence Wenner, and Toby Miller, in particular, have examined this transition. Their research proposes that the post-1990s sports bar is an "extension of domesticated mall design," welcoming female customers, in particular, "with an emphasis on cleanliness, multiple TVs and sites for viewing."[42] Historically, this transition coincides with the completion of the US economy's transformation to a service-based economy. For businesses to thrive in this context, "the greatest opportunity for value creation resides in staging experiences."[43] The "experience economy" is based on having consumers pay for experiences that, in the past, would not have been market-based activities. Finally, but perhaps most critically, the TV that is essential to out-of-home TV sports arguably changed more between 1995 and the present than in its entire prior history. Thanks to the post-1995 availability of restaurant/bar licensing for DirecTV's NFL Sunday Ticket package coupled with the early-2000s availability of HDTV, sports viewing became the ideal and, increasingly, *central* experience upon which to build this promise of community and connection through consumption (particularly of beer, wings, and sports).

Indeed, NFL football remains the most popular out-of-home viewing sport on a weekly, seasonal basis. In 1994, the league made a deal with satellite provider DirecTV to be the exclusive home of "NFL Sunday Ticket," an out-of-market subscription package that allowed subscribers access to all weekly games that were not televised locally. Bars and other commercial establishments were offered the opportunity to purchase Sunday Ticket at a rate based on the bar's size (from occupancy starting at 50 people up to as much as 10,000). According to a bar-owner in Pittsburgh, "You have no Ticket, you have no business. And that's the truth."[44] In its first full out-of-home season in 1995, DirecTV's NFL Sunday Ticket package was featured in over 5,000 bars and restaurants.[45] For venue owners, the DirecTV package mimicked the excitement and boon that had been caused by *Monday Night Football* 30 years earlier. According to one restaurant marketing manager,

> We took a Sunday night and made it like a Thursday or Friday night—pretty awesome. . . . Instead of being empty on a Sunday afternoon in October, we're packed with people who want to watch an NFL game and have lunch or dinner.[46]

Enhancing such newfound access to games, however, was the ability to experience them in high definition. HDTV was too expensive for most consumers to have in their homes until 2009 (which also marked the deadline for broadcasters to finalize the upgrade to digital broadcast signals). Bars and restaurants could not only provide HDTV, but could have multiple screens offering several different channels or a great view of the same game from any seat in the house. In 2004, *Restaurant Hospitality* magazine commented that "for operators who rely on television to attract crowds to the bars and dining rooms of their full-service establishments, a new Golden Age might be at hand." Though "most Average Joes still haven't taken the plunge . . . a come-for-the-HDTV, pay-for-the food experience at a restaurant is a sweet deal."[47] Overall, new TV technology and content providers created a "stickiness" for out-of-home venues, encouraging patrons to stay for the duration of a game, ordering multiple more items than they may have if arriving for a meal alone.

The most successful of these themed restaurant/bar venues has been Buffalo Wild Wings, or BW3. BW3's design, menu, branded apps, and corporate partnerships and sponsorships immerse its patrons in "sportsworld"—a realm of food, drink, sports viewing, and app-driven engagement and gaming that positions them both as spectators and participants, consumers and performers.[48] Founded in 1982 by two college buddies in Ohio, BW3 is now the leading sports bar chain in sales in the US. Its motto—"Beer. Wings. Sports"—succinctly explains its focus and the contours of its intended immersion experience. Each BW3 is designed to appeal across generations, with distinct spaces within the restaurant. Its bar "features a giant TV screen hanging over it—is at the center of the action, and its new horseshoe shape encourages people to talk with each other—a feature that appeals specifically to Millennials."[49] However, since 2013, BW3 has also "made moves to lure more families with its stadium restaurant design, which separates the bar and dining areas . . . while also providing the same viewing options available in the bar area" with over 80 TVs dispersed throughout each venue.[50] The "Stadia" design concept encourages "a more stadium-like feel to watch the game," but, notably, one where "there is really not a bad seat in the house"[51] and the climate is always favorable. BW3 has become a corporate partner to the NCAA and to esports' Team Dignitas, establishing itself as the "Official Hangout" of both and giving its logo presence in gaming livestreams on Twitch and Facebook. Relatedly, here, BW3's design for optimal sports viewing is reinforced by "gamifying" patrons' wait-time at their tables. Currently, BW3 is partnered with DraftKings for a fantasy football game and is collaborating with MGM Resorts international on its sports-betting venture, Roar Digital, "to provide sports gaming experiences at a national scale inside Buffalo Wild Wings."[52] Significantly, however, in spite of nationally available telecasts, fantasy, and betting platforms, each individual BW3 still appeals to local specificity by featuring area high school and college team jerseys, helmets, and posters in order to connect the franchise with the community. It's this broader communal and even *familial* appeal of out-of-home viewing to which I now turn.

According to sports logo wear company, Fanatics, a sizeable majority of each professional sports league's fans "root for teams that do not play in the state where they reside."[53] In a mobile, digitally driven, data-gathering era, the value of this fan community's loyalty is increasingly recognized and monetized by sports media organizations who are urged to "glocalize" their pro sports team clients' thinking by targeting "a strategy for displaced fan" to "Tag them. Follow them. Keep them."[54] For displaced fans, the home stadium can no longer be the focus of belonging, but the "ex pat" club and its game-watch bar provides a powerful site to reconnect with home through communal viewing that

> is, in its sense of shared collective ritual, closer to the stadium experience than to the domestic one. . . . [T]he bar, which facilitates movement, interaction, and profanity, is arguably closer to the traditional football audience experience than is the modern stadium.[55]

In 2008, television historian Jon Kraszewski wrote the only sustained TV studies analysis of the phenomenon of the displaced fan's out-of-home viewing at "expat sports bars" to date. Focused on a Pittsburgh Steelers bar in Fort Worth, Texas, Kraszewski finds that

> [s]ports offer a cultural language to speak about regionalisms and a very coherent notion of home. In this sense, the bar hosting the fans becomes a stage for fans to perform former home identities, and the television screen becomes one part of the mise-en-scene for this performance.[56]

Kraszewski's study analyzes sports' power to forge a profound sense of home among those displaced from it, but also to study the ways in which fluency in local references, geography, slang, food and drink, as well as team history and depth of loyalty are also tested to establish authenticity and belonging. In Kraszewski's study, ex-pat club members staged local identities in four key categories: consumption of regional food and drink; organization of game-watch seating; performance of regionalisms (as seen through Pittsburgh slang and dialect, geographic references, and display of Steeler swag that was only available within that market and, thus, a marker of authenticity and connection to home); and rivalries. Any tensions that might arise among the group (political differences, etc.) acknowledge "that home is a place riddled with social tensions,"[57] but these are displaced, particularly, onto shared geographic references and sporting rivalries. In the remainder of this section, I apply Kraszewski's method and model to a case study of the Philly Phans of Orange County (California), who gather to game-watch at an independently owned neighborhood pub in Costa Mesa, CA, a beach-adjacent community half-way between Los Angeles to the north and San Diego to the south.

At the other end of the state of Pennsylvania from Kraszewski's Pittsburgh Steeler followers, fans of the Philadelphia Eagles have a notoriously tough, even unpalatable, reputation. Anyone who has ever watched national coverage of an Eagles game is intimately familiar with the tales, repeated ad nauseum, of fans pelting Santa Claus with snowballs, cheering at the sight of injured opponents, or beating up opposing team mascots. And yet, Eagles' fans' intense loyalty to their team, win or lose, has also led to a historically deep and respectful bond between the fans and the team's players and has shaped the identity of the city itself. Eagles fandom in "exile" from the City of Brotherly Love is thus marked both by defensiveness and pride at its rough reputation while defining its ex-pat community, above all, as "Phamily."

The Philly Phans of Orange County (PPOC) was formed in 2014 through a merger of two Meetup groups. In 2016, the club expanded again by absorbing an Eagles group that had previously met at a cheesesteak restaurant chain, "Philly's Best." The PPOC thus has three primary organizers, but the majority of the weekly planning falls to one woman who manages the membership, sends out weekly in-season newsletters, and organizes game-watch raffles, swag, and charitable endeavors. Game-watches take place at the Harp, an Irish pub that has been a fixture in the neighborhood for over 30 years. Its owner, John Lyons, had previously owned a bar in "Giants country" in New Jersey that had been "taken over" by Eagles fans. Thereby deeply familiar with the fandom, the club's gracious host calls the PPOC "the best and most loyal fans I have ever seen."[58] The pub offers iconic Philly foods during game-watches, including soft-pretzels, Taylor pork rolls, and cheesesteaks. Doors open at 8:00 a.m. on Sundays, with kickoff generally at 10:30 a.m. Pacific time. At each game, the club hosts a 50/50 raffle with prizes and proceeds going to an Eagles' player's charity or to local organizations such as women's shelters, emergency relief funds, or local kids' programs. The PPOC is known to be one of the most active and dedicated Eagles ex-pat clubs in the nation. This value is recognized in special offers and discounts that also help "tag, follow, and keep" loyalty. In 2019, for example, NBC Sports' Philadelphia offered PPOC members a discounted subscription to the NBC Sports Gold Philly Pass mobile/streaming app, which provides access to the Philadelphia feed of local pre- and post-game talk shows and special features for each of the pro sports teams "back home." Because of the Harp's location adjacent to Newport Beach, which is home to many professional athletes, former Eagles players have also, on occasion, attended game-watch parties. Following the Eagles' Super Bowl victory, the pub temporarily installed a huge outdoor banner thanking off-season neighborhood resident, and championship MVP quarterback, Nick Foles.

Because the Harp is a small, independent neighborhood bar and restaurant, space is at a premium. There is a small outdoor patio, a main room with a small stage, and the bar. Though seating is first-come, first-served, the longest-term regulars and more senior members of the group generally occupy the available tables and booths, with "newbies" and, particularly, "bandwagoners" standing. Non-divisional games and games that are otherwise available nationally are less well attended or, as one regular confided, attended by "only the crazies." Though fair-weather fans are uniformly looked upon with skepticism, one of the PPOC organizers notes,

> what I love about our group is that it is comprised of ex-Philly folks and also born and raised CA folks who just "chose" the Eagles for various reasons. I give them credit for being just as diehard as Philly fans, given they weren't born into it and they had picked a team who had never won a superbowl until last year. [59]

Indeed, the club is a robust mix of primarily Philadelphia and Philly-region natives (including one of the club organizers who grew up in nearby Baltimore), combined with those who lived in Philadelphia long enough to fall in love with its sports teams (including a contingent whose education or work took them to Philly), and those California natives who chose the Phamily, as noted earlier. There is, however, a "vetting" that occurs to confirm fan legitimacy and loyalty in order to access the full features of the club. To join the club's closed and moderated Facebook group, and thus get all club notifications and get on the mailing-list, requires answering questions about one's fan history and Philadelphia knowledge. During game-watches, performances of "authenticity" include wearing gear with historic value (e.g., jerseys that pre-date the club's transition to the "midnight green" color palette), or "insider" references (such as those found on locally made T-shirts by independent retailers like Shibe Sports). Such performances also include mimicking attendance at the stadium and displaying fluency in Lincoln Financial Field rituals in unison—as when the group chants the call-and-response, "And that's another Eagles," "first down!" or sings "Fly, Eagles, Fly" when the team scores.

One unique tension within the group might be characterized as a form of "survivor's guilt." Kraszewski notes that while many in the Steelers club were displaced to Fort Worth because of work and though "[a]ll people in the club felt that western Pennsylvania was a primordial home . . . they also had other identities—professional and personal—well-established in Fort Worth."[60] While the PPOC is valued as a place to reconnect with home and to establish a familiar shorthand in most all conversations, there is also a sense among at least some of the members that—other than the comparatively exorbitant cost of housing—being in California represents an achievement in which to take pride. While visiting friends and relatives "back East" and, especially, getting back to attend an Eagles game in person at "the Linc" is celebrated, there is also a fairly broadly shared and commented-upon joy in having the California weather and SoCal lifestyle now part of everyday life. This "best of both worlds" sensibility extends in both directions: while the "Cali" lifestyle is "easy" or "soft" in relation to the prized grit and resilience of Philadelphia, by being hard-core Eagles fans, the PPOC's faithful can—in spite of their ex-pat locale—remain loyal to hometown values and legitimately claim to represent Philly.

Of the many interventions made by Kraszewski's study, one of the most significant is its challenge to theories of TV's "placelessness" and of contemporary culture's presumed mobility as one experienced as unmoored. From Steelers fans in Fort Worth to Eagles fans in Costa

Mesa, TV serves as the articulating or connecting object that enables shared community focused on local specificity and distinct levels of commitment to place, from the point of "exile." Ex-pat game-watches clearly demonstrate "that sports fandom resonates with the idea of permanence and geographic origins and not just with the idea of temporary communities or lack of traditional communities in this current stage of capitalism."[61] Indeed, in many US cities the professional sports franchise is metonymic of the city itself, serving as the most recognizable "brand" both within the region and to the broader nation. In the final section of this chapter, I focus on this phenomenon through a case-study of St. Louis, Missouri's Ballpark Village and the "sportification" of place.

Sportification of Place: St. Louis's Ballpark Village

The post-2000s phenomenon of the urban sports district is the *civic* expression of the "new media sport order": the brick-and-mortar, experience economy-based realization of the "sportification" of place. Ivo Jirásek and Geoffrey Zain Kohe have defined "sportification" as a context "in which performative, interpretative, and superficial elements of sporting phenomena are transferred beyond the sporting realm."[62] They are particularly focused on an "overarching theatrification of social life"[63] by which sports iconography and sportswear are now prominent across non-sporting populations and sites. We might think, here, of the athleisure phenomenon by which yoga-wear has become the requisite about-town errand-running uniform or the ways that throwback jerseys, hats, or sneakers have become high fashion. Both are examples of sports-based gear now thoroughly disconnected from explicit sporting activity and made performative and a lifestyle. Helen Morgan Parmett and Kate Ranachan have crucially extended the sportification concept to analyze Seattle's and Atlanta's urban sports district developments, where professional sports stadiums are the anchor of master planning for an entire urban neighborhood.[64] Since the 1990s, such developments have occurred across the country, but they have been particularly prominent in non-coastal, historically industrial cities whose population and economic heyday peaked by 1970 and have struggled ever since, including St. Louis, Cleveland, Cincinnati, Louisville, Pittsburgh, and Kansas City. Why does the sportification of *place* emerge so powerfully as a strategy of urban renewal, community pride, branding, and perceived economic engine in the new millennium?

St. Louis's population peaked in 1950, and "[b]y the 1970s, St. Louis was clearly the patron saint of the nation's urban crisis"[65] due to geographic conscription via home rule (dating back to 1876) and the city's own concerted combination of private discrimination and public policy that insistently created and enforced segregated and unequal housing and employment in explicitly Black and white terms. Here, I refer to the fact that St. Louis has, from its inception to the present, been a predominantly African American and "white" city, with residents overwhelmingly identifying as either Black or white, historically. At present, only 4.13 percent of the population self-identifies outside one of those two categories.[66] In the 1950s and 1960s, federal policy and programs exacerbated and encouraged this pattern of private discrimination and segregationist public policy, by making it easier for suburban, county "commuters to get in and out of the city."[67] Compounding St. Louis's own self-destructive, systemically racist policies has been the post-1980s acceleration of regional inequality energized by the clawing back of federal antitrust laws that encouraged unprecedented corporate mergers and takeovers. Economically, this has meant that former local employers including Anheuser-Busch, McDonnell-Douglas, Ralston Purina, TWA, Mallinckrodt, Southwestern Bell, and Express-Scripts each dissolved and disappeared, moved to a coastal or "frontier" city market, or were downsized to a shell of their former selves.[68] Though finance, medicine, and academic campuses continue to lead St. Louis's market profile, these conditions have—both internally and externally—contributed to a sense that the city is dysfunctional and downscale.

Across this history, St. Louis has ritually attempted to "recapture downtown prosperity with tourist attractions—museums, sports facilities, convention centers, and boutique shopping."[69] Sports, in particular, have been promoted as the answer for renewal, restoration, civic togetherness, and pride. Eero Saarinen's St. Louis Arch was completed in 1965, after which the Civic Center/Redevelopment Area blighted and cleared adjacent land for the construction of the multipurpose original Busch Stadium in 1966. A series of blight and redevelopment strategies and projects followed in the Central Business District through the 1990s. George Lipsitz's 2011 *How Racism Takes Place* includes a chapter outlining St. Louis's active destruction of the city's public-school system in order to entice a second soon-to-depart NFL football franchise. Since then, the city has doubled down on its commitment to "renewal" through the sportification of place.

In 2001, the major league baseball St. Louis Cardinals signed a contract with the state, city, and county to build a new, baseball-only ballpark downtown, adjacent to the old Busch Stadium, which would be demolished to be redeveloped as Ballpark Village—a dining, entertainment, residential, and office campus to be built out in three phases, with the first opened in March of 2014 and the final phase completed in the summer of 2020. Developed by Baltimore-based Cordish Companies—whose initial mark was made through the construction of that city's Inner Harbor development—Ballpark Village is one of several of Cordish's "sports-anchored districts" around the country. Ballpark Village is primarily oriented toward indoor and outdoor dining, drinking, and TV sports viewing. It also prominently houses the St. Louis home television studio for Fox Sports Midwest. To the north of Ballpark Village is phase two of the development, featuring the One Cardinal Way residential complex, a OneLife Fitness Center, retail stores, an office tower and a Lowe's Live! hotel.

In the US Midwest, the cities whose economies have been most gutted by neoliberal policies have also been those that have most eagerly embraced the "retro" ballpark and accompanying urban sports districts, particularly as these developments "articulate utopian longings for racial solidarity even as the renewed infrastructure of the city helps to reestablish a color line."[70] Indeed, arguably, Ballpark Village symbolizes the latest example of St. Louis's ritual approach to community renewal through institutionally racist policies and practices

Figure 5.2 St. Louis's Ballpark Village TVs.

Source: Photograph by the author

while it simultaneously stages the possibility of integrated community and celebration through the performance of insistently *local* knowledges and the affective bonds forged by geographically specific team fandoms. In other words, in a fundamentally "Black and white" city largely evacuated of industry, St. Louis has consistently attempted to mystify race-based defunding of public service and housing opportunities through appeals to shared *love* of the Cardinals, Blues, and the short-lived XFL and, now, new pro soccer franchises. This is a love that crosses geographic and demographic borders within the city and extends to the larger region.[71] Here, sports is what theorists of the experience economy refer to as a "great connector," touching people "at a gut level" with "values that seem lacking in today's leaders and missing from day-to-day experiences of life—among them: empathy and optimism; strength and decisiveness; authenticity, faith, and a sense of community, belonging, and purpose."[72]

Indeed, as there is "a growing consensus that stadiums provide little economic advantage for local communities," so development boosters have, instead, increasingly promoted the *intangible*, social benefits of such projects. In particular, they identify the importance of internal and external identification as "a first-rate, major-league city."[73] As one St. Louis civic leader admitted, "Economically, you're better off with a bank or factory . . . but it buys a lot of emotional impact."[74] Here, the unique resonance of sports cannot be underestimated:

> Professional sports truly are different from any other kind of business because much more attention and emotion are attached to the home team. If a nonsports business that employed 150 people left town, hardly anyone would notice. But if that business were a professional sports team, thousands of hours of talk radio, hundreds of pages of print media, and millions of e-mail messages would be devoted to the news.[75]

This is the power of sports as *emotional* capital in an experience economy. The emotional capital of sports helps to answer the question as to why sports stadiums and sports districts are promoted for community identity and renewal rather than any other type of public good. But, it should also be underscored here that while the new media sport order's built-environment is the most visible iteration of this mode of urban renewal, the requisite promotion of "low or nonexistent corporate taxes and generous subsidies" as key to "local economic growth" and its resulting redistribution of wealth upward is not unique to sports, but is "the new normal under neoliberalism."[76]

The St. Louis Cardinals are an economic engine within the local economy. But they are also a uniquely affective and visible site of local and regional success and pride. Beyond the city and region, the Arch, Budweiser, and St. Louis sports teams are, largely, how the city is known. In the current geography of jobs in the US, arguably, communities like St. Louis have far more at stake than a New York or Los Angeles in *both* the success of urban sports districts and the intangible benefits of, for example, winning the Stanley Cup. While I emphasize the willful mystification that Ballpark Village enables—covering over integral aspects of the city's political history in order to revel in visualization of the possibility of togetherness and equity—I am, also, with Krasze-wski, Whannel, and others discussed earlier, here intentionally writing *against* scholarship that imagines such developments to be emblematic of "nonspace," disembodiment, "mall-ification," or touristic cosmopoli-tanism. In spite of the broader phenomenon of sportification and the sports-anchored district—with its often-shared developers and archi-tectural firms, each of these are *unique* city stories with real laborers, visitors, and fans, in daily traversal.

Promotions for Ballpark Village's luxury apartment complex, One Cardinal Way, beckon potential residents to "live like a player." Across this chapter's examples of out-of-home sports viewing we see consis-tent attempts to turn emotional connection and the lived experience of fan loyalty into real, material, economic gains. As the experience econ-omy morphs into an accelerated quest for "immersive entertainment" increasingly "themed to a single franchise,"[77] the significance of *sports* franchises as analogs to televisual, cinematic, and gaming franchises or content universes should be more fully explored. How might television and media studies be extended and renewed by including the sports franchise, its civic brand, televisual extensions, and built-environment in our understanding of fictional universes in which multiple indepen-dent yet mutually informing works are set? As policy entities, textual phenomena, and social and political forces, conceptualizing the sports franchise as media content universe compels an analysis of "the com-plex ways in which media . . . are bound up with wider institutional, technological and political processes in the modern world" and how these "processes and everyday life are interwoven with each other."[78] When we take seriously that "sports is television that matters to people in ways that no other entertainment can," we expand the work of TV studies and significantly reenergize its relevance and value for the future.

Notes

1. Jacqueline L. Salmon, "Bill Would End Separation of Church and Super Bowl," *The Washington Post*, February 7, 2008, A06. Specter's proposal was in response to the National Football League's intention to sue such venues for copyright

infringement. The NFL interceded, stating that it would allow live screenings of the Super Bowl by religious organizations when free-of-charge and held on church premises, preventing the need for the bill.

2. Statistical data from www.census.gov/prod/99pubs/99statab/sec31.pdf 885. Since 1980, US TV ownership rates have held steady at 98 percent of the population.

3. Garry Whannel, "Pregnant With Anticipation: The Pre-History of Television Sport and the Politics of Recycling and Presentation," *International Journal of Cultural Studies* 8, no. 4 (2005): 408.

4. Whannel, "Pregnant With Anticipation," 414.

5. Whannel, 414–415.

6. Joseph B. Pine, II. and James H. Gilmore, *The Experience Economy* (Boston, MA: Harvard Business Review Press, 2011), 62. Pine and Gilmore propose a "third-place opportunity for sports" through which teams might charge fans to "come to a facility designed explicitly for watching away games," a practice that most major league franchises now encourage during playoffs when the home stadium becomes host to large-screen video displays of the away games in each series. Here I think of "third place" as descriptive of the intimate, familial nature of fan game-watch activity in public spaces that simultaneously mimic the crowd energy and rituals of the home team stadium.

7. Brett Hutchins and David Rowe, *Sport Beyond Television: The Internet, Digital Media and the Rise of Networked Media Sport* (New York: Routledge, 2012), 4.

8. Brett Hutchins and David Rowe, "Introduction," in *Digital Media Sport: Technology, Power and Culture in the Network Society*, eds. Brett Hutchins, David Rowe, Peter Morris, and Riki Therivel (New York: Routledge, 2013), 2.

9. Hutchins and Rowe, *Sport Beyond Television*, 10.

10. Hutchins and Rowe, "Introduction," 4.

11. Dennis Deninger, *Sports on Television: The How and Why Behind What You See* (New York: Routledge, 2012), 2.

12. Eva Illouz, *Cold Intimacies: The Making of Emotional Capitalism* (Malden, MA: Polity Press, 2007), 63.

13. Illouz, *Cold Intimacies*, 108.

14. Anna McCarthy, "Closed-Circuit Television," in *Encyclopedia of Television*, 2nd edition, Volume 1, A-C, ed. Horace Newcomb (New York: Fitzroy Dearborn, 2004), 541.

15. "TV's Bonus Aud is 732,400, Tho Not All in Bars," *Billboard* 62, no. 36 (September 9, 1950): 7.

16. It should be noted here that closed-circuit TV is commonly used in non-exhibition contexts, to this day—from in-house residence hall, hospital, or other educational institution channels to factory surveillance technologies and bank surveillance of ATM machines.

17. See Michele Hilmes, *Hollywood and Broadcasting: From Radio to Cable* (Urbana, IL: University of Illinois Press, 1990); Douglas Gomery, "Theatre Television: The Missing Link of Technological Change in the US Motion Picture Industry," *The Velvet Light Trap* 21 (Summer 1985): 54–61; and, Timothy R. White, "Life After

Divorce: The Corporate Strategy of Paramount Pictures Corporation in the 1950s," *Film History* 2, no. 2 (June-July 1988): 99–119.

18. Department of Justice Office of Public Affairs, "Department of Justice Files Motion to Terminate Paramount Consent Decrees," *Justice News,* November 22, 2019, *www.justice.gov/opa/pr/department-justice-files-motion-terminate-paramount-consent-decrees*

19. Hilmes, *Hollywood and Broadcasting*, 121.

20. Hilmes, 122.

21. Anna McCarthy, "'Like an Earthquake!' Theater Television, Boxing, and the Black Public Sphere," *Quarterly Review of Film and Video* 16, nos. 3–4 (1999): 308.

22. In addition to sporting events, symphonic performances, operas, and other special presentations, closed-circuit TV was popular with industrial interests as a means of holding conventions, sales meetings, and other training. In other words, closed-circuit was a precursor (if one-way) to group-conferencing technologies like Zoom or Skype. Early clients included IBM, Chevrolet, Dodge, Sheraton Hotels, and Pan Am Airways. See also Jack Singer, "Theater TV Breaks Big Barrier; Makes Big Tracks for 1954," *The Billboard* 66, no. 34 (August 21, 1954): 1, 15; and Gomery, "Theatre Television."

23. Travis Vogan, "Exhibiting Ali's 'Super Fights': The Contested Politics and Brief History of Closed Circuit Boxing Broadcasts," *Film History* 30, no. 3 (2018): 3.

24. Vogan, "Exhibiting," 3.

25. McCarthy, "'Like an Earthquake!'" 311.

26. Vogan, "Exhibiting," 5.

27. Vogan, 5–6.

28. Vogan, 7.

29. Vogan, 9.

30. "Six-City Report on Exclusive Theatre TV Broadcast: Theatre TV Fight Showings a Sensation at Boxoffice," *Boxoffice* 59, no. 8 (June 23, 1951): 9.

31. "Program Services: Halpern Says Commercial TV, Theatre TV Won't Compete," *Broadcasting* 49, no. 19 (November 7, 1955): 105.

32. "Radio-Television: Halpern Formula for Closed-Circuit Sports Telecasts," *Variety* 200, no. 10 (November 9, 1955): 23.

33. Vogan, "Exhibiting," 27.

34. For example, ESPN+ subscribers can, periodically, pay an additional $64.99 for UFC pay-per-view championship bouts and related undercards.

35. See www.fathomevents.com. Fathom Events is a joint venture of cinema exhibitors AMC Entertainment, Cinemark Holdings, and Regal Entertainment Group. The company exhibits approximately 150 events per year.

36. Nielsen Media Research, "For The Win: Out-of-Home Viewers of Fall Sports on Linear TV Watch in Multiple Locations and Are Engaged," *Insights,* January 24, 2019, www.nielsen.com.

37. Anna McCarthy, *Ambient Television: Visual Culture and Public Space* (Durham, NC: Duke University Press, 2001), 29, 34.

38. McCarthy, *Ambient Television*, 32.

39. Don Page, "Saloon Grid Clubs Pass Tube Test," *Los Angeles Times*, November 14, 1970.

40. Donald Freeman, "Monday Night Football Proved to Be a Big Hit," *San Diego Union-Tribune*, December 16, 1970, n.p.

41. ABC Research Department Memo, January 6, 1971, Roone Arledge Papers, Columbia University, New York.

42. Toby Miller, *Sportsex* (Philadelphia, PA: Temple University Press, 2001), 8. See also: Whannel, "Pregnant with Anticipation"; and Lawrence A. Wenner and Steven J. Jackson, eds., *Sport, Beer, and Gender: Promotional Culture and Contemporary Social Life* (New York: Peter Lang, 2009).

43. Pine, II. and Gilmore, *The Experience Economy*, ix. Pine and Gilmore use the example of birthday parties, which have increasingly become out-of-home, immersive events.

44. Michael Sanserino, "Bars Pay an Arm, a Leg, and a Beer for NFL Content," *Pittsburgh Post-Gazette*, October 18, 2014. Indeed, at the time of this writing, the NFL was being sued by a sports bar in San Francisco for anticompetitive business practices, arguing that the exclusivity deal between the NFL and DirecTV is, effectively, a monopoly that can set prices at any rate, as there is no way to access the content by any other means.

45. Michael Sanson, "Football Fever," *Restaurant Hospitality* 79, no. 8 (August 1995): 34.

46. John Soeder, "Deep Dish," *Restaurant Hospitality* 82, no. 10 (October 1998): 140.

47. "Re-Thinking Your Big Picture," *Restaurant Hospitality* 88, no. 5 (May 2004): 34.

48. John F. Sherry, Jr., et al., "Gendered Behavior in a Male Preserve: Role Playing at ESPN Zone Chicago," *Journal of Consumer Psychology* 14, nos. 1-2 (2004): 153.

49. Lia Jennings, "Leading the Way," *Nation's Restaurant News* 47, no. 8 (April 23, 2013): 3.

50. Vance Cariaga, "Buffalo Wild Wings Eyes Boost from NFL, Easier Comps," *Investors Business Daily*, September 15, 2015, A5.

51. Charlie Duerr, "Having Words With Sally Smith," *Nation's Restaurant News* 48, no. 18 (September 22, 2014): 49.

52. *MarketLine Company Profile: Buffalo Wild Wings, Inc.* (September 26, 2019).

53. Irving Fain, "Displaced Fans Remain Connected—And Valuable—To Teams," *Sports Business Journal*, February 4, 2013, n.p.

54. Rick Burton and Norm O'Reilly, "It's Time to 'Glocalize' Team Thinking," *Sports Business Journal*, March 16–22, 2020, 16.

55. Whannel, "Pregnant With Anticipation," 408.

56. Jon Kraszewski, "Pittsburgh in Fort Worth: Football Bars, Sports Television, Sports Fandom, and the Management of Home," *Journal of Sport & Social Issues* 32, no. 2 (May 2008): 147.

57. Kraszewski, "Pittsburgh in Fort Worth," 142.

58. Harp owner, John Lyons, in a message to the PPOC weekly email update, January 28, 2019.

59. Jennifer McGilloway, email message to author, August 27, 2018.

60. Kraszewski, "Pittsburgh in Fort Worth," 149.

61. Kraszewski, 155.

62. Ivo Jirásek and Geoffrey Zain Kohe, "Readjusting Our Sporting Sites/Sight: Sportification and the Theatricality of Social Life," *Sport, Ethics and Philosophy* 9, no. 3 (July 3, 2015): 257.

63. Jirásek and Kohe, "Readjusting Our Sporting Sites/Sight," 258.

64. Kate Ranachan and Helen Morgan Parmett, "Fortune Favors the Braves? Race and the Suburban Rebranding of Baseball in Atlanta." (Paper presented at the annual meeting of the Society for Cinema and Media Studies, Atlanta, GA, April 2, 2016).

65. Colin Gordon, *Mapping Decline: St. Louis and the Fate of the American City* (Philadelphia: University of Pennsylvania Press, 2008), 156.

66. Deloitte, "St. Louis, MO," *Data USA*, November 16, 2020, https://datausa.io/profile/geo/st.-louis-mo/

67. Gordon, *Mapping Decline*, 157.

68. The 2008 takeover of Anheuser-Busch by Belgian-based InBev led to the layoff of one-fifth of the brewer's local workforce.

69. Gordon, *Mapping Decline*, 155.

70. Daniel Rosensweig, *Retro Ball Parks: Instant History, Baseball, and the New American City* (Knoxville: The University of Tennessee Press, 2005), 19.

71. The greater St. Louis area includes the city, six counties in Missouri, and eight counties in Illinois. The St. Louis Cardinals have a much larger regional television footprint, however, with Fox Sports Midwest telecasts in states including Arkansas, Oklahoma, Tennessee, Kentucky, Kansas, and Iowa.

72. Douglas B. Sosnik, Matthew J. Dowd, and Ron Fournier, *Applebee's America: How Successful Political, Business, and Religious Leaders Connect With the New American Community* (New York: Simon & Schuster, 2006), 2.

73. Rick Eckstein and Kevin Delaney, "New Sports Stadiums, Community Self-Esteem, and Community Collective Conscience," *Journal of Sport & Social Issues* 26, no. 3 (August 2002): 237.

74. Michael Oriard, *Brand NFL: Making and Selling America's Favorite Sport* (Chapel Hill: University of North Carolina Press, 2010), 159.

75. Rick Eckstein and Kevin Delaney, *Public Dollars, Private Stadiums: The Battle Over Building Sports Stadiums* (New Brunswick, NJ: Rutgers University Press, 2006), 192.

76. Sean Dinces, "'Nothing but Net Profit': Property Taxes, Public Dollars, and Corporate Philanthropy at Chicago's United Center," *Radical History Review* 125 (May 2016): 22.

77. Todd Martens, "A Falcon Flight to the Future," *Los Angeles Times*, May 31, 2019, A8.

78. Shaun Moores, *Media, Place, and Mobility* (New York: Palgrave Macmillan, 2012), 108.

QUESTIONS FOR DISCUSSION AND FURTHER RESEARCH

Chapter 1 "Not a Traditional Business": Sports TV as For-Profit Public Good?

1. Scholars have long debated whether sports were foundational to the success of television or whether television fundamentally popularized and changed sports. Which perspective do you find most compelling and why?

2. Can commercial, for-profit endeavors serve "in the public interest, convenience and necessity"? How have professional sports teams historically been conceptualized as a public good?

3. Why is it important to think of communications law and policy as *cultural* phenomena? How does the Sports Broadcasting Act of 1961 exemplify this?

Chapter 2 Sportvision: The Texts and Tech of Sports TV

1. According to Margaret Morse, how does sports TV challenge conventional understandings of gender and objectification? How does sports programming reduce the "threat" of this challenge?

2. Consider onscreen graphics that succeed with audiences (e.g., the 1st & Ten Line) and those that fail (e.g., the glow puck). What distinguishes success from failure, here?

3. How do "videogame graphics" and increasing use of in-game analytic data encourage viewer "interactivity" and second (or third,

or more) screen engagement? Do videogamegraphic aesthetics extend or revise Morse's theorization of sports TV address?

Chapter 3 Generation IX: Sports TV, Gender, and Voice

1. Why is the "film" aesthetic common to "prestige" documentary typically so valued by critics? What types of television are aesthetically *different* from this style? Why have these genres typically been less valued by critics, if not by audiences?
2. How do you identify the "author" of a television text? What different elements make up the "voice" within a television program or series? How is our perception of authorship and voice different in *Being Serena* and in *Nine for IX*, and what contributes to this difference?
3. Scholars have argued that "postfeminism" describes a context in which feminism is simultaneously taken for granted and disavowed. How do episodes of *Nine for IX* exemplify this paradox? See www.espn.com/espnw/w-in-action/nine-for-ix/.

Chapter 4 The Level Playing Field? Sports TV and Cultural Debate

1. Why, historically, have sports been hailed as a venue for the realization of civil rights, or a "level playing field"?
2. Why is the Super Bowl a particularly fraught site for questions of indecency and FCC concern?
3. Sports references are often used as shorthand to identify presumed political affiliations (e.g., NASCAR Dads, hockey Moms, Roller Derby women, etc.). Why are certain sports associated with particular political leanings? How do such terms, further, connect to geographic mythologies and imagined capital relations?

Chapter 5 The Sports Media Ecosystem: Sports TV's Out-of-Home Communities

1. While out-of-home TV is often discussed as a contemporary phenomenon, how has it, in fact, been part of TV's history from its inception? How has out-of-home TV changed from the 1940s to the present?

2. Even though we now have more and more opportunities for individualized sports content to be delivered directly to our mobile devices, sports bars and team-sponsored watch parties—not to mention esports arenas—are thriving. Why might sport's built-environment be surging in popularity in the "TV everywhere" era?

3. Beyond the urban sports district and sports bars, what are some everyday examples of "sportification"?

A SELECT TIMELINE OF US SPORTS TELEVISION EVENTS

1927   In an experimental television transmission, Philo T. Farnsworth uses previously filmed footage of a Jack Dempsey v. Gene Tunney boxing match

1939   Television is introduced to the general public at the New York World's Fair. Display of the technology at the Fair includes broadcasts of a Columbia-Princeton baseball game, a Brooklyn Dodgers v. Cincinnati Reds baseball game, a Philadelphia Eagles v. Brooklyn Dodgers football game, and excerpts of wrestling, boxing, and ice-skating, captured by NBC-TV's mobile production unit

1946–1949   NBC's sports digest series *Gillette Cavalcade of Sports* comes to TV (the series premiered on radio in 1944)

1949   CBS telecasts the Preakness (horse race) live from Pimlico racetrack (May 14)

1951   CBS broadcasts the first color sports event from Monmouth Park, NJ (horse racing, July 14); National Football League championship game is first telecast on DuMont (December 23)

1952   First live coverage of the Kentucky Derby on CBS (May 3)

1959   NBC broadcasts the first color telecast of an indoor sporting event (basketball, November 1)

1960   ABC secures American Football League telecast rights

1961   The Sports Broadcasting Act grants professional sports leagues limited exemption from antitrust laws, allowing them to pool broadcast rights and to negotiate single television packages to sell to networks. This exemption is later applied to the NCAA for college sports; CBS secures National Football League telecast rights for $28 million; slow-motion replay is tested during an ABC telecast of a Boston College–Syracuse football game

1961–1997   ABC's weekly digest series, *Wide World of Sports*

1963   In-game use of instant replay debuts at CBS telecast of the Army-Navy football game (December 7)

1964–1965   CBS pays $28 million for NFL television rights

1966   The AFL and NFL merge, creating the National Football League. CBS is granted National League telecast rights; NBC is granted American League telecast rights

1967   Super Bowl I between Green Bay and Kansas City is telecast on CBS and NBC (January 15)

1968   Tommie Smith's and John Carlos's anti-imperialist, anti-racist, social justice protest from the awards podium at the Olympics in Mexico City is telecast worldwide (ABC, October 16); "The Heidi Game" (NBC) creates controversy when the decisive minutes of a New York Jets v. Oakland Raiders game are unaired as NBC begins telecast of the film *Heidi* on time (November 17)

1970–2005   ABC's *Monday Night Football* (moves to ESPN, 2005–present)

1971   *Brian's Song* is ABC's Movie of the Week (November 30)

1972   The Summer Olympics in Munich become a news event as 11 Israeli athletes are murdered after being taken hostage by Palestinian terrorists. For two days, viewers watched as events unfolded, prior to the resumption of the Games (August 26–September 10). HBO (Home Box Office) is launched with telecast of a National Hockey League game between the New York Rangers and the Vancouver Canucks, from Madison Square Garden

1973   Billie Jean King v. Bobby Riggs in the "Battle of the Sexes" tennis match on ABC (September 20)

1975   HBO telecasts "The Thrilla from Manila" World Heavyweight Title fight between Joe Frazier and Muhammad Ali, via satellite (October 1)

1977–2008   HBO weekly football series (in season), *Inside the NFL*, featuring content provided by NFL Films (from 2008–present, the series airs on Showtime)

1978   Launch of Superstation WGN-TV makes Chicago Cubs baseball nationally available

1979   Launch of Ted Turner's Superstation WTBS makes Atlanta Braves baseball nationally available. Launch of ESPN (Entertainment and Sports Programming Network)

1980   ABC telecast of the "Miracle on Ice" from the Lake Placid, NY Olympics (February 22); NBC Telecast of Miami Dolphins v. NY Jets NFL game without play-by-play or commentary (December 20)

1982   The "CBS Chalkboard," allowing commentators to "draw" plays on the screen debuts in NFL football coverage

1984   Capital Cities/ABC becomes a majority owner of ESPN

1989   The Cablecam is developed by Jim Rodnunsky; the World Series telecast between the San Francisco Giants and the Oakland A's is interrupted by the Loma Prieta earthquake (October 17)

1991   FOX outbids CBS for NFL telecast rights

1994   The "Fox Box" first appears offering digital, real-time, onscreen information during NFL games and, later, Major League Baseball games. Each sports outlet develops a version of the Fox Box through the 1990s and 2010s and the box alternates its placement onscreen, in part to adapt to HDTV aspect ratios (at top of screen, bottom of screen, bottom-left corner, bottom-right corner)

1995   The Walt Disney Company purchases Capital Cities/ABC (and, therefore, ESPN)

1996   Fox Sports Regional Networks launch as cable's FSN; Sport-Vision creates the "FOX Trax" infrared "comet-trail" puck for hockey coverage (lasts until the 1998 season)

1997   FOX, NBC, and Lifetime networks share broadcast rights for the inaugural season of the WNBA

1998   NBA TV is the first league-owned network to launch on cable; SportVision's electronic 1st & Ten Line premieres in NFL game coverage

1998–2004   Fox Entertainment Group owns the Los Angeles Dodgers

1999   US Women's World Cup Soccer victory at the Rose Bowl in Pasadena, CA on ABC (July 10)

2000   MLB Advanced Media is formed

2001   SportVision's graphics enter NASCAR coverage, highlighting driver position and indicating intervals between cars; *Sunday Night Baseball* premieres the "K zone" on ESPN (followed soon after by FOX with "FOX Trax" and TBS with "Pitch Trax")

2002   MLB.TV livestreams its first game; SportVision's stromotion allows for frame by frame capture of athletes in motion; CBS Sports Network launches

2003   The NFL Network launches; out-of-market subscription service MLB.TV is offered for the first time, for an entire season

2004   Super Bowl XXXVIII (CBS) features Janet Jackson's "wardrobe malfunction" during MTV produced half-time performance with Justin Timberlake; Skycam (competitor to Cablecam) is developed by Garrett Brown

2005–present   *Monday Night Football* moves from ABC to ESPN

2005   The NFL hosts its first regular season game outside the US with a Mexico City matchup between the Arizona Cardinals and the San Francisco 49ers; MLB Advanced Media supports CBS's March Madness; Cleatus the Robot makes its first appearance on FOX *NFL Sunday*

2006   Google enters sports streaming with a video download deal with the NBA; NBC is the first Olympics rights holder to stream live action from the Olympics (Turin)

2007   NHL Network launches as cable network; the NFL holds its first overseas game in London (Miami Dolphins v. New York Giants, October); the MLB "At Bat" app is launched

2008   The Beijing Olympics demonstrate power of multiplatform sports media, with online, hand-held, and "classic" TV delivery (NBC); the NFL initiates streaming of all regular season games on NFL.com and NBCSports.com

2009–present   ESPN documentary series, *30 for 30*; *Inside the NFL* moves to Showtime from HBO; MLB Network launches as a cable network

2010   LeBron James's "Decision" to leave Cleveland for Miami takes place as a live TV event on ESPN (July 8)

2011   MLB.com reports that, for the first time, a majority of its traffic takes place on mobile devices

2011–present   Ultimate Fighting Championship (UFC) is featured in mainstream TV coverage (vs. only pay-per-view; on FX, FOX)

2012   NBC Sports Network is launched on cable; the Super Bowl is both televised and streamed for the first time

2013   FOX Sports Network is launched on cable

2015   BAMTECH is spun off from MLB Advanced Media; BAMTECH takes over NHL app, NHL.com, and operation of the NHL Network; the Olympics include more hours of coverage on digital platforms than on traditional/linear TV for the first time

2016   The Philadelphia 76ers become the first professional US sports franchise to own controlling interest in a professional gaming entity (with majority stake in esports franchises, Team Dignitas and Team Apex); BAMTECH and FOX Sports launch Fox Sports Go

2017   The Walt Disney Company acquires majority ownership of BAMTECH; the NFL launches its "nextgen stats" portal with Amazon Web Services (AWS); Twitter announces a multi-year deal to livestream WNBA regular season games and highlight packages

2018   Major League Soccer team Los Angeles Football Club partners with YouTube TV to offer all of its locally televised matches via livestreaming

2020   COVID-19 pandemic shuts down most all live sports coverage on TV from March through July 2020; livestreaming of video-game play (NBA, NASCAR, Indycar) briefly substitutes for live telecasts; sports documentary surges in popularity with new content, including the Michael Jordan–focused *The Last Dance* on ESPN and Netflix; the WNBA and NBA postpone games to recognize ongoing systemic injustices and violence against Black Americans (August); the NFL "Kickoff" weekend games and season are themed "It Takes All of Us" to acknowledge "important causes vital to our players and fans" (September); Naomi Osaka wins the US Open tennis tournament, throughout which she wears facemasks honoring individuals killed at the hands of the police (September); #SayTheirNames2020; www.sayevery. name.

SCHOLARLY BIBLIOGRAPHY

Alexander, Michelle. *The New Jim Crow: Mass Incarceration in the Age of Colorblindness*. New York: The New Press, 2011.

Anderson, Christopher and Michael Curtin. "Mapping the Ethereal City: Chicago Television, the FCC, and the Politics of Place." *Quarterly Review of Film and Video* 16, nos. 3–4 (1997): 289–305.

Arledge, Roone. *Roone: A Memoir*. New York: Harper Collins, 2003.

Baker, Aaron and Todd Boyd, eds. *Out of Bounds: Sports, Media, and the Politics of Identity*. Bloomington: Indiana University Press, 1997.

Banet-Weiser, Sarah. *Empowered: Popular Feminism and Popular Misogyny*. Durham, NC: Duke University Press, 2018.

——————. "Hoop Dreams: Professional Basketball and the Politics of Race and Gender." *Journal of Sport & Social Issues* 23, no. 4 (November 1999): 403–420.

——————. "Keynote Address: Media, Markets, Gender-Economics of Visibility in a Neoliberal Moment." *The Communication Review* 18, no. 1 (2015): 53–70.

Banet-Weiser, Sarah and Laura Portwood-Stacer. "The Traffic in Feminism: An Introduction to the Commentary and Criticism on Popular Feminism." *Feminist Media Studies* 17, no. 5 (2017): 884–906.

Becker, Ron. *Gay TV and Straight America*. New Brunswick, NJ: Rutgers University Press, 2006.

Bennett, Michael and Dave Zirin. *Things That Make White People Uncomfortable*. Chicago, IL: Haymarket Books, 2018.

Berger, John. *Ways of Seeing*. New York: Penguin Books, 1972.

Birrell, Susan and Cheryl L. Cole. *Women, Sport, and Culture*. Champaign, IL: Human Kinetics, 1994.

Blumenthal, Karen. *Let Me Play: The Story of Title IX, The Law That Changed the Future of Girls in America*. New York: Atheneum, 2005.

Bodroghkozy, Aniko, ed. *A Companion to the History of American Broadcasting*. Hoboken, NJ: John Wiley & Sons, 2018.

Boyd, Todd. *Am I Black Enough for You? Popular Culture from the 'Hood and Beyond.* Bloomington: Indiana University Press, 1997.

Boyd, Todd and Kenneth L. Shropshire, eds. *Basketball Jones: America Above the Rim.* New York: New York University Press, 2000.

Brooks, Peter. *The Melodramatic Imagination: Balzac, Henry James, Melodrama, and the Mode of Excess.* New Haven, CT: Yale University Press, 1976.

Burstyn, Varda. "Sport as Secular Sacrament." In *Sport in Contemporary Society*, 7th edition, edited by Stanley Eitzen, 11–20. Boulder, CO: Paradigm Publishers, 2005.

Butler, Judith. "Athletic Genders: Hyperbolic Instance and/or the Overcoming of Sexual Binarism." *Stanford Humanities Review* 6, no. 2 (1998). https://web.stanford.edu/group/SHR/6-2/html/butler.html

Butterworth, Michael L. and Stormi D. Moskal. "American Football, Flags and 'Fun': The Bell Helicopter Armed Forces Bowl and the Rhetorical Production of Militarism." *Communication, Culture, & Critique* 2 (2009): 411–433.

Caldwell, John Thornton. "Critical Industrial Practice: Branding, Repurposing, and the Migratory Power of Industrial Texts." *Television & New Media* 7, no. 2 (May 2006): 99–134.

―――. *Televisuality: Style, Crisis, and Authority in American Television.* New Brunswick, NJ: Rutgers University Press, 1995.

Consalvo, Mia, Konstantin Mitgutsch and Abe Stein, eds. *Sports Videogames.* New York: Routledge, 2013.

Cooky, Cheryl and Michael A. Messner, eds. *No Slam Dunk: Gender, Sport and the Unevenness of Social Change.* New Brunswick, NJ: Rutgers University Press, 2018.

Crawford, Susan. *Captive Audience: The Telecom Industry and Monopoly Power in the New Gilded Age.* New Haven, CT: Yale University Press, 2013.

Creedon, Pamela J., ed. *Women, Media and Sport: Challenging Gender Values.* Thousand Oaks, CA: Sage Publications, 1994.

Curtin, Michael. *Redeeming the Wasteland: Television Documentary and Cold War Politics.* New Brunswick, NJ: Rutgers University Press, 1995.

D'Acci, Julie. *Defining Women: Television and the Case of Cagney & Lacey.* Chapel Hill: University of North Carolina Press, 1994.

Deninger, Dennis. *Sports on Television: The How and Why Behind What You See.* New York: Routledge, 2012.

Dinces, Sean. "'Nothing But Net Profit': Property Taxes, Public Dollars, and Corporate Philanthropy at Chicago's United Center." *Radical History Review* 125 (May 2016): 13–34.

Dyer, Richard. *Only Entertainment.* 2nd edition. New York: Routledge, 2002.

―――. *Stars.* London: British Film Institute, 1998.

Eckel, Julia, Jens Ruchatz and Sabine Wirth, eds. *Exploring the Selfie: Historical, Theoretical, and Analytical Approaches to Digital Self-Photography.* Cham, Switzerland: Palgrave Macmillan, 2018.

Eckstein, Rick and Kevin Delaney. "New Sport Stadiums, Community Self-Esteem, and Community Collective Conscience." *Journal of Sport & Social Issues* 26, no. 3 (August 2002): 235–247.

————. *Public Dollars, Private Stadiums: The Battle Over Building Sports Stadiums*. New Brunswick, NJ: Rutgers University Press, 2006.

Edgerton, Gary and Jeffrey P. Jones, eds. *The Essential HBO Reader*. Lexington: University of Kentucky Press, 2008.

Edwards, Harry. *Sociology of Sport*. Homewood, IL: The Dorsey Press, 1973.

Ellcessor, Elizabeth. "'One Tweet to Make So Much Noise': Connected Celebrity Activism in the Case of Marlee Matlin." *New Media & Society* 20, no. 1 (2018): 255–271.

————. "Tweeting @feliciaday: Online Social Media, Convergence, and Subcultural Stardom." *Cinema Journal* 51, no. 2 (Winter 2012): 46–66.

Feuer, Jane. "HBO and the Concept of Quality TV." In *Quality TV: Contemporary American Television and Beyond*, edited by Janet McCabe and Kim Akass, 145–157. New York: I.B. Tauris & Co., Ltd., 2007.

Feuer, Jane, Paul Kerr and Tise Vahimagi, eds. *MTM: Quality Television*. London: BFI Publishing, 1984.

Fiske, John. *Television Culture*. New York: Routledge, 1989.

Fiske, John and John Hartley. *Reading Television*. New York: Routledge, 1990.

Fleetwood, Nicole. *On Racial Icons: Blackness and the Public Imagination*. New Brunswick, NJ: Rutgers University Press, 2015.

Freedman, Eric. "Software." In *The Craft of Criticism: Critical Media Studies in Practice*, edited by Michael Kackman and Mary C. Kearney, 318–330. New York: Routledge, 2018.

Gates, Racquel. *Double Negative: The Black Image and Popular Culture*. Durham, NC: Duke University Press, 2018.

Gomery, Douglas. "Theatre Television: The Missing Link of Technological Change in the U.S. Motion Picture Industry." *The Velvet Light Trap* 21 (Summer 1985): 54–61.

Gordon, Colin. *Mapping Decline: St. Louis and the Fate of the American City*. Philadelphia: University of Pennsylvania Press, 2008.

Gray, Herman. *Watching Race: Television and the Struggle for 'Blackness.'* Minneapolis: University of Minnesota Press, 1995.

Gray, Jonathan. "Antifandom and the Moral Text: Television Without Pity and Textual Dislike." *American Behavioral Scientist* 48, no. 7 (2005): 840–858.

Gray, Jonathan and Amanda D. Lotz. *Television Studies*. Malden, MA: Polity Press, 2012.

Haggins, Bambi and Julia Himberg. "The Multi-Channel Transition Period: 1980s-1990s." In *A Companion to the History of American Broadcasting*, edited by Aniko Bodroghkozy, 111–134. Hoboken, NJ: John Wiley & Sons, 2018.

Hargreaves, Jennifer, ed. *Sport, Culture, and Ideology*. London: Routledge & Kegan Paul, 1982.

Heywood, Leslie and Shari Dworkin. *Built to Win: The Female Athlete as Cultural Icon.* Minneapolis: University of Minnesota Press, 2003.

Hilmes, Michele. *Hollywood and Broadcasting: From Radio to Cable.* Urbana, IL: University of Illinois Press, 1990.

Hogshead-Makar, Nancy and Andrew Zimbalist, eds. *Equal Play: Title IX and Social Change.* Philadelphia, PA: Temple University Press, 2007.

Holland, Sharon Patricia. *The Erotic Life of Racism.* Durham, NC: Duke University Press, 2012.

Holmlund, Chris. *Impossible Bodies: Femininity and Masculinity at the Movies.* New York: Routledge, 2002.

Holt, Jennifer. *Empires of Entertainment: Media Industries and the Politics of Deregulation, 1980–1996.* New Brunswick, NJ: Rutgers University Press, 2011.

———. "NYPD Blue: Content Regulation." In *How to Watch Television*, edited by Ethan Thompson and Jason Mittell, 271–280. New York: New York University Press, 2013.

Holt, Jennifer and Kevin Sanson, eds. *Connected Viewing: Selling, Streaming, & Sharing Media in the Digital Era.* New York: Routledge, 2014.

Hutchins, Brett and David Rowe. *Sport Beyond Television: The Internet, Digital Media and the Rise of Networked Media Sport.* New York: Routledge, 2012.

Hutchins, Brett, David Rowe, Peter Morris and Riki Therivel, eds. *Digital Media Sport: Technology, Power and Culture in the Network Society.* New York: Routledge, 2013.

Illouz, Eva. *Cold Intimacies: The Making of Emotional Capitalism.* Malden, MA: Polity Press, 2007.

Jhally, Sut. "The Spectacle of Accumulation: Material and Cultural Factors in the Evolution of the Sports/Media Complex." *Insurgent Sociologist* 12, no. 3 (July 1984): 41–57.

Jirasek, Ivo and Geoffrey Zain Kohe. "Readjusting Our Sporting Sites/Sight: Sportification and the Theatricality of Social Life." *Sport, Ethics and Philosophy* 9, no. 3 (2015): 257–270.

Johnson, Arthur T. and James H. Frey, eds. *Government and Sport: The Public Policy Issues.* Totowa, NJ: Rowman & Allanheld, 1985.

Johnson, Catherine. "Tele-Branding in TVIII." *New Review of Film and Television Studies* 5, no. 1 (2007): 8–9.

Johnson, Victoria E. "Everything New Is Old Again: Sport Television, Innovation, and Tradition for a Multi-Platform Era." In *Beyond Prime Time: Television Programming in the Post-Network Era*, edited by Amanda D. Lotz, 114–137. New York: Routledge, 2009.

———. *Heartland TV: Prime Time Television and the Struggle for U.S. Identity.* New York: New York University Press, 2008.

———. "Historicizing TV Networking: Broadcasting, Cable, and the Case of ESPN." In *Media Industries: History, Theory, and Method*, edited by Jennifer Holt and Alisa Perren, 57–68. Malden, MA: Wiley-Blackwell, 2009.

————. "'Monday Night Football': Brand Identity." In *How to Watch Television*, edited by Ethan Thompson and Jason Mittell, 262–270. New York: New York University Press, 2013.

————. "More Than a Game: LeBron James and the Affective Economy of Place." In *Racism Postrace*, edited by Roopali Mukherjee, Sarah Banet-Weiser, and Herman Gray, 154–177. Durham, NC: Duke University Press, 2019.

Joseph, Ralina L. *Postracial Resistance: Black Women, Media, and the Uses of Strategic Ambiguity*. New York: New York University Press, 2018.

Kahn, Frank J., ed. *Documents of American Broadcasting*. Englewood Cliffs, NJ: Prentice-Hall, 1984.

Kaiser, Lacie L. "Revisiting the Sports Broadcasting Act of 1961: A Call for Equitable Antitrust Immunity from Section One of the Sherman Act for All Professional Sports Leagues." *DePaul Law Review* 54 (2005): 1237–1276.

Kaplan, E. Ann, ed. *Regarding Television: Critical Approaches-An Anthology*. Frederick, MD: University Publications of America, Inc., 1983.

Katz, Elihu. "And Deliver Us from Segmentation." *Annals of the American Academy of Political and Social Science* 546 (July 1996): 22–33.

Khan, Abraham Iqbal. "A Rant Good for Business: Communicative Capitalism and the Capture of Anti Racist Resistance." *Popular Communication: The International Journal of Media and Culture* 14, no. 1 (2016): 39–48.

King, Samantha. *Pink Ribbons, Inc.: Breast Cancer and the Politics of Philanthropy*. Minneapolis: University of Minnesota Press, 2006.

Kraszewski, Jon. "Pittsburgh in Fort Worth: Football Bars, Sports Television, Sports Fandom, and the Management of Home." *Journal of Sport and Social Issues* 32, no. 2 (May 2008): 1–19.

Leonard, Suzanne. *Wife, Inc.: The Business of Marriage in the Twenty-First Century*. New York: New York University Press, 2018.

Lipsitz, George. "The Struggle for Hegemony." *The Journal of American History* 75, no. 1 (June 1988): 146–150.

Lotz, Amanda D. *Portals: A Treatise on Internet-Distributed Television*. Ann Arbor: Michigan Publishing, 2017.

Marshall, David P. "The Promotion and Presentation of the Self: Celebrity as Marker of Presentational Media." *Celebrity Studies* 1, no. 1 (2010): 35–48.

McCarthy, Anna. *Ambient Television: Visual Culture and Public Space*. Durham, NC: Duke University Press, 2001.

————. "'Like An Earthquake!' Theater Television, Boxing, and the Black Public Sphere." *Quarterly Review of Film and Video* 16, nos. 3–4 (1999): 307–323.

McChesney, Robert W. *The Political Economy of Media: Enduring Issues, Emerging Dilemmas*. New York: Monthly Review Press, 2008.

McClearen, Jennifer. "'We Are All Fighters': The Transmedia Marketing of Difference in the Ultimate Fighting Championship." *International Journal of Communication* (August 2017): 3224–3242.

McRobbie, Angela. "Post-Feminism and Popular Culture." *Feminist Media Studies* 4, no. 3 (2004): 255–264.

Meer, Zubin, ed. *Individualism: The Cultural Logic of Modernity*. New York: Lexington Books, 2011.

Miller, Toby. *Sportsex*. Philadelphia, PA: Temple University Press, 2001.

Mitchell, Nicole and Lisa A. Ennis. *Encyclopedia of Title IX and Sports*. Westport, CT: Greenwood Press, 2007.

Modleski, Tania. *Feminism Without Women: Culture and Criticism in a 'Postfeminist' Age*. New York: Routledge, 1991.

———. *Loving With a Vengeance: Mass-Produced Fantasies for Women*. 2nd edition. New York: Routledge, 2008. Kindle.

———. "Misogynist Films: Teaching 'Top Gun.'" *Cinema Journal* 47, no. 1 (Autumn 2007): 101–105.

———. "The Rhythms of Reception: Daytime Television and Women's Work." In *Regarding Television: Critical Approaches-An Anthology*, edited by E. Ann Kaplan, 67–75. Frederick, MD: University Publications of America, Inc., 1983.

Moores, Shaun. *Media, Place, and Mobility*. New York: Palgrave Macmillan, 2012.

Morse, Margaret. "Sport on Television: Replay and Display." In *Regarding Television*, edited by E. Ann Kaplan, 44–66. Frederick, MD: University Publications of America, Inc., 1983.

Mullen, Megan. *The Rise of Cable Programming in the United States: Revolution or Evolution?* Austin: University of Texas Press, 2003.

Mulvey, Laura. "Visual Pleasure and Narrative Cinema." *Screen* 16, no. 3 (1975): 6–18.

Murray, Susan. *Bright Signals: A History of Color Television*. Durham, NC: Duke University Press, 2018.

Murray, Susan and Laurie Ouellette, eds. *Reality TV: Remaking Television Culture*. New York: New York University Press, 2009.

Newcomb, Horace, ed. *Encyclopedia of Television*. 2nd edition. New York: Fitzroy Dearborn, 2004.

———. "Studying Television: Same Questions, Different Contexts." *Cinema Journal* 45, no. 1 (Autumn 2005): 107–111.

———, ed. *Television: The Critical View*. 4th edition. New York: Oxford University Press, 1987.

———. *TV: The Most Popular Art*. New York: Anchor Books, 1974.

Newman, Michael Z. "Is Football Our Fault?" *Antenna*, September 17, 2014. http:// blog.commarts.wisc.edu/2014/09/17/is-football-our-fault/

Oates, Thomas P. *Football and Manliness: An Unauthorized Feminist Account of the NFL*. Urbana, IL: University of Illinois Press, 2017.

Oates, Thomas P. and Robert Allen Brookey, eds. *Playing to Win: Sports, Video Games, and the Culture of Play*. Bloomington: Indiana University Press, 2015.

Oates, Thomas P. and Zack Furness, eds. *The NFL: Critical and Cultural Perspectives*. Philadelphia, PA: Temple University Press, 2014.

Oriard, Michael. *Brand NFL: Making and Selling America's Favorite Sport*. Chapel Hill: University of North Carolina Press, 2007.

——. *King Football: Sport and Spectacle in the Golden Age of Radio and Newsreels, Movies and Magazines, the Weekly & the Daily Press*. Chapel Hill: University of North Carolina Press, 2001.

Ouellette, Laurie. *Lifestyle TV*. New York: Routledge, 2016.

Ouellette, Laurie and Jonathan Gray, eds. *Keywords for Media Studies*. New York: New York University Press, 2017.

Ouellette, Laurie and James Hay. *Better Living Through Reality TV: Television and Post-Welfare Citizenship*. Malden, MA: Blackwell, 2008.

Peck, Reece. *Fox Populism: Branding Conservatism as Working Class*. New York: Cambridge University Press, 2019.

Perlman, Allison. *Public Interests: Media Advocacy and Struggles Over Television*. New Brunswick, NJ: Rutgers University Press, 2016.

Pine, Joseph B. II. and James H. Gilmore. *The Experience Economy*. Boston, MA: Harvard University Press, 2011.

Piper, Timothy. "Transition Game: Television and the National Basketball Association During the Multichannel Shift, 1970–1984." Ph.D. dissertation, University of Texas, Austin, 2020.

Ranachan, Kate and Helen Morgan Parmett. "Fortune Favors the Braves? Race and the Suburban Rebranding of Baseball in Atlanta." Paper presented at the annual meeting of the Society for Cinema and Media Studies, Atlanta, GA, March 2016.

Rankine, Claudia. *Citizen: An American Lyric*. Minneapolis, MN: Graywolf Press, 2014.

Rapping, Elayne. *The Looking Glass World of Nonfiction TV*. Boston, MA: South End Press, 1987.

——. *The Movie of the Week: Private Stories, Public Events*. Minneapolis: University of Minnesota Press, 1992.

Real, Michael R. "Super Bowl: Mythic Spectacle." *Journal of Communication* 25, no. 1 (Winter 1975): 31–43.

Rose, Ava and James Friedman. "Television Sport as Mas(s)culine Cult of Distraction." *Screen* 35 (Spring 1994): 22–35.

Rosensweig, Daniel. *Retro Ball Parks: Instant History, Baseball, and the New American City*. Knoxville: The University of Tennessee Press, 2005.

Roth, Amanda and Susan A. Basow. "Femininity, Sports, and Feminism: Developing a Theory of Physical Liberation." *Journal of Sports & Social Issues* 28, no. 3 (August 2004): 245–265.

Ruberg, Bonnie. *Video Games Have Always Been Queer*. New York: New York University Press, 2019.

Rugg, Adam. "America's Game: The NFL's 'Salute to Service' Campaign, the Diffused Military Presence and Corporate Social Responsibility." *Popular Communication: The International Journal of Media and Culture* 14, no. 1 (2016): 21–29.

————. "Incorporating the Protests: The NFL, Social Justice and the Constrained Activism of the 'Inspire Change' Campaign." *Communication & Sport* (2019): 1–18.

Schultz, Jaime. "Reading the Catsuit: Serena Williams and the Production of Blackness at the 2002 U.S. Open." *Journal of Sport & Social Issues* 29 (2005): 338–357.

Secular, Steven. "Hoop Streams: The Rise of the NBA, Multiplatform Television, and Sports as Media Content, 1982 to 2015." Ph.D. dissertation, University of California, Santa Barbara, 2019. ProQuest ID: Secular_ucsb_0035D_14311.

Serazio, Michael and Emily Thorson. "Weaponized Patriotism and Racial Subtext in Kaepernick's Aftermath: The Anti-Politics of American Sports Fandom." *Television & New Media* 21, no. 1 (2016): 21–29.

Shea, Stuart. *Calling the Game: Baseball Broadcasting from 1920 to the Present*. Phoenix, AZ: Society for American Baseball Research, Inc., 2015.

Sheppard, Samantha N. "Give and Go: The Double Movement of 'Shut Up and Dribble'." *Los Angeles Review of Books*, February 12, 2019. https://lareviewofbooks.org/article/give-go-double-movement-shut-dribble/

————. "Historical Contestants: African American Documentary Traditions in 'On the Shoulders of Giants'." *Journal of Sport & Social Issues* 4, no. 6 (2017): 462–477.

————. *Sporting Blackness: Race, Embodiment, and Critical Muscle Memory on Screen*. Berkeley: University of California Press, 2020.

————. "Structuring Absences Revealed." *Journal of Sport History* 44, no. 3 (Fall 2017): 481–483.

Sherry, John F., Robert V. Kozinets, Adam Dubacheck, Benet DeBerry-Spence, Krittinee Nuttavuthisit and Diana Storm. "Gendered Behavior in a Male Preserve: Role Playing at ESPN Sports Zone Chicago." *Journal of Consumer Psychology* 14, nos. 1-2 (2004): 151–158.

Solloway, Jill. "The Female Gaze." *TIFF Master Class*, September 11, 2016. www.topple productions.com/the-female-gaze

Sosnik, Douglas B., Matthew J. Dowd and Ron Fournier. *Applebee's America: How Successful Political, Business, and Religious Leaders Connect With the New American Community*. New York: Simon & Schuster, 2006.

Spigel, Lynn. *Make Room for TV: Television and the Family Ideal in Postwar America*. Chicago, IL: University of Chicago Press, 1992.

————. "TV's Next Season?" *Cinema Journal* 45, no. 1 (Fall 2005): 83.

Spigel, Lynn and Denise Mann, eds. *Private Screenings: Television and the Female Consumer*. Minneapolis: University of Minnesota Press, 1992.

Spigel, Lynn and Jan Olsson, eds. *Television After TV: Essays on a Medium in Transition*. Durham, NC: Duke University Press, 2004.

Stauff, Markus. "Smartphone Referees: Social Media and Sports' Politics of Visibility." Paper presented at the annual meeting of the Society for Cinema and Media Studies, Seattle, WA, March 2014.

————. "Taming Distraction: The Second Screen Assemblage, Television and the Classroom." *Media and Communication* 4, no. 3 (2016): 185–198.

————. "The Accountability of Performance in Media Sports-Slow-Motion Replay, the 'Phantom Punch,' and the Mediated Body." *Body Politics* 2 (2014): 101–123.

————. "The Faces of Athletes: Visibility and Knowledge Production in Media Sport." *Flow*, October 16, 2009. www.flowjournal.org/author/markus-stauff/

Streeter, Thomas. *Selling the Air: A Critique of the Policy of Commercial Broadcasting in the United States*. Chicago, IL: University of Chicago Press, 1996.

Surdam, David G. *The Big Leagues Go to Washington: Congress and Sports Antitrust, 1951 1989*. Urbana, IL: University of Illinois Press, 2015.

Terranova, Tiziana. "Free Labor: Producing Culture for the Digital Economy." In *The Media Studies Reader*, edited by Laurie Ouellette, 331–349. New York: Routledge, 2013.

Tussey, Ethan. *The Procrastination Economy: The Big Business of Downtime*. New York: New York University Press, 2018.

Vogan, Travis. *ABC Sports: The Rise and Fall of Network Sports Television*. Berkeley: University of California Press, 2018.

————. "ESPN: Live Sports, Documentary Prestige, and On-Demand Culture." In *From Networks to Netflix: A Guide to Changing Channels*, edited by Derek Johnson, 107–115. New York: Routledge, 2018.

————. *ESPN: The Making of a Sports Media Empire*. Urbana, IL: University of Illinois Press, 2015.

————. "Exhibiting Ali's 'Super Fights': The Contested Politics and Brief History of Closed Circuit Boxing Broadcasts." *Film History* 30, no. 3 (2018): 1–31.

————. *Keepers of the Flame: NFL Films and the Rise of Sports Media*. Urbana, IL: University of Illinois Press, 2014.

————. "LeRoy Neiman and the Art of Network Sports Television." *American Art* 30, no. 3 (Fall 2016): 54–75.

————. "'Monday Night Football' and the Racial Roots of the Network TV Event." *Television & New Media* (2016): 1–17.

Wanzo, Rebecca. "African American Acafandom and Other Strangers: New Genealogies of Fan Studies." *Transformative Works and Cultures* 20 (2015). http://journal.transformativeworks.org

Warner, Kristen J. "ABC's 'Scandal' and Black Women's Fandom." In *Cupcakes, Pinterest, and Ladyporn: Feminized Popular Culture in the Early Twenty-First Century*, edited by Elana Levine, 32–50. Urbana, IL: University of Illinois Press, 2015.

Wenner, Lawrence A., ed. *Media, Sports, & Society*. Newbury Park, CA: Sage Publications, 1989.

Wenner, Lawrence A. and Steven J. Jackson, eds. *Sport, Beer, and Gender*. New York: Peter Lang, 2009.

Whannel, Garry. "Pregnant With Anticipation: The Pre-History of Television Sport and the Politics of Recycling and Preservation." *International Journal of Cultural Studies* 8, no. 4 (2005): 405–426.

White, Timothy R. "Life After Divorce: The Corporate Strategy of Paramount Pictures Corporation in the 1950s." *Film History* 2, no. 2 (June-July 1988): 99–119.

Williams, Linda. "Melodrama Revised." In *Refiguring American Film Genres: History and Theory*, edited by Nick Browne, 42–88. Berkeley: University of California Press, 1998.

Williams, Mark. "Issue Introduction: U.S. Regional and Non-Network Television History." *Quarterly Review of Film and Video* 16, nos. 3–4 (1997): 221–228.

Wilson, Julie A. *Neoliberalism*. New York: Routledge, 2018.

Zoller Seitz, Matt. "Avengers, MCU, Game of Thrones, and the Content Endgame." April 29, 2019. www.rogerebert.com/mzs/avengers-mcu-and-the-content-endgame

Archival Collections

Pat Weaver Papers, Wisconsin Historical Society, Madison, WI.

Roone Arledge Papers, Columbia University, New York, NY.

INDEX

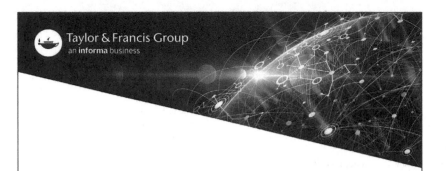

9780415722940